FORESHADOWS
OF THE LAW

FORESHADOWS OF THE LAW

Supreme Court Dissents and Constitutional Development

DONALD E. LIVELY

Westport, Connecticut
London

Library of Congress Cataloging-in-Publication Data

Lively, Donald E., 1947–
    Foreshadows of the law : Supreme Court dissents and constitutional
development / Donald E. Lively.
        p.   cm.
    Includes bibliographical references and index.
    ISBN 0–275–94382–8 (hc : alk. paper). — ISBN 0–275–94383–6 (pb :
alk. paper)
    1. Dissenting opinions—United States.   2. United States—
Constitutional law—Interpretation and construction.   3. United
States.   Supreme Court.   I. Title.
KF4550.L58   1993
342.73—dc20
[347.302]   92–19827

British Library Cataloguing in Publication Data is available.

Library of Congress Catalog Card Number: 92-19827
ISBN: 0-275-94382-8
ISBN: 0-275-94383-6 (pbk.)

First published in 1992

Praeger Publishers, 88 Post Road West, Westport, Connecticut 06881
An imprint of Greenwood Publishing Group, Inc.

Printed in the United States of America

∞™

The paper used in this book complies with the
Permanent Paper Standard issued by the National
Information Standards Organization (Z39.48-1984).

10 9 8 7 6 5 4 3 2 1

To Jim R. Carrigan, a great role model and, when necessary, a great dissenter; and to Pam and Rico for their endless love and support.

CONTENTS

PREFACE

The U.S. Constitution, as originally framed and ratified, plotted a structure of governance, delineated political powers and itemized certain individual rights and liberties. The chartering of the republic resolved the formal challenge of establishing a union but, with respect to the nation's evolution, was more a starting than an ending point. The framing process itself left open the possibility of further constitutional development. The potential for the document's own growth and change was anticipated specifically by Article V, which sets forth the conditions and procedures for amendment. Multiple amendments over two hundred years, including the Bill of Rights which was appended to secure ratification, have helped to redefine the Constitution. Still, the relatively cumbersome process of such change, requiring supermajorities of the Congress or states to propose and of the states to ratify an amendment, is not the only or even the most profound source of constitutional development.

For nearly two centuries, the U.S. Supreme Court has been the primary interpreter of the Constitution's meaning. Although not specifically provided by the document itself, the power of the judiciary to interpret the Constitution has existed since Chief Justice Marshall asserted it in *Marbury v. Madison.* As the ultimate authority on the Constitution's meaning, the Supreme Court exercises the power to define, amplify and steer the document's operative terms and conditions. Constitutional law, as a consequence, comprises not only broad and imprecise terms of the charter itself, but also a massive body of case law expounding principle, doctrine and sometimes contradiction.

For practical purposes, the Constitution is animated by the resolution of cases that work their way through the judicial process. The Supreme

Court is the final arbiter of constitutional claims, which are the raw material from which decisions are rendered, precedent is defined and meaning is established. Because cases seldom present facts and circumstances that are precisely identical, subsequent decisions may embellish, distinguish or qualify previously articulated principle. The judicially established proposition that formal racial discrimination offends the equal protection guarantee of the Fourteenth Amendment, for instance, has been a departure point for some decisions extending the principle to defeat affirmative action plans and others distinguishing the premise when such programs are reviewed. Even when presented with essentially the same issue, the Court may overturn precedent if it determines that its prior interpretation was misplaced. Minus the capacity to modify, abandon or repudiate past principle, constitutional law would be unbending even as initial errors in judgment compounded.

The development of constitutional law in a flexible rather than fixed manner has proved crucial to the society's legal and moral progress. In 1896, for instance, the Supreme Court rendered the separate but equal doctrine and accordingly determined that official segregation was a reasonable and permissible exercise of legislative power. More than half a century later, the Court determined that separate inherently was unequal and thus constitutionally offensive. The decision, which invalidated official segregation in public schools and was a catalyst eventually for comprehensive civil rights legislation, repudiated long-established practice and precedent. Within that abandoned past was the precursor of future doctrine.

When the Court originally upheld official segregation a century ago, as discussed in Chapter 5, the majority decision elicited a single dissenting opinion. Justice Harlan, begging to differ, advanced the notion that the "Constitution is color-blind" and allows "no superior, dominant, ruling class of citizens." Harlan's understanding of the Constitution, which was rejected when first espoused, several decades later became central to the Fourteenth Amendment's meaning. The guarantee of equal protection, which in 1896 countenanced color-conscious policies, by 1954 was redirected into a requirement of official color blindness. Although the Court did not specifically mention Harlan when it invalidated official segregation, in *Brown v. Board of Education,* his dissenting view afforded a source of inspiration for eventual redirection of constitutional principle. Contemporary restatement of the law thus cites both to *Brown* and to Harlan for the same proposition.

The retrieval of originally rejected principle, in the undoing of segregation, is notable but not entirely exceptional. It is significant because the Constitution's meaning was profoundly redefined. The process was not unique, however, insofar as many important constitutional developments derive from a past that initially was discredited. A basic purpose of this book is to demonstrate the influence of dissenting opinions in the evolution of constitutional law. Although at odds with dominant understanding of the Constitution when first articulated, dissents facilitate the law's development while providing a linkage that establishes a source of continuity. What appears to be settled principle, therefore, may preface but not necessarily predict future law. Not infrequently, dissents have been the foundation for future constitutional landmarks.

The dissenting opinions focused on in this book do not exhaust the instances in which constitutional law has been foreshadowed by an originally repudiated vision. For every opinion considered, it may be possible to contend that another has been neglected. The past few decades in particular have offered powerful and significant dissents for and against enlarging and narrowing the scope of enumerated rights and liberties, developing and refraining from establishing new freedoms and allowing and prohibiting race or gender-based preferences. Although recent opinions are discussed in the broader context of constitutional development, the primary focus is on seminal contributions with historically settled consequences. The opinions examined express views that not only influenced the law's direction but, in so doing, also proved especially and indisputably influential to society's development.

Several people deserve recognition for their contributions to this book. Fran Molnar and Peggye Cummings were indispensable in the processing of the manuscript. Faye Ransom provided valuable research assistance. Professor William Richman shared his knowledge and insight into jurisprudence, history and constitutional law. A special debt is owed to the University of Toledo College of Law, which provided a grant to support the research and writing processes, and to the administration, faculty and staff that in innumerable ways have contributed to my professional and personal development and satisfaction.

INTRODUCTION: JUDICIAL REVIEW AND CONSTITUTIONAL DEVELOPMENT

The U.S. Constitution is notable for both its adaptability and its durability. Over the course of its existence, the Constitution has accommodated and invalidated slavery, survived disunion and civil war, allowed and prohibited racial segregation, specified freedoms and rights that government may not abridge and been a departure point for identifying liberties not itemized by the document itself. Although time has passed, circumstances have changed and understanding has evolved since its ratification, the Constitution in form remains unaltered except for twenty-six amendments to it since 1791. Appearances are deceiving, however, to the extent that limited textual revision might suggest minimal development or even consistency of principle and understanding. As evidenced by volumes of case law that have accumulated over two centuries, including more than five hundred compiled by the U.S. Supreme Court, the Constitution itself has been a source of controversy and debate from which doctrine and principle have evolved. Because it is not always self-defining, especially with respect to its most profound but broadly stated passages, the Constitution challenges and effectively requires each generation to contribute to its development and consequent meaning.

The Power of Judicial Review

The judiciary's primacy in construing the Constitution, and consequent power to define and gloss its meaning, was established in 1803. Chief Justice Marshall, in *Marbury v. Madison*, determined that it was the Court's power "to say what the law is." Few decisions in constitutional history rival

Marbury in significance. The Constitution by its terms does not assign to the judiciary eminence in defining its meaning. Such a paramount role at the time was not ordained by precedent or tradition. Nor was it a function conceded by President Jefferson, whose interest in voiding last-minute judicial appointments of his predecessor was at the core of the *Marbury* litigation. Although Marshall ruled in favor of Jefferson's immediate interests, the characterization of judicial power is what proved to be of long-term significance. What was established in *Marbury* and survived the political dispute underlying the case was the principle that when the Constitution's meaning is disputed, the judiciary not only resolves the immediate controversy, but also establishes principles for general purposes.

The practical significance of the *Marbury* decision has evidenced itself repeatedly over the course of history. A decision that a state law interferes with Congress's power to regulate interstate commerce, for instance, not only declares the rights of litigants, but also determines the relation between federal and state government. A ruling that expression may not be prohibited absent a clear and present danger, besides resolving rights of litigants, charts general perimeters for freedom of speech. Likewise, a decision that official segregation is unconstitutional establishes a principle of both specific and general application. Such power to expound the Constitution in a universal manner actually may be a more significant influence on the charter's evolution than the amendment process itself. Judicial review is a more frequent source of constitutional development that not only may redefine the document's meaning but, like amendments themselves, may exceed or deviate from original expectations or purposes.

Constitutional Interpretation and Evolution

Although the Constitution is the preeminent law of the land, the litigative and interpretive processes do not always generate certainty and consistency of principle or fidelity to original design or precedent. Over the course of its history, the Constitution as interpreted has accommodated and precluded slavery, broadened and narrowed congressional power to regulate interstate commerce, allowed and prohibited racial segregation, cramped and expanded expressive freedom, enhanced and curtailed rights of suspects and the accused, and developed and abandoned fundamental rights not specified by the charter itself. Such variation in or vacillation between principle suggests that interpretation may be final in resolving a particular controversy but not necessarily indefeasible as a statement of general law. A consequence of such functional qualification may be uncertainty of future principle. Doctrinal unpredictability, however, is critical to a developmental scheme valuing both adaptability and durability.

The evolutionary nature of constitutional law evidenced itself even before the charter was ratified. During the ratification process, a controversy arose over perceived dangers presented by the proposed national government. The argument advanced by Antifederalists, that a central government would endanger individual rights and liberties, presented a serious obstacle to ratification. To facilitate the Constitution's adoption, Federalists supported an itemization of rights and liberties that the national government could not abridge. What became the Bill of Rights essentially was considered superfluous by the Federalists, who believed that assignment of limited powers to the federal government obviated the need for such guarantees. Either as a matter of convenience or as a sensed need, broad support materialized for the Bill of Rights. Ratification and amendment thus were contemporaneous and interdependent processes resulting in express limitations on the exercise of federal power.

Since ratified, the text of the Bill of Rights has remained unchanged. The scope of its coverage, however, has expanded significantly. Although the Bill of Rights initially was conceived as a check solely on federal power, many of its guarantees subsequently have been applied against the states. Such an extension of its operation has resulted from the introduction of the Fourteenth Amendment and the incorporation of many provisions of the Bill of Rights through it. The Fourteenth Amendment, as discussed in Chapters 2 and 3, was framed and ratified in the aftermath of the Civil War primarily for purposes of confirming citizenship, civil rights and equality for persons of African origin. Its adoption reflected new concepts of national citizenship and interests. Among other things, the amendment prohibited any "State [from] depriv[ing] any person of life, liberty, or property without due process of law."

As the twentieth century progressed, the Supreme Court increasingly used the Fourteenth Amendment as a medium for expanding enumerated rights and freedoms so that they operated against not only federal government but state government as well. Through the process of judicial review, provisions including First Amendment freedoms of expression, religion, assembly and petition; Fourth Amendment protection against unreasonable searches and seizures; Fifth Amendment provisions against double jeopardy, compelled self-incrimination and taking of property without just compensation; Sixth Amendment guarantees of speedy, public and jury trial, access to counsel, compulsory process to secure witnesses and opportunity to confront witnesses; and the Eighth Amendment right against cruel and unusual punishment have been incorporated through the Fourteenth Amendment. Provisions not applicable to the states include the Second, Third, and Seventh Amendments and the Fifth Amendment requirement of indictment by a grand jury. For practical purposes, therefore, the Bill of Rights, as a consequence of judicially supervised development rather than initial design, has evolved as a check on both national and state power.

During the same period that the Fourteenth Amendment has been used to extend and amplify constitutionally enumerated guarantees, it has functioned as an independent source of fundamental rights. Despite its relatively limited initial purpose in reconstructing a union within which citizenship and civil rights previously denied would be secured, much more has been achieved in the name of the Fourteenth Amendment. Over the course of its existence, the amendment has been not only a means for expanding the protective scope of the Bill of Rights, but also a basis for introducing rights identified as fundamental even though they are not enumerated by the Constitution. A general liberty of contract, for example, was proposed in litigation soon after the Fourteenth Amendment was ratified and, as discussed in Chapter 4, became a defining feature of constitutional jurisprudence during the first third of this century. Since then, as discussed in Chapter 7, the Fourteenth Amendment has been the source of privacy rights comprehending such interests as liberty to elect an abortion, marital rights and family integrity.

Judicial Review and Critics

As used to extend existing rights and freedoms and to identify new ones, the Fourteenth Amendment is unrivaled as a source of constitutional development. Judicial review responsible for such results, however, has engendered extensive controversy and criticism. A fundamental objection is that application of the Bill of Rights to the states and recognition of rights not specified by the Constitution itself circumvent the requirements set forth in the document for amendment. Robert Bork has asserted that "[w]hen constitutional law is judge-made and not rooted in the text or structure of the constitution, . . . it *is* illegitimate, root and branch." Bork's argument is consistent with a critical perspective of judicial review as counter-majoritarian and anti-democratic. Competing against such concerns are arguments that the Constitution, presented in broad and general terms with a history that itself may be debated, must be developed with attention to values and their prioritization. The debate over how activist or restrained constitutional interpretation should be is as old as the American judiciary itself. Even as the controversy persists, judicial review seems well established as a prolific and primary source of constitutional development.

Judicial primacy in interpreting the Constitution, as noted previously, is a result of evolution rather than the document's own command. The framers themselves were ambivalent and imprecise about the role of the judiciary. Discerning their expectations of the judicial function is problematic, given the absence of any specific textual charge or clear indication by the historical record. As Leonard Levy has noted, with respect to enduring dispute over the judiciary's role, "[t]he people who say the framers intended [judicial primacy] are talking nonsense, and the people who say they did not intend it are talking nonsense."

Even if the judiciary's eventual role was not specifically contemplated by the Constitution's architects, they nonetheless created a political structure from which modern powers of review emerged. The Supreme Court's interpretive eminence, as noted previously, was established in *Marbury v. Madison*. The case itself arose from the intense rivalry between political parties competing to shape the republic in its formative years. Specifically at issue was whether a newly elected Republican president was required to deliver commissions to last-minute judicial appointments of his Federalist predecessor. From the clash of competing ideologies emerged not only a resolution of the immediate controversy, but a further definition of the government itself as well. Jefferson's warning that he would not deliver the commissions, even if ordered, presented Marshall with the challenge of asserting the Court's power without sacrificing it. By determining that executive action could be judicially reviewed but that legislation giving the Court jurisdiction over the case at hand was unconstitutional, Marshall resolved the controversy, defused a significant challenge to the judiciary's legitimacy and filled a breach in the Constitution's assignment of governmental powers.

The critical passage in Chief Justice Marshall's opinion, at least for durational purposes, was the conclusion that "it is, emphatically, the province and duty of the judiciary department, to say what the law is." Justice Frankfurter later characterized the Court's self-described role as "an indispensable, implied characteristic of a written Constitution." The power of judicial review, even as so depicted, nonetheless is a function of progress rather than ordination. Establishment of the Court's primacy in defining the Constitution's meaning was significant not only as a development itself, but also as a source of further evolution. Over nearly two centuries, the judiciary's power "to say what the law is" has not been entirely unchallenged. In response to the Court's determination that the Constitution established a right to slavery, Abraham Lincoln maintained that Supreme Court decisions did not establish general law unless and until they commanded consensual societal support. Franklin Roosevelt attempted to expand and pack the Court in an effort to reshape its ideology and enable him to influence—at least indirectly—"what the law is." Lincoln's argument that the Court resolved the case but not necessarily general policy descended from perspectives advanced by Presidents Jefferson and Jackson and revived under President Reagan. Attorney General Meese thus proposed a distinction between "the Constitution . . . as . . . 'the supreme Law of the Land'" and "constitutional law [which] is what the Supreme Court says about the Constitution in its decisions resolving the cases and controversies that come before it."

Notwithstanding opposition to or disregard of the Court's rulings, and theories to lessen its influence, sometimes resistance may enhance rather than diminish the judiciary's primacy in defining the Constitution. Initial response to the desegregation mandate, enunciated in *Brown v. Board of Education,* was characterized by widespread intransigence, evasion and delay by state and local officials ordered to implement it. One state even passed a law declaring the *Brown* decision unconstitutional and prohibiting school desegregation. Although his personal conviction was that judicially ordered desegregation was miscalculated and unwise, President Eisenhower dispatched federal troops to enforce the Court's mandate. Interpretation had defined "what the law is" for theoretical purposes, but enforcement, especially against a backdrop of opposition and hostility, determined its practical meaning. The net result was effectuation of newly identified constitutional demands and fortification of the judiciary's interpretive eminence.

The Court's authority likewise was enhanced when President Nixon asserted that his recorded conversations, subpoenaed for use as evidence in a criminal proceeding, were protected from disclosure by executive privilege. The resultant case of *United States v. Nixon* was reminiscent of the *Marbury* controversy insofar as it presented a constitutional conflict between the executive and judicial branches. Unlike the posture struck by Jefferson in 1803, who promised to disregard any order to deliver contested judicial commissions, Nixon complied with the Court's demand that he produce his tapes. The president's obedience of the Court's command confirmed again the judiciary's power "to say what the law is."

The Nature of the Constitution

Authority to review legislative output and executive action is a responsibility of significant proportion magnified further by the Constitution's nature. In delineating federal powers and enumerating basic rights and liberties, the document itself speaks in broad generalities rather than with detailed precision. Although granting Congress power "[t]o regulate Commerce . . . among the several States," for instance, the Constitution does not define critical terms of the clause. Commerce itself is not explained, nor are standards offered to distinguish interstate and intrastate activity. When controversy or dispute arises over a provision's meaning, it is the judiciary that has supplied authoritative definition and practical content. The process of interpretation, however, does not necessarily yield fixed meaning for all times. In *Gibbons v. Ogden,* Chief Justice Marshall originally construed the commerce power in terms that accounted for a broad range of activity and dismissed the Tenth Amendment as a specific check on federal authority. For the first third of this century, the Court narrowed the scope of the power by distinguishing between processes of production and transportation and identifying the Tenth Amendment as a restraint. Since then, the Court has reverted to the analytical model established by Marshall and again construed the commerce power expansively.

Likewise neither self-defining nor self-actualizing, but subject to interpretive change, are the rights and liberties enumerated by the Constitution. Such concepts as "freedom of speech . . . and of the press," "unreasonable searches and seizures," "just compensation," "double jeopardy," "speedy trial," "impartial jury," "assistance of counsel," "excessive bail," "cruel and unusual punishments," "privileges and immunities," "due process," and "equal protection," as evidenced by their inclusion in the nation's charter, represent profound interests. The litigative record of such provisions demonstrates, however, that each is subject to debate with respect to meaning. Like other terms suceptible to varying interpretation, their practical significance is less a function of predetermined certainty than of interpretive development.

Judicial Review and Constitutional Development

Evolution of constitutional law seldom proceeds in a straight or unbroken manner or in a consistent direction. As doctrinal underpinnings may develop or be displaced, the principles premised on them invariably are affected. Theory and law may appear, disappear and even reappear, as evidenced by the aforementioned expansion, constriction and rebroadening of the federal commerce power. The uncertain course of judicial review reflects the reality that jurists of different generations, background and experience have diverging values, priorities and perspectives. When President Adams appointed John Marshall as chief justice, it was with anticipation that Marshall would facilitate the Federalist agenda. Consistent with Adams's expectation, Marshall's tenure is notable for decisions that defined national authority broadly. By the end of the nineteenth century, other presidents steeped in laissez-faire economic principles nominated and secured the confirmation of justices committed to the preservation of marketplace freedom. As a consequence, and as discussed in Chapter 4, congressional authority to regulate commerce during the first third of this century was delineated narrowly, and liberty of contract simultaneously was identified as a basic freedom that checked the economic regulatory power of states.

Like most redirection of constitutional law, such change did not materialize without background or history. Sometimes development of the law is a logical or predictable extension of existing principle. Once the Court prohibited segregation in public education, for instance, it followed that discrimination could not survive constitutional scrutiny in other public

venues. Case law quickly developed, therefore, to expand the anti-discrimination principle in a broad spectrum of public contexts. Even when the
Supreme Court displaces precedent and establishes new law, the change
may have been previewed by earlier jurisprudence. Particularly relevant
for purposes of such constitutional development are dissenting opinions.
The practice of dissent is well established and probably implicit in a process of collective decision-making. It is a custom enabling a jurist not only
to disagree with and disclaim the majority's work but also to provide a
reference point of reason for future consideration. As described by Chief
Justice Hughes, a dissent represents "an appeal to the brooding spirit of
the law, to the intelligence of a later day."

The Nature and Function of Dissenting Opinions

   The dissenting opinion has evolved as a term of art. Typically, a judicial
decision consists of a judgment supported by an opinion that provides
explanatory reasoning for the result reached. When the judicial process is
a collective rather than individual enterprise, as it is with the Supreme
Court and other appellate tribunals, disagreement may exist and be expressed with respect to one or both aspects of the decision. A dissent in
its purest form departs from both the holding and the opinion. A concurring opinion, although agreeing with the decisional result, expresses disagreement with respect to the reason why the conclusion should be reached.
For practical purposes, such analysis concurs in the Court's judgment but
dissents from its opinion. The nature of a concurring opinion is typified
by Justice Scalia's separate statement in *City of Richmond v. J. A. Croson
Co.* that expressed agreement with the outcome but also objected to the
reasoning used by his colleagues to reach the same result. Scalia joined
four other justices in support of a judgment that a city policy establishing
preferences for minority contractors was unconstitutional. Although concurring that the program at issue offended the Fourteenth Amendment's
equal protection guarantee, Scalia disagreed with reasoning that race
sometimes could be taken into account to remedy proven discrimination.
He thus wrote separately to express his sense that racial preferences were
prohibited under virtually all circumstances. Scalia thereby concurred in
the judgment but identified his own reasons in support of the result.
   The line between a concurring and a dissenting opinion at times may be
rather fine. In *Branzburg v. Hayes,* for instance, the Court refused to establish a First Amendment privilege that would have immunized journalists
from disclosing their sources to a grand jury. Justice Powell authored a
concurring opinion that effectively supported a qualified privilege akin to
what was sought by the news media. What the dissenters described in
Branzburg as an "enigmatic concurring opinion," therefore, indicated a dis-

sent in substance and concurrence mainly in form. Two opinions discussed in subsequent chapters, Chief Justice Taney's in *Prigg v. Pennsylvania* and Justice Brandeis's in *Whitney v. California,* are styled as concurring opinions. Because the views they expressed were so profoundly divergent from the Court's, however, it is their dissenting spirit that is most notable.

Whether responding to the Court's judgment or reasoning, a dissenting opinion establishes an alternative model of logic or understanding for future reference. The potential for competing constitutional understandings and expoundments historically has seemed proportionate to the magnitude and profundity of the controversy at hand. As the following chapters illustrate, jurisprudential history is suffused with perspective that, although initially rejected, eventually defined the meaning of the Constitution. Taney's opinion in *Prigg* (see Chapter 1) deviated from the majority's sense that Congress had exclusive power to regulate fugitive slave issues. In emphasizing that slave owner rights were rooted in the Constitution, Taney presaged the Court's determination in *Dred Scott v. Sandford* (see Chapter 2) that the federal interest in slavery was limited and the Fifth Amendment secured slave owner property interests. The *Dred Scott* decision itself contained dissenting opinions that previewed the eventual displacement of the Court's holding, pursuant to constitutional amendments ratified after the Civil War. Arguments that the Fourteenth Amendment incorporated a broad spectrum of rights and liberties, including guarantees associated with the Bill of Rights, the Declaration of Independence and natural law, initially were rejected in the *Slaughter-House Cases* (see Chapter 3). Even before the end of reconstruction, analysis increasingly was driven by sentiment expressed by the *Slaughter-House* dissenters who favored an expansive interpretation of the Fourteenth Amendment. As the dissenting perspective of the *Slaughter-House Cases* hardened into constitutional principle emphasizing economic liberty, by the beginning of this century, it was not without a competing viewpoint of long-term significance. In disputing the Court's development of economic liberty as a check on legislative power, in *Lochner v. New York* (see Chapter 4), Justice Holmes maintained that the Court was impeding the democratic process. More than three decades later, the Court echoed much of his sentiment in abandoning its focus on economic rights. While expanding the Fourteenth Amendment to account for marketplace liberty during the late nineteenth and early twentieth centuries, the Court simultaneously limited its potential utility in responding to racial discrimination. The Court in the *Civil Rights Cases* and *Plessy v. Ferguson* (see Chapter 5), respectively, denied Congress the power to prohibit private discrimination and endorsed the separate but equal doctrine. It did so despite Justice Harlan's arguments for a more liberal concept of state action and a color-blind constitution. By the middle of the twentieth century, as the Court eliminated segregation of public schools and other contexts, Harlan's originally repudiated notions prevailed. Constitutional development also was slow but eventual with respect to speech-protective First Amendment theory advanced by Justices Holmes and Brandeis in several cases earlier this century (see Chapter 6). Their introduction of clear and present danger principles, which failed to command a majority when articulated in the 1920s, became settled doctrine by the 1960s. Finally, Justice Brandeis's notion of a right to privacy, proposed in *Olmstead v. United States* (see Chapter 7), failed initially to define Fourth Amendment protection against unreasonable searches and seizures. A few decades later, his thinking had inspired decisions that not only expanded Fourth Amendment protection against invasive investigative technologies, but also created new constitutional zones of privacy for personal decisions concerning family, marriage, sexual activity, and abortion.

A Long Tradition of Dissent

As constitutional law itself has evolved over two centuries, so too have the nature and significance of dissenting opinions. Before 1801, Supreme Court decisions were not rendered with an "Opinion of the Court." Because early American practice followed the English custom, allowing each justice to author an individual opinion, early procedure was especially conducive to the articulation of analytical differences. Dissent initially manifested itself in *Georgia v. Brailsford,* one of the earliest officially reported Supreme Court decisions and the first in which opinions were set forth. The *Brailsford* case concerned a state's effort to secure an injunction to prevent payment of a debt to a British company. Under pertinent state law, money and property used to pay obligations to British citizens or their government were subject to confiscation. A majority of the Court supported injunctive relief. Justice Cushing disagreed and maintained that such a remedy was inapt. Cushing's dissenting view was expressed in a single paragraph. The difference of opinion, although relatively inconsequential with respect to substantive significance or impact, commenced a tradition that has survived and been strengthened over the course of time.

Early discord of more lasting pertinence manifested itself in the case of *Calder v. Bull.* The competing opinions of Justices Iredell and Chase are significant because they previewed the persisting debate, discussed in Chapters 4 and 7, over the judiciary's power to identify fundamental rights not specified by the Constitution. At issue in *Calder* was whether a state enactment, setting aside a judicial decree and providing for a new hearing, was an *ex post facto* law in violation of the Constitution. The Court was unanimous in its judgment that the enactment was unconstitutional as applied. More significant for long-term purposes were Iredell's and Chase's conflicting views with respect to the Court's power of review.

Iredell advocated a model of analysis characterized by restraint. Emphasizing the need for deference to the legislative process, he maintained:

It is true, that some speculative jurists have held, that a legislative act against natural justice must, in itself, be void; but I cannot think that, under such a government any court of justice would possess a power to declare it so. . . .

In order, therefore, to guard against so great an evil, it has been the policy of all the American states, which have, individually, framed their state constitutions, since the revolution, and of the people of the United States, when they framed the federal constitution, to define with precision the objects of the legislative power, and to restrain its exercise within marked and settled boundaries. If any act of congress, or of the legislature of a state, violates those constitutional provisions, it is unquestionably void; though, I admit, that as the authority to declare it void is of a delicate and awful nature, the court will never resort to that authority, but in a clear and urgent case. If, on the other hand, the legislature of the Union, or the legislature of any member of the Union, shall pass a law, within the general scope of their constitutional power, the court cannot pronounce it to be void, merely because it is, in their judgment, contrary to the principles of natural justice. The ideas of natural justice are regulated by no fixed standard: the ablest and the purest men have differed upon the subject; and all that the court could properly say, in such an event, would be, that the legislature (possessed of an equal right of opinion) had passed an act which, in the opinion of the judges, was inconsistent with the abstract principles of natural justice. There are then but two lights, in which the subject can be viewed: 1st. If the legislature pursue the authority delegated to them, their acts are valid. 2d. If they transgress the boundaries of that authority, their acts are invalid. In the former case, they exercise the discretion vested in them by the people, to whom alone they are responsible for the faithful discharge of their trust.

Iredell's view effectively summarized the arguments that have been advanced since by exponents of judicial restraint. In *Griswold v. Connecticut,* for instance, Justice Black dissented from the Court's recognition of a right to privacy on grounds that it was unsupported by "some specific constitutional" provision. Modern criticism of the judicially identified liberty to elect an abortion reflects a like sense, as Justice White has complained, that the result flows from the exercise of "raw power" rather than from constitutional prescription. Such perspective of the judicial function reflects Iredell's sense that a law cannot "be void, merely because it is, in [the Court's] judgment, contrary to the principles of natural justice."

A counterpoint to Iredell's analytical model was presented by Justice Chase. From Chase's perspective, judicial review could factor in not only constitutional text and history, but also natural rights. What Iredell considered antidemocratic represented to Chase another means of accounting for the people's will.

I cannot subscribe to the omnipotence of a state legislature, or that it is absolute and without control; although its authority should not be expressly restrained by the constitution, or fundamental law of the state. The people of the United States erected their constitutions or forms of government, to establish justice, to promote the general welfare, to secure the blessings of liberty, and to protect their persons and property from violence. The purposes for which men enter into society will determine the nature and terms of the social compact; and as they are the foundation of the legislative power, they will decide what are the proper objects of it. The nature, and ends of legislative power will limit the exercise of it. This fundamental principle flows from the very nature of our free republican governments, that no man should be compelled to do what the laws do not require; nor to refrain from acts which the laws permit. There are acts which the federal, or state legislature cannot do, without exceeding their authority. There are certain vital principles in our free republican governments, which will determine and overrule an apparent and flagrant abuse of legislative power; as to authorize manifest injustice by positive law; or to take away that security for personal liberty, or private property, for the protection whereof the government was established. An act of the legislature (for I cannot call it a law), contrary to the great first principles of the social compact, cannot be considered a rightful exercise of legislative authority. The obligation of a law, in governments established on express compact, and on republican principles, must be determined by the nature of the power on which it is founded. . . .

The legislature may enjoin, permit, forbid and punish; they may declare new crimes; and establish rules of conduct for all its citizens in future cases; they may command what is right, and prohibit what is wrong; but they cannot change innocence into guilt; or punish innocence as a crime; or violate the right of an antecedent lawful private contract; or the right of private property. To maintain that our federal, or state legislature possesses such powers, if they had not been expressly restrained; would, in my opinion, be a political heresy, altogether inadmissible in our free republican governments.

The tension between Iredell's and Chase's concepts of constitutional review remains largely unresolved. Consistent with Iredell in theory, the Court frequently has emphasized that it does not function as a super legislature to determine the wisdom of policy. In reality, the Court has developed a multitude of fundamental rights that are unenumerated by the Constitution and within the natural law tradition favored by Chase. The long-term significance of *Calder* thus includes contributions not only to principle, but also to the legacy of dissent.

The two centuries since *Calder* have yielded literally thousands of dissenting opinions. A study of the Court's first 183 years disclosed that a total of 27,916 decisions included 3,915 dissenting opinions and 1,322 concurring opinions. During Chief Justice Marshall's tenure, dissenting opinions were relatively rare. From 1801 to 1835, the Court rendered 1,244 opinions that elicited only seventy dissenting opinions. The low rate of dissonance reflected Marshall's own influence on the Court's procedures and direction. On becoming chief justice, Marshall abandoned the custom of individual opinions. By introducing a single opinion of the Court, he promoted analytical common ground and consensuality. The procedural change enabled the Court to speak in a single voice and significantly enhanced its institutional influence and status. So committed was Marshall to establishing unanimity that he reportedly changed his own vote on occasion to achieve it.

Marshall's concessions to appearance may have been sensible at a time when the judiciary was trying to establish its identity and consolidate its power. Once the Court's role was secured, such trade-offs could not be so easily justified. As Chief Justice Hughes noted:

When unanimity can be obtained without sacrifice of conviction, it strongly commends the decision to public confidence. But unanimity which is merely formal, which is recorded at the expense of strong, conflicting views, is not desirable in a court of last resort, whatever may be the effect upon public opinion at the time. This is so because what must ultimately sustain the court in public confidence is the character and independence of the judges. They are not there simply to decide cases, but to decide them as they think they should be decided, and while it may be regrettable that they cannot always agree, it is better that their independence should be maintained and recognized than that unanimity should be secured through its sacrifice.

Dissent became a more common phenomenon in the post-Marshall era. Factors that contributed to the increased discord were personnel change and the nature of issues presented to the Court. Slavery, for instance, posed questions that the Constitution's framers deliberately had left open in an effort to accommodate North and South and establish a viable union. Confronted eventually with the Constitutional Convention's unfinished business, as sectional antagonisms multiplied and hardened, unanimity proved increasingly elusive. Also contributing to competition rather than to consensuality of principle was Chief Justice Taney's factoring of state sovereignty and police powers in ways that qualified his predecessor's staunchly nationalist doctrine. The rate of dissent during Taney's era, which lasted for almost three decades, was nearly double that of Marshall's.

Even then, dissents were relatively infrequent by modern standards. The proportion of dissenting opinions, which constituted about five per cent of the written opinions during the Marshall period, neared ten per cent during Taney's tenure. Through the first third of the twentieth century, the ratio declined to about the level of the Marshall years. In the post–New Deal era, the rate of dissent has doubled that of the Taney era and quadrupled that of the Marshall period. The increase corresponds to the Court's expansion of individual rights, attention to equality interests and spirited debate over the validity and scope of such developments. Such dispute, given the nature of the issues and concerns, should be neither surprising nor unsettling. As Chief Justice Hughes observed:

Dissents in important controversies may be expected because they are cases in which it would be difficult for any body of lawyers freely selected to reach an accord. While the public may not understand division in the Court, because of an illusion as to attainable certitude in opinions as to the law, which is notably absent in other fields, it must be remembered that conviction must have its say and that the conservatism of the Court as a judicial body furnishes all the protection that is needed in the long run against capricious overturning of decisions.

As the following chapters demonstrate, the tradition of dissent has facilitated rather than challenged the interest of reason. In so doing, it has contributed to a balance between constitutional stability and change.

Bibliography

Cases

Branzburg v. Hayes, 408 U.S. 665 (1972).
Brown v. Board of Education, 347 U.S. 483 (1954).
Calder v. Bull, 3 U.S. 386 (1798).
Civil Rights Cases, 109 U.S. 3 (1883).
Dred Scott v. Sandford, 60 U.S. 393 (1857).
Georgia v. Brailsford, 2 U.S. 415 (1793).
Gibbons v. Ogden, 22 U.S. 1 (1824).
Griswold v. Connecticut, 381 U.S. 479 (1969).
Lochner v. New York, 198 U.S. 45 (1905).
Marbury v. Madison, 5 U.S. 137 (1803).
Olmstead v. United States, 277 U.S. 438 (1928).
Plessy v. Ferguson, 163 U.S. 537 (1896).
Prigg v. Pennsylvania, 41 U.S. 539 (1842).
Richmond, City of, v. J. A. Croson Co., 488 U.S. 469 (1989).
Slaughter-House Cases, 83 U.S. 36 (1873).
United States v. Carolene Products Co., 304 U.S. 144 (1938).
United States v. Nixon, 418 U.S. 683 (1974).
Whitney v. California, 274 U.S. 357 (1927).

Books and Articles

Blaustein, A., & Mersky, R., The First One Hundred Justices (1978).
Bork, R., The Tempting of America (1990).
Choper, J. (ed.), The Supreme Court and Its Justices (1987).
Frankfurter, F., *John Marshall and the Judicial Function*, 69 Harv. L. Rev. 217 (1955).
Hughes, C., The Supreme Court of the United States (1928).
Levy, L., Judicial Review and the Supreme Court (1967).
Meese, E., *The Law of the Constitution*, 61 Tul. L. Rev. 979 (1987).
Pfeffer, L., This Honorable Court (1965).

FORESHADOWS
OF THE LAW

Chapter 1

A CONSTITUTIONAL RIGHT IN SLAVERY

Ratification of the Constitution created a new political union. Even when consisting of only thirteen states, as it did in the immediate aftermath of revolution, the nation comprised many interests and competing priorities. The rivalries, differences and chauvinism of the several states were an impediment to but ultimately a reason for establishing a viable national union. Under the Articles of Confederation, which governed the nation in the years immediately after the American Revolution, the federal government had no power over interstate commerce. Minus centralized authority and uniformity of standards, the various states sought to maximize their respective advantage by means of taxation, tariffs and other trade barriers. As economic warfare devolved into economic chaos, it became apparent that the fledgling union would not prosper and might not survive without structural revision. A commonly sensed need to enhance national economic powers soon expanded into inspiration for the Constitutional Convention which, in 1787, generated the plan for a new political system.

Compromise and the Constitution

Not all differences among the states were resolved in the framing and ratification process. Brokering a new nation required compromise, the success of which depended on calculated ambiguity and manipulability of terms. Agreement with respect to the contents of the Constitution thus did not resolve all aspects of the document's meaning or even its general purpose. Even now, perceptions vary with respect to what the Constitutional Convention achieved and the charter it produced signifies. For some, the Constitution is notable as a source of individual rights and liberties that check the exercise of assigned governmental powers. For others, the document is essentially a blueprint of governmental structure and authority subject to specific restrictions on official action.

The establishment clause typifies how text was adapted to varying demands and interests two centuries ago, but has presented an interpretive problem since. The First Amendment provides, among other things, that "Congress shall make no law respecting an establishment of religion." When proposed and ratified, the establishment clause had diverse constituencies that shared little ideological common ground. The Virginia delegation favored the clause as a means of erecting a wall between church and state. Pennsylvania and Maryland saw it as a prohibition of sectarian discrimination essential to the maintenance of religious tolerance. Rhode Island and Connecticut supported the guarantee as a device for preserving their established state religions. A successful framing process depended on the generation of terms that accommodated such diverse and even incongruous concerns. For modern controversies that have arisen with respect to school prayer, bible reading and other religious practices or influences in public contexts, the original record yields conflicting possibilities for resolution. Such interpretive complications derive from the original need to bypass or defer differences that otherwise might have impeded the Constitution's creation.

As evidenced by its survival for over two centuries, the Constitution in its framing, ratification and interpretation has been largely successful in reconciling or resolving contradiction and conflict. Since establishing its power "to say what the law is," the Supreme Court has been the primary source of constitutional detail and animation. To the extent that the framing process left the scope of governmental power or personal guarantees uncertain, it has been the Court that has provided resolution. The interests of compromise, as noted previously, favored the drafting of broad principles. Once consensus was established, hard specifics still had to be worked out through the political and adjudicative processes. Although it may have been assumed that such debate and conflict would be negotiated within the system that the Constitution created, one aspect of unfinished business ultimately led to the union's undoing.

Slavery: The Cost of a Union

The institution of slavery presented an especially vexing problem to the chartering of the republic. The tension between the theory and the reality of personal freedom and equality was especially well evidenced by the words and actions of Thomas Jefferson. It was Jefferson who wrote the Declaration of Independence, which, in its opening paragraph, asserts that "[w]e hold these truths to be self-evident, that all men are created equal, that they are endowed by their Creator with certain unalienable Rights, that among these are Life, Liberty, and the Pursuit of Happiness." The self-evident truths so identified coexisted with the practice of slavery in which Jefferson himself engaged. On its face, the Declaration of Independence may have seemed irreconcilable with slavery. It stated a concept nonetheless that was subject to a subtle if not hidden qualifier. Contemporaneous with the Declaration of Independence, Virginia adopted its own Declaration of Rights in comparable terms. The notion "[t]hat all men are by nature equally free and independent" emphasized a status that attached only "when they enter into a state of society." The loophole in the Virginia declaration suggested an understanding that, if not universal at the time, denoted for many an implicit racial qualification applicable also to the Declaration of Independence. As the Supreme Court observed, just before the Civil War, the reference to "all men" translated into "white men."

By 1787, when the Constitutional Convention was held, the Virginia declaration had become the model for similar resolutions by other states. Gradual or immediate abolition by constitutional or legislative enactment, however, had been or was in the process of being achieved by then in New England, Pennsylvania, New York and New Jersey. At the convention itself, the legitimacy of slavery was a debated proposition that presented a question of legal and moral dimension. Jefferson himself, who was posted in France at the time, expressed concern that slavery was premised on "the most unremitting despotism on the one part, and degrading submissions on the other." Several delegates articulated antislavery positions and were prepared to risk the alienation of states such as Georgia and South Carolina, which demanded accommodation of the institution as the cost of joining the union. Differences with respect to slavery, although not the source of national apoplexy that it eventually became, were a significant cause of friction and uncertainty in 1787. As James Madison observed, sectional dispute at the convention arose

principally from the effects of . . . having or not having slaves. These two causes concur in forming the great division of interests in the U. States. It did not lie between the large [and] small states; it lay, between the Northern [and] Southern.

Although a slave owner himself at the time, Madison thought it "wrong to admit in the Constitution the idea that there could be property in men." Even if not directly referring to slavery by name, the framers in the interest of establishing a union nonetheless agreed at least to accommodate it. The premise in 1787, therefore, was that each state could decide for itself whether to allow slavery within its jurisdiction. Slavery was not to be a concern of the national government, except to the extent that the Constitution assigned it an interest as it did, for instance, in prohibiting the slave trade after 1807 and somewhat less clearly in accounting for fugitive slaves. By such a distribution of responsibility and interest, it was anticipated that the differences among states could be reconciled and a viable union established.

The solution of self-determination by each state represented a conscious and calculated accommodation that ultimately was a concession to slavery itself. National policy established a safe harbor within which the institution could flourish. Actual maintenance of that zone of security, as future events demonstrated, required not merely complicity of but eventual nurturing by free states, the federal government and the nation itself. By its terms, the Constitution specifically prohibited federal interference with the slave trade until 1808, at which time Congress's general power to regulate foreign commerce would no longer be qualified. It also reckoned, at least indirectly, with the legal status of slaves for the purpose of ascertaining how they should be counted for purposes of taxation and political representation. Consistent with the logic of compromise, rather than with perceptions of slaves as exclusively persons or property, apportionment provisions established the hybrid status of "three-fifths" of a person. Finally, the fugitive slave clause seems to have anticipated a basic problem inherent in a system housing both free and slave jurisdictions. Although no record exists to clearly define the clause's full purpose, the provision suggests the obligation of all states to cooperate in returning runaway slaves to their owners. Within a few years of ratification, Congress enacted fugitive slave legislation that confirmed slaveowners' rights to reclaim runaways as a matter of national policy. As discussed later, the fugitive slave clause and federal law it engendered were critical aspects of accommodation that eventually proved critical to the perception of slavery as a pervasive rather than localized condition.

The compromise of northern and southern agendas, although leaving significant loose ends, made possible the Constitution's ratification and the union's formation. The early assumption and premise for compromise was that free and slave states could coexist. Contributing to the credibility of a long-term accord was the sense that slavery was a dying institution that eventually would expire of natural causes. Even if not concurring in the diagnosis, the Georgia and South Carolina delegations had no interest in disabusing such notions. Optimistic calculations of slavery's ultimate demise made rationalization of it in the meantime that much easier. Subsequent history disclosed that perceptions of slavery as a terminal institution were as misplaced as expectations that free and slave states could endure in the same union.

The Loose Ends of Slavery

The unfinished business of the framers, as the nineteenth century unfolded, became an increasingly significant preoccupation of Congress and the Supreme Court. Two factors of greater and lesser predictability when the union was formed proved especially influential in the postratification definition and development of the slavery issue. Both territorial acquisition and fugitive slave problems were specifically anticipated by the Constitution. Less comprehended in 1787 perhaps was the nation's rapid geographical expansion during the early eighteenth century and the intense sectional competition it bred to define standards for the nation's growth and governance. In the same year the Constitution was framed, Congress enacted the Northwest Ordinance which created the Northwest Territory and prohibited slavery therein. The process of enactment contained few hints of the controversy and antagonism future territorial questions would present. Throughout the first half of the nineteenth century, territorial acquisition and development presented serial opportunities for increasingly divisive revisitings of the slavery issue. For each territory's proposed creation and each state's proposed admission, slavery became a pivotal and complicating factor. What divided the Constitutional Convention in 1787 became a continuous and compounding challenge to the political process.

The Missouri Compromise, which in 1820 provided for the admission of Missouri and Maine respectively as slave and free states and established a geographical bright line between slave and free territory, was a model of resolution grounded in past experience. Compromise is a workable option to the extent that disputing parties perceive an acceptable rate of return from the agreement. As expectations and demands escalate to the point that agendas are mutually exclusive, the capacity for compromise eventually is exceeded. Despite the centrality of territorial and statehood issues to sectional conflict, they were not directly addressed by the judiciary until a few years before the Civil War. At least through the first half of the nineteenth century, both sides looked to the political process as the primary means of negotiating advantage and protecting interests. A notable aspect of that process were efforts by North and South respectively to shape the territories in their own images. Given a finite number of territories and states that eventually would emerge, controversy over extension or restriction of slavery was perceived as a zero sum game. As recognition of the ultimate stakes heightened, each side became motivated to fortify the ideological underpinnings of their respective positions. Because the Constitution is the supreme statement of society's law, North and South alike had strong incentive to capture its meaning for their respective interests. What eventually became central to doctrinal development for or against slavery, therefore, was the Constitution itself.

Although further slave importation was foreclosed by federal law in 1808, the nation's slave population continued to grow. By 1830, it totaled two million. Such numbers demonstrated how misplaced earlier calculations were of slavery's natural demise. Consistent with and reflective of excessive optimism about slavery's ultimate destiny were early concepts for ridding the nation of the institution. The African Colonization Society and like organizations, for instance, advocated repatriation and resettlement programs. The first generation of abolitionists, in the late eighteenth and early nineteenth centuries, pushed gradual emancipation which often represented a compromise between slavery and freedom. Slavery was entirely abolished in some states, but in others emancipation was provided only after a certain number of years of service. Both movements assumed slavery's eventual and natural devolution, and thus made no demands that were unsettling to slave interests.

As the slave population swelled, notions of slavery as a terminal institution and of gradual emancipation became demonstrably illusory. Responding to those circumstances in the early 1830s was another wave of abolitionist sentiment that sought total and prompt eradication of slavery. The new strain of abolitionism differed from its ideological forebears in two significant ways, as it demanded immediate rather than gradual emancipation and contemplated assimilation rather than expatriation of former slaves. The call for immediate rather than gradual abolition never became a dominant movement, at least before the Civil War. The impact of second-generation abolitionism, however, was profound. Abolitionists challenged the proposition of accommodation, which assumed that slavery was legal where authorized by state law. The direct attack on slavery, coupled with fears of slave rebellion exacerbated by actual uprisings, prompted the South to fortify the institution. Among other things, southern states prohibited dissemination of anti-slavery literature, and representatives secured a House rule providing for automatic tabling of anti-slavery petitions. Responding in even more defensive terms, some legislators argued that abolitionists had no right to petition the national legislature in anti-slavery terms and Congress had no jurisdiction to receive such grievances.

Fortifying the premises at both poles of the debate were revisionist readings of the Constitution. The more radical abolitionists, typified by William Lloyd Garrison, regarded the Constitution as a pro-slavery document. So defective was it, at least from the Garrisonian perspective, that the only remedy was disunion of the nation. An equally significant strand of abolitionist thought favored development of the Constitution to defeat slavery. From the moderate abolitionist point of view, provisions such as the due process clause and the privileges and immunities clause presented interpretive opportunities for securing liberty and equality. Like the abolitionists, the South also looked to the Constitution for counterargument and vindication. In a Senate speech delivered in 1836, John C. Calhoun referred to slaves as property and an interest thereby protected by the Fifth Amendment guarantee against deprivation without due process of law.

Two decades before the Supreme Court upheld slavery in *Dred Scott v. Sandford*, indications thus were of an issue evolving from a political into a constitutional controversy. Demographics and ideology had contributed to slavery's status as a durable phenomenon rather than a terminal institution. Rationalization of slavery's demise or gradual abolition, which enabled free and slave systems to coexist in relatively satisfactory terms, had been displaced by realities and premises that eventually necessitated refocusing on the nation's fundamental law. Arrangements that were premised on continuity of a static order had been destabilized by territorial expansion, which reminded the South of its political vulnerability, and abolitionism, which stressed the region's moral vulnerability. Despite a substantial middle ground that favored maintenance of the union and original premises of accommodation, a significant new dimension of the slavery debate suggested mutually exclusive propositions. For abolitionists, the union and slavery could not exist together. The Southern counterpoint was that the union and abolition were incompatible.

The progress of slavery from an issue of political compromise toward one of constitutional resolution injected a new institutional factor into the controversy. As the case for and against slavery acquired increasingly significant constitutional overtones, it became the function of the Supreme Court to "say what the law is." Before the 1840s, the Court had addressed issues relating to slavery but not implicating its general legitimacy or the premises of sectional accommodation. In verifying Congress's power to prohibit further importing of slaves, the Court had described the slave trade itself as "inhuman traffic that was contrary to the laws of nature." Prior to abolition itself, however, it never translated any moral reservations about slavery into a general anti-slavery principle.

As competition over the meaning of the Constitution intensified, the Court was called on to resolve questions that were perceived as crucial to slavery's legitimacy and viability. Even if slavery had to be accommodated, debate existed with respect to the extent of cooperation required. Dispute over the allowability or impermissibility of slavery in the territories, as the nation's frontier pushed westward, was a persistent source and reminder of sectional differences and frictions that were compounded by the negotiation of each new territory or state. Rivaling controversies over territory and statehood as a source of mutual antagonism was the fugitive slave controversy.

Fugitive Slave Controversy

The dispute over the status of fugitive slaves probably had more symbolic than practical significance. From an economic standpoint, a runaway slave even if recaptured had diminished market value attributable to demonstrated unreliability. The willingness of Northern states to facilitate the return of runaway slaves was a significant indicator to the South of sincerity and cooperative spirit in accommodating slavery. For North and South alike, the fugitive slave controversy became graphic evidence of systemic incompatibility.

Runaway slave problems drew the attention of the Constitutional Convention, which drafted the fugitive clause, and Congress, which passed the Fugitive Slave Act of 1793. The enactment actually was prompted less by specific runaway slave problems than by a dispute among states over general criminal extradition. The law affirmed the duty of one state to return a fugitive from justice to another and established the right of a slave owner to recapture a runaway slave. Although the measure was based on the fugitive slave clause, the linkage was at least questionable. The Constitution provides that:

No Person held to Service or Labour in one State, under the laws thereof, escaping into another, shall, in Consequence of any Law or Regulation therein, be discharged from such Service or Labour, but shall be delivered up on Claim of the Party to whom such Service or Labour may be due.

Although identifying a duty of returning runaway slaves, the fugitive slave clause assigned to Congress no power to enforce it by legislation. Because the clause is housed in Article IV, Section 2, which concerns interstate relations, rather than in Article I, which enumerates the powers of the national legislature, congressional implementation of it was at least a debatable proposition.

Despite its dubious constitutional pedigree, the Fugitive Slave Act of 1793 was passed without significant controversy or opposition. By its terms, it allowed a slave owner to pursue and seize a slave in a free jurisdiction and on proof of ownership obtain a judicial order providing for the slave's return to captivity. Missing from the act was any semblance of rudimentary due process for the alleged slave. At best, the law superseded basic guarantees relating to a jury trial, habeas corpus and presentation of evidence. The process, at worst, invited fraud, mistake and blatant disregard of procedure in favor of outright kidnapping.

Given the absence of meaningful procedural guarantees under the federal law, several Northern states passed personal liberty laws. Common enactments included provisions for writs of habeas corpus, anti-kidnapping laws and specified procedures for recapture that demanded more detailed proof of ownership. Such legislation enhanced protection for runaway slaves and free blacks but did not create insurmountable obstacles to recapture. Even though the state laws were not necessarily inimical to recovery of fugitive slaves, the South perceived them as a peril to slavery itself. From the Southern perspective, personal liberty laws and their ilk raised doubt about the North's good faith.

Because federal legislation derived from the fugitive slave clause, it was possible to argue that the action of Northern states compromised not only the interests of slave owners but also the Constitution itself. Even though the connection to the Constitution was dubious, strong incentive existed to exploit it. By 1840, the fugitive slave clause was being described by Southerners as having been essential to the Constitution's ratification and the union's formation. Overlooked was the fact that the historical record is largely empty with respect to why the clause was included and that it seems to have been adopted without much reflection toward the convention's end. Implicit in the Southern position nonetheless was the notion that default on fugitive slave obligations was equivalent to breach of the union's premise itself.

The concept of the fugitive slave clause as a critical condition of the Constitution's passage initially tapped effectively into Northern understanding of union obligations. Consistent with premises of sectional cooperation essential to the union's maintenance, Northern jurisprudence responded sympathetically to the interests of slave owners in reclaiming runaways. The Supreme Judicial Court of Massachusetts in *Commonwealth v. Aves,* for instance, ruled in favor of a slave who claimed freedom based on mere sojourner status in a free state. In distinguishing the sojourner question, however, the court referred to the fugitive slave clause as the virtual linchpin of the union. As related by Chief Justice Lemuel Shaw in 1836, it was

manifestly the intent and the object of one party to this compact to enlarge, extend and secure, as far as possible, the rights and powers of the owners of slaves, within their own limits, as well as in other States, and of the other party to limit and restrain them. Under these circumstances the clause in question was agreed on and introduced into the constitution; . . . was intended to secure future peace and harmony . . . [and should be interpreted] to afford effectual security to the owners of slaves. The States have a plenary power to make all laws necessary for the regulation of slavery and the rights of the slave owners, while the slaves remain within their territorial limits; and it is only when they escape, without the consent of their owners, into other States, that they require the aid of other States, to enable them to regain their dominion over the fugitives.

The *Aves* decision enhanced constitutional mythology with respect to the fugitive slave clause and acknowledged the incidental responsibilities as a fundamental condition of the union itself. It also previewed how the fugitive slave controversy would be resolved by the U.S. Supreme Court.

Prigg v. Pennsylvania

The Fugitive Slave Act itself became a focal point of review in 1842, after a slave catcher convicted for violation of a state anti-kidnapping law challenged the enactment's constitutionality. The circumstances resulting in *Prigg v. Pennsylvania* disclosed precisely the abuses that had prompted legislative concern and action in free states. The case arose when a Pennsylvania woman and her children were claimed by a slave owner in Maryland. Although her parents had been slaves, the woman had not been claimed as such until after having moved to Pennsylvania. There she married a free man, had children and resided for several years. The Pennsylvania court refused to provide a certificate of removal, but the woman and her children were captured and returned to Maryland anyway. The slave catcher's conviction under the Pennsylvania anti-kidnapping law prompted a challenge to the constitutionality of the Fugitive Slave Act and consequent allowability of conflicting state law.

In resolving the controversy, the Court determined that (1) the federal act was constitutional, (2) state law in conflict with it was impermissible and (3) slave owners or their agents could seize and recover fugitive slaves largely by their own devices. The Court's opinion was authored by Justice Story, who reiterated the notion that the fugitive slave clause was indispensable to the Constitution's very being. The provision's inclusion in the nation's charter, from the Court's perspective, established an unqualified right of slave owners to recapture a runaway in any jurisdiction. Such a determination essentially extended the law of the South into the North for fugitive slave purposes. As noted previously, the fugitive slave clause did not expressly vest Congress with enforcement authority. Still, the Court found that congressional power to enact the federal law could be reasonably inferred. The Court also dismissed arguments that the provision violated rights secured by the privileges and immunities clause and the due process clause as well as the guarantee against unreasonable seizures afforded by the Fourth Amendment. Even if a free black person was wrongfully seized, the *Prigg* decision affirmed that he or she had no claim to constitutional protection.

A critical aspect of the decision, insofar as it caused division within the Court, was the determination that Congress had an exclusive interest in accounting for slave owner rights with respect to runaways. Although not essential to the disposition of the case, such a finding was consistent with jurisprudence that in the half century before *Dred Scott* struck down not a single federal law. The dubious status of the fugitive slave clause, as a source of enforcement power, at least offered the possibility of a different result. The principle of federal exclusivity, even though supportive of slavery interests in *Prigg* itself, was a perilous proposition for the South. Even if federal power had been exercised to secure slave owner interests in recapturing runaway slaves, no guarantee existed that congressional priorities would remain unaltered. The South's worst fear, compounded by the fear of abolitionism and political isolation, was that federal policy might tilt against slavery and the states would be powerless to protect it. The *Prigg* opinion instead of ameliorating slave state concern, therefore, actually exacerbated mistrust and suspicion.

Further contributing to Southern dissatisfaction was the Court's observation that, although Congress could authorize state courts to enforce the federal act, it could not compel them to do so. Combined with his comment that state judges could enforce the law, unless prohibited by state legislation, Story related what in another context might have been regarded as an acceptable principle of federalism. In the aftermath of *Prigg*, however, many Northern states cited to the decision for purposes of passing laws prohibiting their courts from implementing federal policy. A ruling cast in terms that largely accounted for the rights of slave owners thus was converted into the services of anti-slavery objectives.

Story's characterization of the federal interest, and its potentially unsettling consequences, did not escape critical notice within the Court itself. Chief Justice Taney recognized that an exclusive federal function, even if favorable to slavery in *Prigg*, could mutate into hostility later. Dissatisfied with the Court's depiction of Congress's role, Taney stressed that the Constitution not only prohibited state interference with a slave owner's rights, but obligated the states to protect them as well. Even though concurring in the judgment, Taney disagreed with the Court's reasoning and advanced the theory of a diminished federal interest and slave owner interests grounded in the Constitution itself.

Roger B. Taney

As slavery became an increasingly significant constitutional issue, Taney emerged as a vigorous defender of the culture that maintained the institution. Taney himself was born and raised on a Maryland plantation but eventually liberated his own slaves. He commenced his political career as a Federalist which, barring other considerations and influences, might have suggested a more sympathetic response to the nationalist overtones of the *Prigg* majority. His response to slavery questions, however, ultimately was consistent with the hallmarks of his personal and professional development. Like many others who manumitted their slaves, Taney maintained the conviction that blacks were inferior and did not merit the civil and political status afforded whites. Despite his Federalist roots, Taney by the mid-1820s had become an ardent Jacksonian Democrat and aligned himself with the national party's pro-slavery wing.

In 1831, President Jackson rewarded Taney for his political service by appointing him attorney general of the United States. In that capacity, Taney furnished counsel on the status of free blacks that effectively previewed the conclusions he reached in the *Dred Scott* case a quarter of a century later. Particularly relevant was his opinion on the status of black crew members aboard ships using ports in Southern states. Previous attorney general opinions had reached conflicting results. One had determined that federal power over foreign and interstate commerce preempted a South Carolina law prohibiting black sailors from the state's ports. Another had found that such exclusions were a legitimate exercise of state power under the Tenth Amendment.

Neither opinion addressed the possibility that free blacks might have a claim to equality of treatment as citizens of other states. The privileges and immunities clause of Article IV, Section 2, providing that "[t]he Citizens of each State shall be entitled to all Privileges and Immunities of Citizens in the several States," arguably offered a basis for requiring that free blacks from other jurisdictions be accorded the same rights and protections that a slave state afforded its own citizens. Taney's counsel to the president, consistent with the later premise of *Dred Scott,* was that the Constitution neither afforded citizenship to nor conferred rights on free blacks. As he put it:

The African race in the United States even when free, are everywhere a degraded class, and exercise no political influence. The privileges they are allowed to enjoy, are accorded to them as a matter of kindness and benevolence rather than of right. They are the only class of persons who can be held as mere property, as slaves. . . . They were never regarded as a constituent portion of the sovereignty of any state. . . . They were not looked upon as citizens by the contracting parties who formed the Constitution. They were evidently not supposed to be included by the term *citizens.* And were not intended to be embraced in any of the provisions of that Constitution but those which point to them in terms not to be mistaken.

When Taney first was nominated to the Supreme Court in 1835, the Senate refused to confirm him. On Chief Justice Marshall's death, President Jackson again nominated Taney. As in the previous confirmation proceeding, partisan opposition arose based on Taney's role in helping Jackson eliminate the national bank. Despite significant Senate opposition that included some pro-slavery legislators, Taney secured enough votes to succeed Marshall as chief justice.

Preview of *Dred Scott*

Unlike his predecessor, Taney envisioned a Constitution that was less tilted to the interests of nationalism. He made especially notable contributions to doctrine that accommodates exercises of state police power not directly conflicting with the federal authority over interstate commerce. His disagreement with the majority in *Prigg,* however, reflected the sense that Congress's interest in slavery was not exclusive and that all states had an obligation to help slave owners secure their interests. He accordingly observed that

The opinion of the court maintains, that the power over this subject is so exclusively vested in congress, that no state, since the adoption of the constitution, can pass any law in relation to it. In other words, according to the opinion just delivered, the state authorities are prohibited from interfering, for the purpose of protecting the right of the master, and aiding him in the recovery of his property. I think, the states are not prohibited; and that, on the contrary, it is enjoined upon them as a duty, to protect and support the owner, when he is endeavoring to obtain possession of his property found within their respective territories. The language used in the constitution does not, in my judgment, justify the construction given to it by the court. It contains no words prohibiting the several states from passing laws to enforce this right. They are, in express terms, forbidden to make any regulation that shall impair it; but there the prohibition stops. And according to the settled rules of construction for all written instruments, the prohibition being confined to laws injurious to the right, the power to pass laws to support and enforce it, is necessarily implied. And the words of the article which direct that the fugitive "shall be delivered up" seem evidently designed to impose it as a duty upon the people of the several states, to pass laws to carry into execution, in good faith, the compact into which they thus solemnly entered with each other.

Also advanced by Taney in *Prigg,* to be developed more fully in *Dred Scott,* was the notion that slave owner rights not only were accommodated but also secured by the Constitution. As Taney put it:

The constitution of the United States, and every article and clause in it, is a part of the law of every state in the Union; and is the paramount law. The right of the master, therefore, to seize his fugitive slave, is the law of each state; and no state has the power to abrogate or alter it. And why may not a state protect a right of property, acknowledged by its own paramount law? Besides, the laws of the different states, in all other cases, constantly protect the citizens of other states in their rights of property, when it is found within their respective territories; and no one doubts their power to do so. And in the absence of any express prohibition, I perceive no reason for establishing, by implication, a different rule in this instance; where, by the national compact, this right of property is recognized as an existing right in every state of the Union.

The intimation that slavery was a property right of constitutional significance reflected the inexorable hardening of Southern ideology. It initially had been accepted, both in the North and in the South, that slavery was allowable only to the extent provided for by local law. Taney suggested a right that was grounded in the Constitution and, at least for fugitive slave purposes, extended into every state of the union. His argument against federal exclusivity on fugitive slave questions was paralleled and extended in *Dred Scott,* when the Court denied Congress any authority over slavery in the territories. Taney's opinion also presaged decisions that, over the next fifteen years, increasingly emphasized slave owner rights, identified duties to protect those interests and linked them to the Constitution itself.

The *Prigg* decision also revealed a divided Court presiding over an increasingly divided nation. Story's judgment and opinion had elicited disagreement from Justice McLean who, as discussed in Chapter 2, also dissented in *Dred Scott.* McLean was concerned with the failure of federal law to protect free blacks who might be wrongly seized. He maintained that personal liberty laws accounted for a legitimate state interest and were not incompatible with federal policy. The Court's division in *Prigg* was not between abolitionism and slavery, therefore, but over the extent of accommodation required to maintain the union.

The *Prigg* decision not only established a precedent in a formal sense. It also introduced a model of review for slavery issues that decided more than was necessary for resolution of a particular case. Normative standards require that a court only reach those questions that are essential for disposition of the controversy. Although such criteria were abandoned in the extreme, in *Dred Scott,* the habit of saying too much with respect to slavery commenced in *Prigg..* The Court's decision in *Strader v. Graham* furthered that dubious tradition. The *Strader* case arose when a slave owner in Kentucky sued persons who had helped his slaves escape. The state court had rejected a defense theory that the slaves were liberated on reaching a free state. The Supreme Court determined that the case did not present a federal question and accordingly dismissed it for lack of jurisdiction. A resolution on procedural grounds should have ended the inquiry, but Taney on behalf the Court addressed the underlying dispute. Despite having determined that the substantive question was beyond the Court's jurisdiction, Taney endorsed the Kentucky court's analysis and conclusion. The Court thus approved the proposition that status was to be determined by the law of the slave state rather than by the law of the free state.

The *Strader* decision also represented a significant extension of Taney's thinking in *Prigg*—at least in spirit. The defense had argued that, because the slaves had escaped to Ohio, they were free pursuant to federal law.

Cited to specifically was the Northwest Ordinance of 1787 which, in creating territory that eventually became the states of Ohio, Michigan and Indiana, prohibited slavery there. Taney noted that the federal law had been superseded by the constitutions and laws of the states. He concluded more importantly that, assuming the federal ordinance still was applicable, it would have no more effect than the law of a free state. Taney thereby made a point, not necessitated by the case itself, of diminishing the asserted federal interest. The gratuitous nature of the observation underscored its significance.

Historical Prelude to *Dred Scott*

Resolution of slavery questions in overbroad terms was a phenomenon that reached its peak in the *Dred Scott* case. The departure from traditional norms of restraint was not entirely surprising under the circumstances. The two decades before *Dred Scott* were characterized by the provocativeness of abolitionism, an escalating Southern sense of vulnerability, a rising consciousness in the North of how fugitive slave obligations involved it in slavery generally and worsening frictions over the status of new territories and states. Such developments presented a severe test for the model of political compromise that was established in 1787 and was reasonably effective in the Missouri statehood controversy. The Compromise of 1850 represented an effort to broker comprehensively the multiplying and widening differences between North and South. Critical aspects of the legislated agreement included a new fugitive slave law, admission of California to the union as a free state, creation of the Utah and New Mexico territories as slave jurisdictions and prohibition of the slave trade in the District of Columbia.

Although the Compromise of 1850 was envisioned as a final solution to the slavery problem, subsequent events demonstrated how illusory such aims were. The compromise in part resolved a controversy fueled a few years earlier by the Wilmot Proviso, which was proposed in Congress to prohibit slavery in any territory acquired from Mexico. Despite attracting widespread support in the House, the measure, which would have applied to a vast expanse of land including what became California, ultimately was defeated. A Southern proposal to extend the Missouri Compromise line to the West Coast also was defeated. The Wilmot Proviso was especially agitating to the South, because it would have sealed off any westward expansion of slavery. The proposal contributed to a mounting sense of siege and perception that Northern objections to slavery were evolving toward a challenge of the institution itself.

The brokering of sectional disputes in 1850 did not resolve the problem of accumulating mutual distrust and suspicion. Divisiveness contributed to the stiffening of ideology, as both sides polished constitutional principles suited to their respective causes. Free soil concepts, supporting the notion of congressional regulation of slavery in the territories, attracted a constituency in the North that was strong enough to support an independent presidential candidacy in 1848. By the mid-1850s, free soil principles had helped to inspire the creation of the Republican Party. Competing against free soil doctrine and abolitionism were principles of popular sovereignty. As touted especially by the Southern wing of the Democratic Party, popular sovereignty maintained that the people of each territory should decide the question of slavery for themselves when they framed their constitutions for statehood. A corollary of popular sovereignty was that Congress had no power under the territory clause of the Constitution to regulate slavery.

Organization of the Nebraska Territory, which covered land from what is now Kansas to the Canadian border, erupted into especially bitter sectional controversy during the early 1850s. In debates over the new territory, the South proposed the extension of slavery north of the Missouri Compromise line. The strategy reversed the position slave states had subscribed to a few years earlier in debates over the Wilmot Proviso, when they proposed a westward extension of the line. The new Southern demand signaled that it was no longer prepared to accept federal preclusion of slavery in the territories. As eventually passed, the Kansas-Nebraska Act allowed for territorial organization pursuant to popular sovereignty and reconfigured the boundary between slavery and freedom etched a few decades earlier by the Missouri Compromise. The immediate aftermath of the legislation was widespread fraud, chicanery and violence as proslavery and anti-slavery forces vied to shape the Kansas constitution in their respective images. Equally if not more significant was political fall-out in the North characterized by widespread purging of representatives who had supported the legislation. The Kansas–Nebraska controversy, resulting in the wholesale loss of congressional seats by Northern Democrats in 1854 and emergence of the Republican Party, proved to be a significant catalyst in the redistribution of political loyalties that further clarified regional differences.

As the decade before the Civil War unfolded, the union's status was in evident peril. With political positions increasingly being defined by competing perspectives of what the Constitution demanded, the Supreme Court became a logical forum in which to address the ultimate question of slavery. Further working toward a judicial resolution were the diminishing returns of compromise and futility of the political process in putting sectional antagonisms to rest. In his inaugural address in 1857, President Buchanan referred to the debate over federal territorial powers as "a judicial question, which legitimately belongs to the Supreme Court of the United States, before whom it is now pending, and will, it is understood, be speedily and finally settled." Buchanan's statement may have been self-interested, insofar as he had advance notice of an impending decision by the Court to his liking, but it at least expressed a common desire for an authoritative resolution.

The *Dred Scott* Decision

What was offered as a comprehensive and conclusive decision on slavery in *Dred Scott v. Sandford* proved anything but final. If not for its political, moral and constitutional significance, the *Dred Scott* case might be noted primarily for its technical complexity and procedural irregularity. Litigation leading to Supreme Court review had commenced in 1846 when Scott sought and received permission to sue for his freedom in a Missouri court. His claim to freedom was premised on having resided for several years with his owner, an army doctor posted in the free territory of Minnesota and the free state of Illinois. Missouri law at the time of original filing actually supported Scott's claims. A jury verdict was returned against him, however, because of an evidentiary oversight of failing to establish that the defendant actually owned him. At a second trial, the jury ruled in Scott's favor. In 1852, the Missouri Supreme Court reversed the verdict. Relying on *Strader v. Graham,* the court determined that it was not bound by the law of another state and concluded that Scott was still a slave.

A year later, Scott filed another suit for freedom in federal court alleging essentially the same facts and theory. Asserting that Scott was of African descent, and thus not a citizen of Missouri, the defendant challenged the court's jurisdiction. The trial judge ruled that, even if not a citizen for general purposes, Scott was qualified to sue in federal court. With respect to the basic issue concerning whether Scott was subject to the defendant's control, the court found that he was.

As presented to the Supreme Court, the *Dred Scott* case could have been resolved on narrow grounds that the law of a slave state rather than of a free state or territory was outcome determinative. The Court also could have decided that, because the litigants were not citizens of different states as required for purposes of federal jurisdiction, it could not reach the merits of the dispute. Instead of deciding the case in such procedural terms, the Court seized the opportunity to expound broadly on the constitutionality of slavery.

The *Dred Scott* decision consists of nine separate opinions, including two dissents. The opinion of the Court was authored by Chief Justice Taney who, in *Prigg,* had challenged the concept of an exclusive federal interest in fugitive slaves and advanced the notion that slave owner rights were constitutionally derived. In *Dred Scott,* Taney extended his reasoning to deny congressional power over slavery in the territories and identify a specific constitutional predicate for the rights of slave owners.

Taney devoted a significant part of his opinion to the proposition that all persons of African descent—not only slaves—had been excluded from citizenship and rights under the Constitution. The determination rested on the premise that when the republic was chartered, black persons were

regarded as beings of an inferior order, and altogether unfit to associate with the white race, either in social or political relations; and so far inferior, that they had no rights which the white man was bound to respect; and that the negro might justly and lawfully be reduced to slavery for his benefit.

The notion that an entire racial class was unqualified for citizenship, possessed no rights and properly was relegated to slavery was at best dubious and at worst a perversion of history. When the Constitution was framed, several states afforded not only citizenship, but also basic civil rights without respect to race.

The determination that blacks possessed neither citizenship nor rights defined constitutional law in precisely the terms Taney had proposed as attorney general in the Jackson administration. Consistent with and even exceeding his argument for reduced federal authority and interest in *Prigg* was Taney's determination that Congress had no power to prohibit slavery in the territories. In determining that the Missouri Compromise was unconstitutional, the Court for the first time since *Marbury v. Madison* struck down a federal law. Article IV, Section 3 [2] of the Constitution enables Congress "to dispose of and make all needful Rules and Regulations respecting the Territory . . . belonging to the United States." Decades of political compromise in the organization and governance of territories had evidenced an understanding in the North and South that the general authority to regulate territories included the lesser authority to regulate slavery therein. Established practice, however, became the casualty of unbending ideology that shaped the Constitution in terms denying such a federal power. Responding to the claim that Scott's freedom was established by the Missouri Compromise, which prohibited slavery in the state and territory in which he had resided, Taney observed that

the difficulty which meets us at the threshold of this part of the inquiry is, whether Congress was authorized to pass this law under any of the powers granted to it by the Constitution; for if the authority is not given by that instrument, it is the duty of this court to declare it void and inoperative, and incapable of conferring freedom upon any one who is held as a slave under the laws of any one of the States.

The counsel for the plaintiff has laid much stress upon that article in the Constitution which confers on Congress the power "to dispose of and make all needful rules and regulations respecting the territory or other property belonging to the United States"; but, in the judgment of the court, that provision has no bearing on the present controversy, and the power there given, whatever it may be, is confined, and was intended to be confined, to the territory which at that time belonged to, or was claimed by, the United States, and was within their boundaries as settled by the treaty with Great Britain, and can have no influence upon a territory afterwards acquired from a foreign Government. It was a special provision for a known and particular territory, and to meet a present emergency, and nothing more.

As Taney described it, the territory clause was a narrow charge authorizing Congress to maintain claims to lands not yet ceded by the states, to regulate only the realty itself and property attached to it and to govern territories that already existed in 1787. As interpreted by the Court, the clause afforded Congress no power to regulate slavery in any territory acquired after the Constitution was ratified.

Having vitiated the Missouri Compromise and denied Congress the power to regulate slavery in what had become the greater part of the nation, Taney depicted slavery as an institution that was secured by the Constitution itself. In *Prigg,* Taney had referred generally to slave owner rights as being constitutionally derived. He reinforced the premise in *Dred Scott* by adverting to constitutional restrictions on congressional interference with the slave trade and the fugitive slave clause. Taken together, they indicated to Taney a "right to purchase and hold this property [that] is directly sanctioned and authorized by the people who framed the Constitution" and a duty "to maintain and uphold the right of the master in the manner specified, as long as the Government shall endure." In referring to what he identified as "the right of property in a slave [being] distinctly and expressly affirmed in the Constitution," Taney maintained that slaves like any other property were protected against federal interference by the due process clause of the Fifth Amendment.

But the power of Congress over the person or property of a citizen can never be a mere discretionary power under our Constitution and form of Government. The powers of the Government and the rights and privileges of the citizen are regulated and plainly defined by the Constitution itself. And when the Territory becomes a part of the United States, the Federal Government enters into possession in the character impressed upon it by those who created it. It enters upon it with its powers over the citizen strictly defined, and limited by the Constitution, from which it derives its own existence, and by virtue of which alone it continues to exist and act as a Government and sovereignty. It has no power of any kind beyond it; and it cannot, when it enters a Territory of the United States, put off its character, and assume discretionary or despotic powers which the Constitution has denied to it. It cannot create for itself a new character separated from the citizens of the United States, and the duties it owes them under the provisions of the Constitution. The Territory being a part of the United States, the Government and the citizen both enter it under the authority of the Constitution, with their respective rights defined and marked out; and the Federal Government can exercise no power over his person or property, beyond what that instrument confers, nor lawfully deny any right which it has reserved.

A reference to a few of the provisions of the Constitution will illustrate this proposition.

For example, no one, we presume, will contend that Congress can make any law in a Territory respecting the establishment of religion, or the free exercise thereof, or abridging the freedom of speech or of the press, or the right of the people of the Territory peaceably to assemble, and to petition the Government for the redress of grievances.

Nor can Congress deny to the people the right to keep and bear arms, nor the right to trial by jury, nor compel any one to be a witness against himself in a criminal proceeding.

These powers, and others, in relation to rights of person, which it is not necessary here to enumerate, are, in express and positive terms, denied to the General Government; and the rights of private property have been guarded with equal care. Thus the rights of property are united with the rights of person, and placed on the same ground by the fifth amendment to the Constitution, which provides that no person shall be deprived of life, liberty, and property, without due process of law. And an act of Congress which deprives a citizen of the United States of his liberty or property, merely because he came himself or brought his property into a particular Territory of the United States, and who had committed no offence against the laws, could hardly be dignified with the name of due process of law. . . .

Now, as we have already said in an earlier part of this opinion, upon a different point, the right of property in a slave is distinctly and expressly affirmed in the Constitution. The right to traffic in it, like an ordinary article of merchandise and property, was guarantied to the citizens of the United States, in every State that might desire it, for twenty years. And the Government in express terms is pledged to protect it in all future time, if the slave escapes from his owner. This is done in plain words—too plain to be misunderstood. And no word can be found in the Constitution which gives Congress a greater power over slave property, or which entitles property of that kind to less protection than property of any other description. The only power conferred is the power coupled with the duty of guarding and protecting the owner in his rights.

Upon these considerations, it is the opinion of the court that the act of Congress which prohibited a citizen from holding and owning property of this kind in the territory of the United States north of the line therein mentioned, is not warranted by the Constitution, and is therefore void; and that neither Dred Scott himself, nor any of his family, were made free by being carried into this territory; even if they had been carried there by the owner, with the intention of becoming a permanent resident.

The Fifth Amendment, providing that "[n]o person shall be . . . deprived of life, liberty, or property, without due process of law," previously had been interpreted as a source of procedural safeguards. The concept of substantive due process, as discussed in Chapters 4 and 7, has since become an established but controversial source of fundamental rights and restraint on legislative power. As introduced by Taney in *Dred Scott,* such analysis affirmatively tied slave owner rights to the Constitution and precluded legislation burdening the use of such property.

Taney's Fifth Amendment premise pushed constitutional principle beyond accommodation of slavery to the point of unqualified security for the institution. The conclusion, that the "right of property in a slave is distinctly and expressly affirmed in the Constitution," disregarded the fact that the document identifies no such right with particularity and pointedly avoids any mention of the term "slavery." It also bypassed the reality that, at the Constitutional Convention, the framers had fashioned a compromise that accepted slavery but did not clearly or indefeasibly stake its vitality to the charter itself. The overarching interest of the framers, bent on establishing a union, was to leave the disruptive slavery question largely open for future resolution. Exactly seventy years later, Taney's response to a question, deliberately left open in 1787, was that the "act of Congress which prohibited a citizen from holding and owning property on this land in the territory of the United States . . . is not warranted by the Constitution, and is therefore void."

Aftermath of *Dred Scott*

The bottom line for Scott, after more than a decade of litigation, was that his status as a slave was reaffirmed. In the broader political context, the decision, even if anticipated by many as a final resolution of the slavery question, had the opposite effect. Given the ideologies, agendas and consequences involved, any decision was bound to enhance rather than diminish sectional antagonism. For all their mutual animosity, radical abolitionists and defenders of slavery at least could agree that the Court had confirmed the Constitution as a pro-slavery document. Instead of resolving the differences between North and South, the *Dred Scott* decision became another milestone on the course toward national disunion and eventual civil war.

Northern reaction to *Dred Scott* was profoundly but selectively negative. Criticism of the ruling focused on the pruning of congressional power rather than on the diminution and belittlement of an entire race. Such qualified objection was consistent with dominant sentiment that considered blacks inferior and insignificant. From a modern perspective, Taney's opinion has been described as "a derelict[] of constitutional law." Dismissal of *Dred Scott* as a "derelict" ignores or discounts the reality that it had a doctrinal past and was an inspiration for future constitutional law. The content and tone of Taney's opinion in significant part are traceable to his earlier work. The significance of the *Dred Scott* decision for the short term was qualified by Lincoln's election in 1860 and his administration's deliberate disregard of it. The ruling's long-term pertinence was formally defeated by the Thirteenth Amendment, which prohibits slavery. Despite formal repudiation of the *Dred Scott* decision, within a decade of its rendition, significant aspects of Taney's opinion endured as a continuing source of constitutional influence. Since the late nineteenth century, as discussed in Chapters 3, 4, and 7, the Supreme Court has referred to due process for purposes of developing rights that although not constitutionally specified have been declared fundamental. The racist spirit of *Dred Scott* survived as a significant factor in constitutional jurisprudence through the middle of the twentieth century. Even after the Fourteenth Amendment was added to the Constitution, the Court denied Congress the power to reach private discrimination in any context and upheld official segregation. Dissenting from the Court's investment in the separate but equal doctrine forty years after *Dred Scott,* in *Plessy v. Ferguson,* Justice Harlan warned that the decision "will, in time, prove to be quite as pernicious as the decision made by this tribunal in the Dred Scott case."

What was offered as a constitutional resolution of the slavery question in 1857 actually compounded the controversy and exacerbated sectional tension. To have expected more, no matter how the Court ruled, seems unrealistic given the almost irreparably divided condition of the union. Even if the Court's judgment with respect to Scott himself was final, its practical effect was not. Two months after the decision, he was manumitted. For Taney, the opinion became a stain on his record that neither time nor the respectability of his jurisprudence otherwise has erased. The Court itself lost prestige and credibility, as some states openly challenged its authority and Republicans flaunted its decision. Derrick Bell has described *Dred Scott* as "being the most frequently overturned decision in history." Even if ultimately discredited, the decision, as discussed in the next chapter, was to be a departure and transfer point rather than an absolute dead end in the development of constitutional law.

Bibliography

Cases

Commonwealth v. Aves, 35 Mass. 193 (1836).
Dred Scott v. Sandford, 60 U.S. 393 (1857).
Josefa Segunda, The, 18 U.S. 338 (1820).
Marbury v. Madison, 5 U.S. 137 (1803).
Plessy v. Ferguson, 163 U.S. 537 (1896).
Prigg v. Pennsylvania, 41 U.S. 536 (1842).
Strader v. Graham, 51 U.S. 82 (1850).

Books and Articles

Bell, D., And We Are Not Saved (1987).
Bell, D., Race, Racism and American Law (1973).

Elliot, J. (ed.), The Debates in the Several State Constitutions of the Adoption of the Federal Constitution (1901).

Farrand, M. (ed.), The Records of the Federal Convention of 1787 (1937).

Fehrenbacher, D., The Dred Scott Case (1978).

Finkelman, P., An Imperfect Union (1981).

Hall, K. (ed.), The Law of American Slavery (1987).

Jordan, W., White over Black: American Attitudes toward the Negro (1968).

Story, J., Commentaries on the Constitution (1905).

Swisher, C., Roger B. Taney (1935).

Tushnet, M., The American Law of Slavery (1981).

Wiecek, W., The Sources of Antislavery Constitutionalism in America, 1760-1848 (1977).

Chapter 2

IMAGES OF A NEW UNION

The *Dred Scott* decision by itself did not cause the union's dissolution and consequent civil war. Nor is it even certain how much of the Republican Party's expanding popularity during the late 1850s was attributable to the *Dred Scott* ruling. The Republicans' explosive growth in the several years before the nation's unraveling reflected the consolidation or transfer of political allegiance pursuant to disintegration of or alienation from other parties. Although impossible to prove Charles Warren's thesis that the *Dred Scott* decision "elected Abraham Lincoln to the Presidency," it is clear that Lincoln's victory prompted secession. As Don Fehrenbacher has suggested, the ruling at least "was a conspicuous and perhaps an integral part of configuration of events and conditions that did produce enough changes of allegiance to make a political revolution and enough intensity of feeling to make that revolution violent."

Limits of Judicial Power

The notion that the Supreme Court somehow could have successfully resolved the slavery controversy was grounded more in political desperation than realism. Although never having reckoned with slavery in its broadest sense, the Court had established enough of a record to suggest that it was an unlikely source for resolving or ameliorating the nation's condition. The case of *Prigg v. Pennsylvania,* for instance, concerned a discrete, albeit significant aspect of the slavery issue. The decision was criticized in the North, where the ruling enhanced sensitivity with respect to the entire nation's involvement in slavery. Even though vindicating the recovery rights of slave owners, the Court's determination, that slavery could exist only by virtue of positive local law and was entitled to no recognition in another state unless extended by principles of comity, established an exclusive federal responsibility on fugitive questions that antagonized Southern interests. The terms of resolution that alienated both sides, and that encouraged rather than defeated resistance, effectively predicted the reality of limited institutional influence in the more heated context of *Dred Scott*.

The practical consequences of the *Prigg* decision warned further against expecting too much from judicial review. New burdens imposed by Northern states on the recovery of runaway slaves were perceived by the South as a calculated evasion of constitutional duties. The failure of *Prigg* to secure Northern cooperation prompted demands for more effective fugitive slave legislation that eventually became part of the Compromise of 1850. Although the new law established special procedures and courts for resolution of fugitive slave claims, that achievement was diminished by understaffing and underfunding of the federal tribunals responsible for hearing such cases. The lesson of *Prigg* and its aftermath, reiterated by *Dred Scott* and consequent events, was that constitutional interpretation by the Court was no competition for unyielding ideology.

By the time of *Dred Scott* itself, continued Southern participation in the union already hinged on the satisfaction of various pro-slavery demands. Given especially a legacy of persistent but futile congressional efforts to balance competing sectional agendas, judicial review presented a possibility for a final resolution that was more wishful than certain. An enduring accommodation of mutually exclusive aims and priorities was increasingly unachievable by the representative process. Once the political branch structured for purposes of brokering competing interests had broken down, reconciliation was even less likely to be attained from a constitutional choice that in favoring one side invariably would antagonize the other.

Political and Cultural Backdrop of *Dred Scott*

The *Dred Scott* case both illuminated and compounded the societal frictions that caused the nation's imminent and inevitable breakdown. The Court's judgment and opinion, however, were not unanimously supported. Given the nature and context of the decision, it is not surprising that Taney's strained accounting for Southern culture prompted a rebuttal. Although the two dissenting opinions in *Dred Scott* argued neither for elimination of slavery nor for unqualified citizenship for blacks, they advanced some formative premises for the union's eventual redemption and reconstruction.

Sentiment toward slavery in the North was more diverse than in the

South where, by the 1830s, abolitionism was subject to severe private and public sanction and essentially had been eradicated. The Northern ideological spectrum was broad enough to include the Democratic Party, moderate and radical abolitionism and an increasingly significant middle ground occupied by free soilers. Except for abolitionists, dominant Northern sentiment, at least until the Civil War, continued to favor accommodation of slavery. The political success of the Democratic Party during the first half of the nineteenth century was attributable to an overriding interest in maintaining organizational harmony and strength, which motivated the Southern wing to soft-pedal its pro-slavery inclinations and the Northern faction to avoid or subordinate the issue. The Whig Party, although rooted in the North, likewise developed a Southern constituency by downplaying slavery and emphasizing common ground on other issues. Maintenance of political coalitions thus borrowed from the model of accommodation that facilitated the union's creation.

By the midpoint of the nineteenth century, established political parties had become casualties of ratcheting sectional intolerance. The Whig Party lost its Southern base and fragmented, as President Taylor's rhetoric and actions with respect to territories and states in the Far West were perceived as inimical to slavery. Northern and Southern Democrats eventually split because of technical differences over the meaning of popular sovereignty. The collapse of the Whigs in particular contributed to an especially fluid political context in which new loyalties were available on a wholesale basis. Fragmentation was accentuated by the emergence of Know-Nothingism, which was notable for its appeal to nativism and bigotry. The primary beneficiary of the shattered political order was the Republican Party. Within several years of its emergence, after the Kansas–Nebraska controversy, the Republican Party had become a dominant force in Northern legislatures and Congress and by 1860 had secured the presidency.

Central to the Republican Party's emergence and development was its qualified anti-slavery position. The party was not abolitionist but vigorously opposed to slavery's expansion. Republican criticism of *Dred Scott* was cautious and defensive, as candidates recognized their vulnerability to Democratic charges that the party was sympathetic to concepts of racial equality and mixing. Racial politics were a substantial part of the fallout from *Dred Scott*, as Democrats sought to capitalize on white supremacist ideology and Republicans worked to protect themselves against charges that they favored racial amalgamation. Consistent with other Republicans who sought to distance themselves from any perceived sympathy toward the victims of *Dred Scott*, Lincoln emphasized the "natural disgust" among whites toward the idea of racial integration.

As the Democratic Party fractured pursuant to intramural differences in the late 1850s, the Republican Party established its capability for housing a relatively broad spectrum of sentiment. A key thread in the Republican fabric was the principle of free soil, which favored prohibition of slavery in territories but allowed it where established. Such doctrine represented a middle ground in the slavery controversy, between the poles of abolitionism and Southern constitutional precepts, and was largely faithful to the original concept of accommodation. Although interested in limiting slavery's extension, Republicans acknowledged a duty on the part of free states to cooperate in and facilitate the return of fugitive slaves. The party's free-soil notions also appealed to an overtly bigoted and racially phobic segment of the population concerned with the impact of slavery on general employment opportunity and wages. Finally, the Republican Party offered an alternative to persons with abolitionist sympathies who were interested in achieving what was feasible under existing political circumstances. Outside the abolitionist movements, little support existed for race-neutral concepts of civil and political rights or equality. A basic reality was that the racial ideology of Taney's opinion in *Dred Scott* reflected dominant attitudes, shared even by its critics, without qualification of party or geography. As noted by Susan B. Anthony, "Taney's decision, infamous as it is, is but a reflection of the spirit and practice of the American people, North and South."

Limited Resources of Dissent

Given the moral, political and ideological backdrop of the *Dred Scott* decision, it was unlikely that a dissenting opinion would have sounded in terms equivalent to what redefined the Constitution after the Civil War. Further militating against such a possibility was the fact that the Constitution itself was a creature and source of slavery's accommodation. To have searched for general antislavery principle in the Constitution, minus a leap toward abolitionist faith, would have been illogical in light of the document's careful acknowledgment of the institution. Missing from the Constitution, at least until the Fourteenth Amendment's ratification, was any basis for establishing indefeasibly the citizenship and rights even of free blacks. In the debate over Missouri statehood, arguments were made that the privileges and immunities clause of Article IV, Section 2, required states to extend the same respect to citizens of other states, regardless of race, afforded its own. The point essentially was bypassed, however, in the course of brokering a general compromise. The same contention was repudiated entirely, as noted in the preceding chapter, in an opinion authored by Taney as attorney general. Early judicial review of the privileges and immunities clause, moreover, assumed citizenship and its incidents to be an exclusive concern of the states and considered state citizenship an essential predicate for national citizenship. Even the proposition that free blacks were protected under the privileges and immunities clause was unsupported by case law and specifically rejected by several state courts.

More significant in the development of formative principles that qualified slavery was an imported legal concept that, as translated, established a presumption against the institution unless the law provided for its existence. Before the American Revolution, a British court released a slave who had been seized in Virginia and brought to England, where he ran away and was recaptured. The court's order rested on grounds that English law did not support his detention. As glossed by anti-slavery interests in the United States, the decision in *Somerset v. Stewart* became associated with the proposition that slavery was offensive to natural law and legitimate only to the extent provided for by positive enactment. Northern and Southern courts alike initially referred to the *Somerset* premise in developing a body of law that tilted toward slave owners in sojourner cases, but upheld freedom claims when residence in a free state was extended enough to constitute domicile. As Northern courts became increasingly resistant toward the extraterritorial effect of slavery, the *Somerset* principle acquired a more ominous meaning for the South. As noted in the preceding chapter, the Supreme Judicial Court of Massachusetts emphasized that slavery was at odds with natural law and depended on positive enactment for legitimacy. Justice Story, in *Prigg v. Pennsylvania,* made a similar point in identifying slavery as a function of local law. By the time of *Dred Scott*— at least in the North—a judicial philosophy had evolved that reinforced political doctrine that if not prepared to extinguish slavery altogether at least was interested in confining its operation and reach.

Before the Civil War and reconstruction, the constitutional potential of such doctrine was never fully developed. At least with respect to the Supreme Court's decisions, moral principle never translated into comprehensive refutation of slavery. Justice Story's opinion for the Court in *Prigg v. Pennsylvania* typified review that subordinated moral reservations about slavery to perceived legal imperative. Story's response to the fugitive slave controversy was consistent not only with the notion that Northern accommodation was a historical necessity, but also with his reputation as an exponent of judicial restraint. Despite his personal conviction that slavery was wrong, Story upheld fugitive slave legislation pursuant to his sense of the North's constitutional obligation to the South and a theory of review that disallowed personal preference from influencing legal judgment. Earlier in his career, Story had joined in the development of doctrine that limited state authority to interfere with contractual and property rights. The Marshall Court's decision in *Dartmouth College v. Woodward,* barring a state legislature's modification of a corporate charter, identified a violation of the Constitution's contract clause. It demonstrated a capacity, in Don Fehrenbacher's words, to "set the Constitution itself like a protective screen, between state legislative power and the people affected by that power."

No justice including Story ever proposed "a protective screen" that would have shielded those victimized by state power to establish slavery.

Dissenting Opinions in *Dred Scott*

Neither Justice McLean nor Justice Curtis, in dissenting from the Court's opinion in *Dred Scott,* predicted or previewed the extensive recasting of the Constitution a decade later. Each broadened the scope of constitutional debate, however, and contributed if not to the fruition then at least to the development of principles central to the document's reformulation. Although disagreeing on the basic procedural question of jurisdiction, McLean and Curtis concurred on the constitutional issues. Both interpreted the territory clause in terms that enabled Congress to provide for or against slavery. In so doing, they rebutted Taney's cramped notions that (1) the federal function in the territories was limited to regulating mere realty, (2) the framers had not contemplated the need to govern new territories and (3) the Northwest Ordinance's pre-constitutional ban on slavery was uniquely allowable. In support of the dissenters' interpretation of federal power were established practice and, in Curtis's words, "the express language of the Constitution."

Curtis also challenged the Fifth Amendment as a check on federal power, noting that the concept of due process predated the Constitution and had not been understood in 1787 as a check on authority to ban slavery then in the Northwest Territory. McLean and Curtis restated the premise that slavery could exist only as a consequence of positive state enactment. Although reiterating the notion that slavery was not allowable, absent provision for it by domestic law, they would have pruned the extraterritorial reach of such legislation by limiting or denying ownership claims with respect to slaves who had established ties to a free state or territory. Both dissenters were satisfied that Scott's presence in a free state and territory was sufficient to establish his permanent liberty. Although Curtis would have required extended presence in a free jurisdiction to extinguish a claim of ownership, McLean may have been satisfied with transient contact. Each rejected the notion that Scott reverted to slave status on leaving a free jurisdiction and returning to Missouri. Such findings reflected differences with the majority on immediate questions concerning Scott's status and the extent to which slavery might impose demands on jurisdictions in which it was not allowed. More pertinent for longer-term purposes was the introduction of principles representing progress toward the elimination of slavery and the extension of citizenship to blacks.

McLean's and Curtis's contributions toward an eventual constitutional reckoning with slavery, citizenship and civil and political rights were significant, even if they were limited by circumstance, history and ideology.

Little more than a decade later, slavery was abolished pursuant to the Thirteenth Amendment, citizenship and civil rights were provided by the Fourteenth Amendment and voting rights were attended to by the Fifteenth Amendment. Such achievements may have been unimaginable at the time of *Dred Scott* when, as noted previously, race-dependent distribution of civil and political rights was the norm even in the North and association with the cause of racial equality was politically suicidal. At least until the Civil War, even the Republican Party stressed saving the union at the cost of preserving slavery where it existed.

Neither McLean nor Curtis was an exponent of constitutional principle that would have entirely banned slavery or that would have secured civil and political rights even as an incident of citizenship. The principles they advanced would not have impaired state practices and policies that, among other things, provided for race-dependent segregation of public schools, denial of civil and political rights, foreclosure of certain trades and occupations and restrictions on migration or residence as a matter of state discretion. McLean and Curtis proposed that the Constitution accounted for a broader citizenry, although not without qualification, and that Congress had authority to prohibit slavery in territories. The possibility of more significant doctrinal development was limited by the Constitution itself. Not until the Thirteenth Amendment was adopted did a clear basis exist for defeating the reality that the document, as originally framed, accommodated slavery. It required the Fourteenth and Fifteenth Amendments and extended interpretive struggles, moreover, for a national interest in civil and political rights to be established and for it to be verified as a direct incident of federal citizenship. Within the context of time, possibility and the considerable political distance that needed to be covered in the decade between *Dred Scott* and reconstruction, McLean's and Curtis's dissents expressed perspectives that helped bridge the vast difference in the Constitution before and after the Civil War.

John McLean

McLean's tenure on the Court largely coincided with Taney's. Like the chief justice, he was appointed by President Jackson. Contrary to Taney's modified federalist convictions, which were more accommodating to state power, McLean subscribed to the ardent nationalism of former Chief Justice Marshall. As a forceful and well-known exponent of free soil principles, McLean's views of slavery also were significantly at variance with Taney's. In *Prigg v. Pennsylvania,* McLean dissented from the Court's affirmance of federal fugitive slave legislation and expressed specific concern for the lack of protection it afforded free blacks. His dissent in *Dred Scott* represented a convergence of federalist and anti-slavery sentiment. During

the three decades he served on the Court, McLean harbored national political aspirations and was seriously considered as a presidential nominee
by various parties. Having failed to secure the Republican nomination for
president in 1856, despite significant support in early balloting, McLean
aimed for another chance in 1860. From his personal ambition, the political significance of the case and McLean's personal correspondence at the
time, historians have deduced an opinion calculated with one eye on the
Constitution and another on political fortune. McLean already had established his fidelity to free soil principles by virtue of published essays and
public statements. Consistent with if not inspired by an interest in expanding his appeal to abolitionists, McLean related sentiment that intimated a
shared moral condemnation of slavery.

We need not refer to the mercenary spirit which introduced the infamous traffic
in slaves, to show the degradation of negro slavery in our country. This system
was imposed upon our colonial settlements by the mother country, and it is due
to truth to say that the commercial colonies and States were chiefly engaged in the
traffic. But we know as a historical fact, that James Madison, that great and good
man, a leading member in the Federal Convention, was solicitous to guard the
language of that instrument so as not to convey the idea that there could be property in man.

I prefer the lights of Madison, Hamilton, and Jay, as a means of construing the
Constitution in all its bearings, rather than to look behind that period, into a traffic
which is now declared to be piracy, and punished with death by Christian nations.
I do not like to draw the sources of our domestic relations from so dark a ground.
Our independence was a great epoch in the history of freedom; and while I admit
the Government was not made especially for the colored race, yet many of them
were citizens of the New England States, and exercised the rights of suffrage when
the Constitution was adopted, and it was not doubted by any intelligent person
that its tendencies would greatly ameliorate their condition.

Many of the States, on the adoption of the Constitution, or shortly afterward,
took measures to abolish slavery within their respective jurisdictions; and it is a
well-known fact that a belief was cherished by the leading men, South as well as
North, that the institution of slavery would gradually decline, until it would become extinct. The increased value of slave labor, in the culture of cotton and
sugar, prevented the realization of this expectation. Like all other communities
and States, the South were influenced by what they considered to be their own
interests.

But if we are to turn our attention to the dark ages of the world, why confine
our view to colored slavery? On the same principles, white men were made slaves.
All slavery has its origin in power, and is against right.

McLean's depiction of slavery as being "against right" was essentially
rhetorical but nonetheless significant in its symbolism. It introduced a tone
that departed from the *Prigg* Court's scrupulous avoidance of moral con-

siderations. McLean himself in *Prigg* and other fugitive slave cases, such as *Miller v. McQuerry,* had emphasized that "[it] is for the people . . . to consider the laws of nature. . . . This is a field which judges cannot explore. . . . They look to the law, and the law only." Even if the *Dred Scott* case afforded no interpretive opportunity to defeat slavery altogether, McLean presented a challenge to slavery's legitimacy. Although some of his observations were referenced primarily to morality rather than to law, the values he emphasized were pertinent to and reflective of thinking that in less than a decade evolved toward securing slavery's abolition pursuant to the Thirteenth Amendment.

Benjamin R. Curtis

Although largely consistent with McLean on substantive questions of law, Justice Curtis's dissent tends to be regarded by historians as more scholarly, less flamboyant and moralistic and especially devastating in refuting Taney's logic. Curtis's tenure on the bench was relatively short-lived, primarily because of a dispute with Taney over the release of his dissent before the Court's opinion was published. He was appointed to the Court in 1851 after a career as a prominent business attorney in Boston. Although regarded as a political conservative, his record discloses significant unpredictability and somewhat of a maverick nature. Two decades before the *Dred Scott* decision, Curtis had represented a slave owner in a case that earned him a pro-slavery reputation. In *Commonwealth v. Aves,* discussed in Chapter 1, he argued that his client retained full rights and control over slaves brought temporarily to Massachusetts. Curtis's argument supported the extraterritorial operation of the law of slavery, even if at odds with the policy of a free state. It thus expressed a reasonably common understanding of the Constitution that, although rejected by the Court in *Aves,* acknowledged duties of accommodation when a slave's contacts with the free jurisdiction were minimal. In dissenting from Taney's judgment and opinion in *Dred Scott,* Curtis maintained that the law of slavery could not reach so far as to govern the status of a slave who had extended contacts with a free jurisdiction. He also emphasized that the federal interest in slavery was limited to fugitive slave renderings, and that the institution was a creature of state law afforded no protection or security beyond what the state itself provided. Contrary to Taney's intimations, Curtis stressed that "[i]n the formation of the Federal Constitution, care was taken to confer no power on the Federal Government to interfere with [slavery] in the States." He thus affirmed the notion that the Constitution was a source of accommodation but not the basis for slavery's existence.

New Visions of Citizenship

Responding to the Court's determination that persons of African descent were not citizens of the United States, Curtis introduced concepts that although formative contributed to future understanding of citizenship. Contrary to Taney's finding that national citizenship was impossible for people denied citizenship by the states in which they resided, Curtis noted that blacks in five states before 1787 had citizenship status and the Constitution did not abrogate it. As he observed, the

Constitution was ordained and established by the people of the United States, through the action, in each State, of those persons who were qualified by its laws to act thereon, in behalf of themselves and all other citizens of that State. In some of the States, as we have seen, colored persons were among those qualified by law to act on this subject. These colored persons were not only included in the body of "the people of the United States," by whom the Constitution was ordained and established, but in at least five of the States they had the power to act, and doubtless did act, by their suffrages, upon the question of its adoption. It would be strange, if we were to find in that instrument anything which deprived of their citizenship any part of the people of the United States who were among those by whom it was established.

I can find nothing in the Constitution which, *proprio vigore,* deprives of their citizenship any class of persons who were citizens of the United States at the time of its adoption, or who should be native-born citizens of any State after its adoption; nor any power enabling Congress to disfranchise persons born on the soil of any State, and entitled to citizenship of such State by its Constitution and laws. And my opinion is, that, under the Constitution of the United States, every free person born on the soil of a State, who is a citizen of that State by force of its Constitution or laws, is also a citizen of the United States.

From Curtis's perspective, the issue of citizenship was reducible to whether any free person of African descent was a citizen of a state when the Constitution was adopted. If so, it followed that the individual was a citizen not only of the state but of the United States as well. In further support of the proposition that national citizenship derived from state citizenship, Curtis maintained

that the Constitution was ordained by the citizens of the several States; that they were "the people of the United States," for whom and whose posterity the Government was declared in the preamble of the Constitution to be made; that each of them was "a citizen of the United States at the time of the adoption of the Constitution," within the meaning of those words in that instrument; that by them the Government was to be and was in fact organized; and that no power is conferred on the Government of the Union to discriminate between them, or to disfranchise any of them—the necessary conclusion is, that those persons born within the several States, who, by force of their respective Constitutions and laws, are citizens of the State, are thereby citizens of the United States.

Curtis's vision of national citizenship, as a factor deriving from state citizenship, represented an order that the Fourteenth Amendment inverted. As provided by that amendment, "[a]ll persons born or naturalized in the United States, and subject to the jurisdiction thereof, are citizens of the United States of the state wherein they reside." Compared with the terms and effect of the Fourteenth Amendment, which establishes national and state citizenship for all people born or naturalized in the United States, Curtis offered an underdeveloped formula. His version was pitched to an understanding of state authority and interest that the Fourteenth Amendment respectively displaced and transferred to federal purview. The eventual redistribution and reordering of citizenship concepts was not to be achieved, however, until civil war had altered perceptions of personal loyalty and identity and catalyzed a sense of national allegiance that vied with or transcended traditional relationships between a state and its people.

Even Curtis's limited concept of citizenship was critical for purposes of rebutting the notion that the Constitution was created on behalf of and accounted only for the interests of whites. Referring to the existence of black citizens in several states, some of whom were afforded the right to vote, Curtis stressed that the Constitution was not an instrument "exclusively by and for the white race." As he viewed it, the notion that the charter

was made exclusively for the white race is, in my opinion, not only an assumption not warranted by anything in the Constitution, but contradicted by its opening declaration, that it was ordained and established by the people of the United States, for themselves and their posterity. And as free colored persons were then citizens of at least five States, and so in every sense part of the people of the United States, they were among those for whom and whose posterity the Constitution was ordained and established.

Curtis's concept of citizenship was significant as a counterpoint to Taney, but also for its limitations. Although enabling a person to sue in federal court as a citizen of the state, citizenship as Curtis related it did not necessarily ensure civil and political rights. As he put it, each state could determine "[w]hat civil rights shall be enjoyed by its citizens, and whether all shall enjoy the same, or how they may be gained or lost." By distinguishing between privileges and immunities incidental to citizenship and those extended by "causes other than mere citizenship," Curtis indicated that restrictions on the basis of race—like denials or limitations based on gender, age or competency—were permissible. Citizenship thus was not a source of civil rights or equality, so long as the states structured their Constitutions and laws as not to attach a particular privilege or immunity to mere naked citizenship. If one of the States will not deny to any of its own citizens a particular privilege or immunity, if it confer it on all of them by reason of mere naked citizenship, then it may be claimed by every citizen of each State by force of the Constitution; and it must be borne in mind, that the difficulties which attend the allowance of the claims of colored persons to be citizens of the United States are not avoided by saying that, though each State may make them its citizens, they are not thereby made citizens of the United States, because the privileges of general citizenship are secured to the citizens of each State. The language of the Constitution is, "The citizens of each State shall be entitled to all privileges and immunities of citizens in the several States." If each State may make such persons its citizens, they become, as such, entitled to the benefits of this article, if there be a native-born citizenship of the United States distinct from a native-born citizenship of the several States.

Summarizing his disagreement with Taney on the citizenship question, Curtis related

First. That the free native-born citizens of each State are citizens of the United States.

Second. That as free colored persons born within some of the States are citizens of those States, such persons are also citizens of the United States.

Third. That every such citizen, residing in any State, has the right to sue and is liable to be sued in the Federal courts, as a citizen of that State in which he resides.

Fourth. That as the plea to the jurisdiction in this case shows no facts, except that the plaintiff was of African descent, and his ancestors were sold as slaves, and as these facts are not inconsistent with his citizenship of the United States, and his residence in the State of Missouri, the plea to the jurisdiction was bad, and the judgment of the Circuit Court overruling it was correct.

I dissent, therefore, from the part of the opinion of the majority of the court, in which it is held that a person of African descent cannot be a citizen of the United States.

Limited Aims and Potential

Neither dissent, notwithstanding McLean's calculated appeal to abolitionist sentiment, stated a case for or even suggested prohibition of slavery as realized in the next decade. Both McLean and Curtis offered a perspective more reflective of Republican Party principles that recognized congressional power to regulate slavery in the territories but would not have extended full civil status or equality to blacks. Despite their limitations, the opinions of McLean and Curtis represented steps toward constitutional developments that in the next decade repudiated *Dred Scott.*

The significance of the dissenting opinions in *Dred Scott* was not in providing a finished template for the reconstruction amendments, which prohibited slavery, established citizenship and secured civil and political rights, but in helping to illuminate the Constitution's limitations. Recognition of the charter's unfinished business heightened in the decade after *Dred Scott*, especially as the Civil War progressed. Until the document's actual amendment, the possibility of more significant constitutional achievement was limited by textual and political realities. Despite abolitionist arguments for interpretation that would have transformed the privileges and immunities clause and the due process clause into anti-slavery and anti-discrimination levers, and the limited development of national citizenship concepts, general understanding before the Civil War was that federal citizenship derived from state citizenship. The most that could have been accomplished through the privileges and immunities clause, under such circumstances, was the limited protection of some free blacks. Even that relatively narrow concept had been rejected by state courts in both the North and the South. Given a violent reaction to Northern efforts to test the premise in Southern courts during the 1840s, implementation and enforcement may have been impracticable anyway. Emphasis on the due process clause was problematic, insofar as the Fifth Amendment was a check only on the exercise of federal power. Even if the provision was applied to the states, competition would have been intense over whether it protected the liberty interest of slaves or the property interest of slave owners. Constitutional achievement beyond what McLean and Curtis had suggested thus was to be the work not of the Court, but of the president, Congress and ultimately the nation itself.

Disunion and the Undoing of *Dred Scott*

Although the Republicans reaffirmed free soil principles in their 1860 party platform, potential for further territorial dispute largely had been exhausted by the limits of geography. More critical to the nation's future was the significant possibility of secession, which Southern states had promised in the event a Republican was elected president. Lincoln's triumph was widely perceived in the South as an indication that the North had fully abandoned its obligations to slavery and had slipped a noose around the institution's neck that eventually would choke it altogether. Despite assurances that his administration did not intend to tamper with slavery where established, Lincoln's election was the prompt for transforming the warning of secessionism into reality.

Disunion was not without a final effort to keep the nation intact. Drawing on the model of compromise and accommodation, a senate committee drafted several constitutional amendments that would have established the Constitution as a manifestly pro-slavery document. The amendments, among other things, would have reintroduced the Missouri Compromise line between free and slave jurisdictions and extended it to the West Coast; provided federal compensation for slave owners who were denied by force the right to recover runaway slaves; prohibited abolition of slavery in the District of Columbia, unless it was ended in Maryland and Virginia; precluded abolition on federal land in the South; barred federal interference with the interstate movement of slaves; and precluded any amendment enabling Congress to abolish interference with slavery where established by law. What was offered as a final solution actually would have divided the nation permanently into free and slave jurisdictions and would have made the constitutional provisions for slavery unamendable. Because the die of secession largely had been cast, it is doubtful whether the amendment package had a realistic chance of saving the union. Republican opposition, in any event, killed the proposal in committee. A modified version that would have secured slavery in states where it existed attracted more support and, despite indications that Lincoln might approve it, was defeated and forgotten with the outbreak of war.

Dissolution of the union and civil war demonstrated the futility of attempting to accommodate such fundamentally irreconcilable social systems. The rupture also presented the opportunity, once the North prevailed, for national reconstruction and constitutional redefinition. By the end of the Civil War, Northern objectives that originally had been defined as saving the union had expanded to include slavery's abolition. Although the *Dred Scott* decision remained the Court's statement of "what the law is," at least until the early stages of reconstruction, the Lincoln administration and Republican Congress had rendered it a practical nullity. Capitalizing on the fact that most of Taney's opinion in *Dred Scott* was unnecessary for resolution of the litigation, many Republicans had argued that his defense of slavery was mere dicta and thus not binding as a principle of law. Lincoln's position was that judicial decisions bound parties to the litigation but did not establish general constitutional principle until the issue was "fully settled."

The merger of Republican legal theory with personnel turnover and unionist sentiment on the Court, plus the turn of national events, effectively defeated much of *Dred Scott*'s significance. In obvious disregard of the Court's meaning, Congress in 1862 enacted legislation abolishing slavery in federal territories. It also repealed fugitive slave legislation and abolished slavery in the District of Columbia. The attorney general, in the same year, authored an opinion to the effect that persons of African descent acquired national citizenship by virtue of being born in the United States. Lincoln himself announced the Emancipation Proclamation, which freed slaves in states at war with the union. Such developments mocked Taney's assertion that federal power could not be used to compromise slavery and, on the territorial question in particular, followed the line of McLean and Curtis.

Toward a Reconstructed Union

Actual and comprehensive abolition of slavery awaited a more secure footing than was afforded by the Constitution as then structured. The Emancipation Proclamation had limited credibility and force, because it rested on Lincoln's authority as commander in chief and did not govern loyal or occupied jurisdictions. Given the limited basis and reach of the president's constitutional power, attention turned toward identification of a more adequate predicate for abolition. The search for sufficient authorization originally focused on the Constitution itself. Some Republicans suggested that the institution was incompatible with Article IV, Section 4, which provides that "[t]he United States shall guarantee to every State in this Union a Republican Form of Government." Such a contention was disputable and even defeasible, given a historical record of accommodation and support of slavery. Southerners for some time had maintained that slavery and republican systems of government were compatible. As the reconstruction process proceeded, the dominant sense was that the Constitution afforded no real basis for abolishing slavery. To change a constitutional culture that had evolved on the premise that concessions to slavery were a historical necessity, it became necessary to restructure the Constitution itself. In 1865, 1868 and 1870, therefore, the Thirteenth, Fourteenth and Fifteenth Amendments were ratified. The Constitution, accordingly, was amended in terms that specifically prohibited slavery, established the citizenship of all people born or naturalized in the United States and provided for basic civil and political rights and equality.

By its specific terms, the Thirteenth Amendment provides that "[n]either slavery nor involuntary servitude . . . shall exist within the United States, or any place subject to their jurisdiction." Prohibition of slavery by itself did not alter for practical purposes the relationship between many slaves and their former owners. Responding to the Thirteenth Amendment, Southern states enacted Black Codes that imposed legal disabilities so burdensome as to establish the functional equivalent of slavery. An effective accounting for the status of freedmen, therefore, required further political action. Toward that end, Congress passed the Civil Rights Act of 1866 which, among other things, guaranteed freedom to contract, buy, sell and own property, sue and be sued, and travel; personal security; and equal standing before the law. The civil rights bill originally was premised on Congress's power to enforce the Thirteenth Amendment. Given the South's reaction to the first reconstruction amendment and concern that the 1866 act might be susceptible to repeal when Southern states returned to the union, attention was directed to the need for more effectively securing civil rights and equality.

The Fourteenth Amendment thus was proposed and ratified as a means of translating the aims of the Civil Rights Act of 1866 into a constitutional prescription. In pertinent terms, it provides that "[a]ll persons born or naturalized in the United States, and subject to the jurisdiction thereof, are citizens of the United States and of the State wherein they reside." Although not expressly itemizing the incidents of citizenship, the amendment further relates that

No State shall make or enforce any law which shall abridge the privileges or immunities of citizens of the United States; nor shall any State deprive any person of life, liberty, or property, without due process of law; nor deny to any person within its jurisdiction the equal protection of the laws.

Considerable debate existed among the Fourteenth Amendment's supporters with respect to what rights and freedoms it secured. Some favored stretching the amendment into a broad incorporation of guarantees that included rights and liberties identified by the Declaration of Independence and the Bill of Rights. At minimum, it established as a function of national constitutional policy the rights and guarantees provided for by the Civil Rights Act of 1866.

Despite disagreement over its scope, the Fourteenth Amendment profoundly restructured the nation's political system. Civil rights before the amendment were considered to be an exclusive concern of states that, respectively and idiosyncratically, accorded privileges and immunities to their citizens. The Fourteenth Amendment established a superseding national concern in basic rights and equality and thereby effected a major redistribution of interest and power from state to federal government. Instead of national citizenship deriving from state citizenship, as Justice Curtis had assumed, the amendment established federal and state citizenship from birth or naturalization in the United States. Given the abolition of slavery as a consequence of the Thirteenth Amendment and the achievements of the Fourteenth Amendment, personhood, national citizenship and its incidents were established comprehensively rather than selectively.

Some Historical Footnotes

Unlike other developments of the law discussed in this book, the repudiation of *Dred Scott* was not primarily the work of the Supreme Court. It was Congress that proposed and a reorganized nation that ratified amendments that, at least on paper, displaced the decision's central meaning. Nearly another century passed, as discussed in Chapter 5, until the racist spirit of *Dred Scott* was disowned. As the reconstruction process wound down, congressional and judicial interest waned with respect to realities that diminished the significance of abolition, citizenship and the civil and political rights secured by the reconstruction amendments. Not until the Court struck down official segregation in *Brown v. Board of Education* did the Court finally excise from constitutional law the premise of racial supremacy.

Justice McLean, who died in 1861, did not survive to witness the formal undoing of *Dred Scott*. After resigning from the Court in 1858, Justice Curtis became a vocal critic of developments that ultimately led to abolition and reconstruction. Curtis accused the Lincoln administration of exceeding its constitutional powers and objected in particular to the Emancipation Proclamation. Despite having advanced a notion of national citizenship deriving from state citizenship, he objected to the inverse proposition that state citizenship was established by virtue of national citizenship. Curtis also opposed the Fourteenth Amendment for imposing demands on the South that he considered excessive. Like the other reconstruction amendments, the Fourteenth Amendment became a cost of readmission to the union and was ratified as a function of post-war realities, of governance rather than popular sentiment in the South. Given the widespread resistance and evasion that the Fourteenth Amendment prompted, reflecting a sense similar to Curtis's that the provision was harsh and unacceptable, it is not surprising that ratification proved a much easier task than actualization.

The reconstruction amendments revised the Constitution so as to disclaim, at least formally, the core legal premises of *Dred Scott*. Their introduction commenced a new and enduring debate over the quality of freedom and nature of rights established and the extent to which power had been redistributed from state to national government. Over the course of its history, the Fourteenth Amendment's practical meaning has evolved according to judicial interpretation and has become the most prolific source of constitutional litigation. The Fourteenth Amendment redefined the Constitution and political system in a way that the dissenters in *Dred Scott* may not have contemplated. It since has become a source of constitutional development that the framers themselves may not have imagined.

Bibliography

Cases

Brown v. Board of Education, 347 U.S. 483 (1954).
Commonwealth v. Aves, 35 Mass. 191 (1836).
Dartmouth College v. Woodward, 17 U.S. 518 (1819).
Dred Scott v. Sandford, 60 U.S. 393 (1857).
Miller v. McQuerry, 17 F. Cas. 332 (C.C.D. Ohio, 1853).
Plessy v. Ferguson, 163 U.S. 537 (1896).

Prigg v. Pennsylvania, 41 U.S. 539 (1842).
Somerset v. Stewart, 1 Lofft's Rep. 1, 98 Eng. Rep. 499 (1772).

Books and Articles

Cover, R., Justice Accused (1975).
Fehrenbacher, D., The Dred Scott Case (1978).
Finkleman, P., An Imperfect Union (1981).
Hyman, H., A More Perfect Union (1973).
Hyman, H., & Wiecek, W., Equal Justice under the Law (1982).
Story, J., Commentaries on the Constitution of the United States (1905).
tenBroek, J., Antislavery Origins of the Fourteenth Amendment (1951).
Warren, C., The Supreme Court in United States History (1932).
Wiecek, W., The Sources of Anti-Slavery Constitutionalism in America, 1760–
1848 (1977).
Woodward, C., The Burden of Southern History (1960).

Chapter 3

CONSTITUTIONAL REDEFINITION AND NATIONAL RECONSTRUCTION

The Fourteenth Amendment restructured the nation in a way that radically realigned state and federal powers and redistributed their respective interests. As formulated in 1868, the Constitution implemented a new model of governance for the union that supplanted the plan of 1787. In its virgin state, the Constitution anticipated a federal government with limited powers specifically allocated to it by the document itself. The Fourteenth Amendment's assignment of enforcement power to Congress did not deviate from that premise. By vesting the federal government with paramount responsibility for managing and protecting basic civil rights, however, the amendment effected a transfer of power and interest previously reserved to the states.

Transfer of Governmental Power

The Bill of Rights, which resolved the conflict between Federalist and anti-Federalist agendas when the Constitution was being debated for purposes of ratification, evidenced an initial sense that centralized national authority presented the paramount risk to personal freedom. The itemization of specific guarantees in the first eight amendments, and reservation of unenumerated rights and powers respectively to the people and the states by the Ninth and Tenth Amendments, reflected the deep concern with the potential perils of centralized authority. The unhappy experience with slavery compounded by Southern resistance to reconstruction demonstrated that the federal government was not the sole threat to individual rights and liberties. The Fourteenth Amendment responded to post-slav-

ery systems of oppression that included the Black Codes, official harass-
ment of unionists and other state devices interfering with reconstruction.
It did so by establishing the concept of national citizenship, providing for
its incidents and giving Congress the responsibility of accounting for those
new federal interests.

The redistribution of governmental power and interests by the Fourteenth Amendment was not achieved without reservations even by its exponents and second thoughts by those responsible for interpreting it. The
debates over the amendment evidence concern by many Republican supporters who worried that Congress might use its authority to intrude into
areas of essentially municipal concern. The mixed impulses identifiable
even on the part of the amendment's framers established a record of commitment qualified by uncertainty. It is not surprising that since the Fourteenth Amendment's ratification, interpretation has reflected an abiding
tension in the charting of federal and state functions and interests.

Minus federal supervision of Southern political processes and the demands of reconstruction, the Fourteenth Amendment would not have
eventuated when it did. Like the other reconstruction amendments, ratification was the cost of readmission to the union. Unlike other constitutional amendments when adopted, the amendments did not reflect broad
popular preference normally required for ratification. The reconstruction
process afforded a window of opportunity for extraordinary constitutional
achievements unattainable under normal circumstances when popular sentiment was accurately represented. Consistent with its unusual beginnings
and the somewhat ambivalent expectations it generated, the Fourteenth
Amendment over the course of its existence has been a source of un-
usually extensive jurisprudential controversy and attention. Initial review
of the Fourteenth Amendment predictably concerned itself with the actual
reach of federal power, as the judiciary became a primary forum for arguments to maximize the provision's potential or fasten a backlash against
it.

The earliest interpretation of the Fourteenth Amendment indicated caution if not resistance in accepting the consequences of constitutional change.
In the *Slaughter-House Cases,* decided five years after ratification, the Supreme Court determined that the provision was concerned essentially with
the civil rights and equality of the nation's newest class of citizens. The
analysis and result, although acknowledging a new federal interest, were
notable for the reservations they disclosed with respect to the Fourteenth
Amendment itself. What is especially striking about the first judicial reading of the amendment is how sparingly federal citizenship and its incidents
were defined and how limited the amendment thus was in its significance.
The Fourteenth Amendment eventually became a source of fundamental
rights, identified neither by the amendment nor elsewhere in the Constitution, that exceeded its immediate agenda. Such results, opposed by the

Slaughter-House Court, required eventual reinterpretation in response to persisting debate over how the Fourteenth Amendment redefined the nation's political system. Apparent at the outset was a reluctance by a majority of the Court to allow significant inroads into concerns traditionally reserved for the states.

Previewing the Court's chilly response to the Fourteenth Amendment was its reaction to federal law enacted pursuant to congressional authority newly assigned by the Constitution. As described by one of its proponents, the Fourteenth Amendment was intended to secure the provisions of the Civil Rights Act of 1866 and specifically "fix [them] in the serene sky, in the eternal firmament of the Constitution where no storm of passion can shake . . . and no cloud can obscure." In less hyperbolic terms, the Fourteenth Amendment represented an effort to enhance the security of basic civil rights and interests by insulating them from future repeal at the whim of a simple majority. Concern for such consequences reflected the sense of risk that reconstruction achievements might be endangered as Southern states returned to the union and exercised their influence in the process of representative governance. The need for special protection was verified as reconstruction terminated, legislative activity with respect to civil rights ceased and Congress repealed voting rights legislation it had enacted in the post–Civil War years.

A Chill Interpretive Wind

Judicial response to the Civil Rights Act of 1866, evidenced in *Blylew v. United States,* provided an accurate forecast of the Fourteenth Amendment's future interpretation. At issue in *Blylew* was a challenge to the federal prosecution of a white man charged with the murder of a black woman. Under the 1866 act, federal courts were empowered to hear all criminal and civil cases "affecting persons who are denied or cannot enforce in the courts or judicial tribunals of the state or locality where they may be, any of the rights secured by the first section of this Act." The first section set out basic civil rights secured by the enactment. Under relevant state law, a person of one race could not testify against a defendant of another race. Because all witnesses to the incident were black, the state would not prosecute. A majority in *Blylew* determined that, despite the gap in the state's criminal justice system, a federal court did not have jurisdiction to hear the case. As the Court related it, the witnesses were not "affected persons" denied access to a state court. Nor did the victim qualify as an "affected person," from the Court's perspective, because she was deceased. The practical consequence of the *Blylew* decision, as noted by Justice Bradley, was that it "deprive[d] a whole class of the community of this right, . . . brand[ed] them with a badge of slavery, . . . expose[d] them to wanton insults and fiendish assaults, . . . [and left] their lives, their families, and their property unprotected by law." Also revealed was an institutional resistance toward acknowledging the policy of the Fourteenth Amendment and an indication that the process of establishing its significance beyond theory had hardly commenced.

Seminal Construction of the Fourteenth Amendment: The *Slaughter-House Cases*

The Supreme Court's first assessment of the Fourteenth Amendment itself arose in a context that seemed significantly removed from concerns that were central to the Constitution's revision. At issue in the *Slaughter-House Cases* was whether a state anti-nuisance law restricting the location of animal slaughtering operations was unconstitutional. Challenged specifically, as a violation of the Fourteenth Amendment, was a Louisiana statute prohibiting all slaughterhouses in New Orleans except for one. Because the law created a monopoly, aggrieved butchers maintained that the state interfered with their right to pursue a trade.

The notion that the Fourteenth Amendment secured a general economic liberty reflected an expansion of the provision beyond its obvious reconstruction roots. Insofar as some congressional supporters and some notable constitutional theorists urged an understanding of the Fourteenth Amendment as a repository for the Bill of Rights and natural freedoms, the concept was not entirely alien or unprincipled. The broad notion was not widely endorsed by the amendment's framers, however, who to a large extent had reservations about the displacement of state power. The limited aims of the Fourteenth Amendment were acknowledged even by those who favored a grander achievement. As one exponent observed, in acknowledging the need to limit the amendment's scope, "we shall be obliged to be content with patching up the worst portions of the ancient edifice."

The case for expansive reading of the Fourteenth Amendment, in the *Slaughter-House Cases,* at first elicited a favorable response. Justice Bradley, who dissented from the majority judgment and opinion, initially considered the case in his capacity as a circuit justice. Bradley found the privileges and immunities clause broad enough to comprehend freedom to pursue a "lawful industrial pursuit." A divided Supreme Court refused to develop the Fourteenth Amendment so liberally. It instead emphasized the provision's concern with securing "the freedom of the slave race, the security of and firm establishment of that freedom, and the protection of the newly made free man and citizen from the oppressions of those who had formerly exercised unlimited dominion over him." The majority opinion, authored by Justice Miller, defined the Fourteenth Amendment restrictively and thus narrowed the significance of national citizenship and the scope of its incidents. Miller focused on the four key provisions of Section 1, which respectively provided for citizenship; the privileges and immunities thereof; due process in the deprivation of life, liberty and property; and equal protection of the laws.

In reviewing the citizenship clause, the Court determined that national and state citizenship were independently significant. The distinction prefaced a parsimonious reading of the incidents of federal citizenship secured by the Fourteenth Amendment privileges and immunities clause. Having identified national citizenship as a unique and separate concept, the Court determined that states were prohibited only from abridging privileges and immunities appurtenant to it. Reserved to the states was authority to regulate the incidents of state citizenship. Crucial to the nature and significance of federal versus state citizenship was how the Court defined the respective privileges and immunities. Rather than acknowledging a meaningful redistribution of power and interest from the state to federal level, the Court depicted the incidents of national citizenship as relatively technical and mundane. Representative guarantees that the Court acknowledged as privileges and immunities of federal citizenship were the rights to assert claims against, transact business with or seek protection from the government; of access to seaports; to receive federal care and protection of life, liberty or property when in a foreign land; to peaceably assemble and petition for redress of grievances; to assert the writ of habeas corpus; to use navigable waters and those rights secured by the reconstruction amendments.

Although recognizing that incidents of federal citizenship were established by the Fourteenth Amendment, the Court did not amplify their nature or content. The amendment's precursor, the Civil Rights Act of 1866, legislatively had secured contractual, property and travel rights, personal security and equal standing before the law. In describing the incidents of state citizenship, the Court referred to antebellum jurisprudence that described such privileges and immunities as including "free ingress and regress to and from any other State and the right to acquire and possess property of every kind, and to pursue and obtain happiness and safety." The characterization of state privileges and immunities, in terms that were largely coextensive with the Civil Rights Act of 1866, illuminated reticence in acknowledging even a minimal redistribution of federal and state interests. Predictably excluded from the privileges and immunities of national citizenship, given the Court's restrictive interpretation, was the Bill of Rights.

The breadth of federal privileges and immunities determined for practical purposes the extent of national interest established by the Fourteenth Amendment. Despite the amendment's reallotment of federal and state concerns, and the national interest it established particularly with respect to civil rights, the Court refused to sanction "transfer [of] the security and protection of all the civil rights we have mentioned, from the States to the Federal Government." The majority opinion thus resonated with concerns that a broader interpretation of the amendment would engender a federal code of civil and criminal law displacing the powers and interests of the states. Although some of the Fourteenth Amendment's exponents had expressed misgivings about its impact, as noted previously, the Court's reasoning was reminiscent primarily of the arguments by critics and opponents during the framing process. Even if obstinate and misplaced, the majority's interpretation of the privileges and immunities clause has endured. The clause was relied on to strike down a state law in the 1930s, but even that decision was soon overruled. The legacy of the *Slaughter-House* decision has included a persisting distortion of the Fourteenth Amendment. Although most of the Bill of Rights eventually was incorporated through the due process clause, and thereby made applicable to the states, the privileges and immunities clause seemed a more logical source for housing them. The *Slaughter-House* majority, however, effectively foreclosed such an option.

Having greatly limited if not preempted the doctrinal potential of the privileges and immunities clause, the Court considered the due process and equal protection guarantees. In examining the due process clause, the Court had two basic interpretive choices. The first was to define it in substantive terms as a check on legislative judgment and policy. The other was to construe it as a guarantee of procedural fairness of processes implicating "life, liberty, or property." The most notable development of substantive due process, at the time, had been Justice Taney's use of it to establish slave owner rights and prohibit congressional interference with them. In the *Slaughter-House Cases,* the Court rejected the notion that the due process clause functioned as a check on legislative power. With respect to the guarantee, as a surety of procedural fairness, the Court recognized that the Fourteenth "Amendment may place the restraining power over the States in this matter in the hands of the Federal Government."

As contrasted with its eventual expansion to account for various types of official discrimination, pertaining to gender, alienage, parental marital status and certain fundamental interests, the equal protection clause's initial interpretation was pinched. The Court understood the clause to be specifically responsive to the Black Codes, which essentially had reestablished slavery in fact after it was prohibited in theory. It acknowledged Congress's power to enforce the provision by appropriate legislation but emphasized that equal protection was exclusively concerned with racially significant official action. The majority thus doubted that the guarantee ever would comprehend state action "not directed by way of discrimination against the negroes as a class, or on account of their race."

Unlike the majority's reading of the privileges and immunities clause that has endured, its interpretations of the due process and equal protection guarantees have been debated and deviated from since. The equal protection clause has evolved to account for various types of discrimination unrelated to race. As discussed later, the due process clause became a source of rights unenumerated by the Constitution that nonetheless checked the exercise of legislative power. The foundation for that result was poured by the dissenting opinions in the *Slaughter-House Cases.*

Dissenting Opinions in *Slaughter-House*

At odds with the Court's judgment and opinion were Justices Swayne, Bradley and Field. Swayne's dissent largely emphasized agreement with the positions staked out by Bradley and Field. Bradley had presided over the trial court proceedings and had endorsed the privileges and immunities clause as broad enough to secure the freedom to engage in a "lawful industrial pursuit" and the protection to the "enjoyment of [one's] property." In his dissent from the majority's judgment and opinion, Bradley maintained that the Fourteenth Amendment secured a panoply of guarantees including those expressed by the Declaration of Independence and the Bill of Rights. Field related a sense of the Fourteenth Amendment somewhat less detailed than Bradley's and more focused on general economic rights. Each contributed significantly to the amendment's development as a restraint on the legislative process.

Joseph P. Bradley

Bradley had recently been appointed to the Court when the *Slaughter-House Cases* was reviewed. He was nominated by President Grant and confirmed as an associate justice in 1870. As a Republican before the Civil War, his primary interest was in preservation of the union rather than the abolition of slavery. Bradley's professional experience included service as an attorney for a New Jersey railroad that had a reputation for dominating state politics by means of corruption and undue influence. Consistent with his background, Bradley was favorably disposed toward economic rights doctrine that evolved during the final quarter of the nineteenth century.

Unlike Justice Field, whose theory of the Fourteenth Amendment is discussed later, Bradley was somewhat more supportive of constitutional doctrine accounting for the remnants of slavery and racial discrimination. In *Blylew v. United States,* discussed previously, the Court denied federal jurisdiction under the Civil Rights Act of 1866 for the murder of a black woman by a white man. Dissenting from the majority's judgment and reasoning, Bradley accurately warned of the consequences if blacks were denied access to the courts for grievous and racially motivated wrongs. As he related it, their consequent vulnerability

gives unrestricted license and impunity to vindictive outlaws and felons to rush upon these helpless people and kill and slay them at will, as was done in this case. To say that actions or prosecutions intended for the redress of such outrages are not "causes affecting the persons" who are the victims of them, is to take, it seems to me, a view of the law too narrow, too technical, and too forgetful of the liberal objects it had in view.

Bradley also authored an opinion for the Court validating congressional power to secure voting rights against racially motivated imperilment and joined other decisions striking down state action excluding blacks from juries. A decade after the *Slaughter-House Cases,* in what was perhaps the most significant opinion he authored, Bradley seriously cramped the federal interest in accounting for the incidents of slavery and citizenship pursuant to the Thirteenth and Fourteenth Amendments. His decision in the *Civil Rights Cases,* discussed in Chapter 5, foreclosed congressional power to reach private discrimination and characterized racially inspired exclusion from various public accommodations as "mere discriminations" that were constitutionally insignificant.

In his *Slaughter-House* dissent, Bradley urged a reading of the Fourteenth Amendment that recognized a significant rechanneling of federal and state interests. Although acknowledging broad state regulatory authority, he maintained that it was conditioned by "certain traditionary rights." For Bradley, such rights derived not only from state but also national citizenship.

The right of a State to regulate the conduct of its citizens is undoubtedly a very broad and extensive one, and not to be lightly restricted. But there are certain fundamental rights which this right of regulation cannot infringe. It may prescribe the manner of their exercise, but it cannot subvert the rights themselves. I speak now of the rights of citizens of any free government. Granting for the present that the citizens of one government cannot claim the privileges of citizens in another government; that prior to the union of our North American States the citizens of one State could not claim the privileges of citizens in another State; or, that after the union was formed the citizens of the United States, as such, could not claim the privileges of citizens in any particular State; yet the citizens of each of the States and the citizens of the United States would be entitled to certain privileges and immunities as citizens, at the hands of their own government—privileges and immunities which their own governments respectively would be bound to respect and maintain. In this free country, the people of which inherited certain traditionary rights and privileges from their ancestors, citizenship means something. It has certain privileges and immunities attached to it which the government, whether restricted by express or implied limitations, cannot take away or impair. It may do so temporarily by force, but it cannot do so by right. And these privileges and immunities attach as well to citizenship of the United States as to citizenship of the States.

Bradley's understanding of the significance of national citizenship and the scope of its incidents was as expansive as the majority's was narrow. In his view, fundamental privileges and immunities of national citizenship were defined by the Constitution itself, including the Bill of Rights:

But we are not bound to resort to implication, or to the constitutional history of England, to find an authoritative declaration of some of the most important privileges and immunities of citizens of the United States. It is in the Constitution itself. The Constitution, it is true, as it stood prior to the recent amendments, specifies, in terms, only a few of the personal privileges and immunities of citizens, but they are very comprehensive in their character. The States were merely prohibited from passing bills of attainder, *ex post facto* laws, laws impairing the obligation of contracts, and perhaps one or two more. But others of the greatest consequence were enumerated, although they were only secured, in express terms, from invasion by the Federal government; such as the right of *habeas corpus,* the right of trial by jury, of free exercise of religious worship, the right of free speech and a free press, the right peaceably to assemble for the discussion of public measures, the right to be secure against unreasonable searches and seizures, and above all, and including almost all the rest, the right of *not being deprived of life, liberty, or property, without due process of law.* These, and still others are specified in the original Constitution, or in the early amendments of it, as among the privileges and immunities of citizens of the United States, or, what is still stronger for the force of the argument, the rights of all persons, whether citizens or not.

From Bradley's perspective, the Bill of Rights did not exhaust the privileges and immunities of national citizenship. What the majority described as basic privileges of state citizenship in his opinion derived, even if not itemized by the Fourteenth Amendment, from the concept of national citizenship:

But even if the Constitution were silent, the fundamental privileges and immunities of citizens, as such, would be no less real and no less inviolable than they now are. It was not necessary to say in words that the citizens of the United States should have and exercise all the privileges of citizens; the privilege of buying, selling, and enjoying property; the privilege of engaging in any lawful employment for a livelihood; the privilege of resorting to the laws for redress of injuries, and the like. Their very citizenship conferred these privileges, if they did not possess them before. And these privileges they would enjoy whether they were citizens of any State or not. Inhabitants of Federal territories and new citizens, made such by annexation of territory or naturalization, though without any status as citizens of a State, could, nevertheless, as citizens of the United States, lay claim to every one of the privileges and immunities which have been enumerated; and among these none is more essential and fundamental than the right to follow such profession or employment as each one may choose, subject only to uniform regulations equally applicable to all.

Finally, Bradley emphasized that persons of African descent were not the sole beneficiaries of the Fourteenth Amendment. Even if their experience had been the primary inducement for the amendment, Bradley found the provision responsive to risks and abuses demonstrated by the states in general.

It is futile to argue that none but persons of the African race are intended to be benefitted by this amendment. They may have been the primary cause of the amendment, but its language is general, embracing all citizens, and I think it was purposely so expressed.

The mischief to be remedied was not merely slavery and its incidents and consequences; but that spirit of insubordination and disloyalty to the National government which had troubled the country for so many years in some of the States, and that intolerance of free speech and free discussion which often rendered life and property insecure, and led to much unequal legislation. The amendment was an attempt to give voice to the strong National yearning for that time and that condition of things, in which American citizenship should be a sure guaranty of safety, and in which every citizen of the United States might stand erect on every portion of its soil, in the full enjoyment of every right and privilege belonging to a freeman, without fear of violence or molestation.

But great fears are expressed that this construction of the amendment will lead to enactments by Congress interfering with the internal affairs of the States, and establishing therein civil and criminal codes of law for the government of the citizens, and thus abolishing the State governments in everything but name; or else, that it will lead the Federal courts to draw to their cognizance the supervision of State tribunals on every subject of judicial inquiry, on the plea of ascertaining whether the privileges and immunities of citizens have not been abridged.

In my judgment no such practical inconveniences would arise. Very little, if any, legislation on the part of Congress would be required to carry the amendment into effect. Like the prohibition against passing a law impairing the obligation of a contract, it would execute itself. The point would be regularly raised, in a suit at law, and settled by final reference to the Federal court. As the privileges and immunities protected are only those fundamental ones which belong to every citizen, they would soon become so far defined as to cause but a slight accumulation of business in the Federal courts. Besides, the recognized existence of the law would prevent its frequent violation. But even if the business of the National courts should be increased, Congress could easily supply the remedy by increasing their number and efficiency. The great question is, What is the true construction of the amendment? When once we find that, we shall find the means of giving it effect. The argument from inconvenience ought not to have a very controlling influence in questions of this sort. The National will and National interest are of far greater importance.

Bradley eventually budged from his conviction that concerns with expanded federal and diluted state interests were exaggerated. A decade later, in the *Civil Rights Cases,* he expressed precisely such reservations in trimming Congress's power to enforce the Fourteenth Amendment.

Bradley's Preview of the Incorporation Controversy

In his *Slaughter-House* dissent, Bradley forecast the result of if not the actual basis for a significant aspect of the amendment's evolution. His suggestion that the Fourteenth Amendment incorporated the Bill of Rights previewed a critical twentieth century debate. The terms of the controversy by then had been skewed by the result in *Slaughter-House.* The notion of incorporating the Bill of Rights, which Bradley had proposed achieving through the privileges and immunities clause, was reintroduced in connection with the due process clause. Consistent with Bradley's theory, Justice Black argued that the amendment incorporated the entire Bill of Rights. The Court, however, rejected the proposition of "total incorporation" in favor of "selective incorporation." Over the course of time, it has incorporated those guarantees perceived to be "implicit in the concept of ordered liberty" or "rooted in the Nation's traditions and conscience." The net result has been the incorporation of nearly the entire Bill of Rights. The meaning and content of "ordered liberty" and societal "traditions and conscience" also evolved as a focal point for purposes of identifying fundamental liberties. The modern right to privacy, although not specifically enumerated by the Constitution itself, nonetheless has been glossed onto the Fourteenth Amendment pursuant to such an inquiry. Bradley's understanding of what rights are fundamental may have varied from contemporary interpretations. What he envisioned as a repository for the Bill of Rights and for incidents of national citizenship materialized, for practical purposes, in twentieth-century interpretations of the Fourteenth Amendment.

Stephen J. Field

Equal to if not more significant than Bradley's input was Justice Field's dissenting opinion. Field ranks as one of the nation's most influential jurists, in significant part because of his contributions to economic rights doctrine. Although Field's views on marketplace liberty did not prevail in the *Slaughter-House Cases,* he lived to see it evolve into accepted constitutional doctrine. Field's background and tenure on the Court were both colorful and controversial. A particularly bizarre footnote to his record occurred toward the end of Field's career, when his bodyguard shot and killed the chief justice of the California Supreme Court. The incident followed a feud between the two jurists exacerbated by Field's having sentenced the chief justice to a six-month prison sentence for contempt. A criminal trial in connection with the incident was avoided on procedural grounds. Field came from an illustrious and accomplished family. His brother, David Dudley Field, was a prominent legal reformer responsible for introducing new codes of pleading that rationalized and streamlined litigation. Before his appointment to the Court, Field had helped to develop and govern a town in California, been disbarred as an attorney, drafted state civil and criminal codes and served in the state legislature and on the California Supreme Court. Although a Democrat, Field supported the union cause. President Lincoln nominated him to the high bench and the Senate confirmed him in 1863.

A primary feature of Field's jurisprudential legacy is his contribution to the Fourteenth Amendment's development as a source of economic rights. With respect to the immediate concerns of reconstruction, Field had little sympathy. He concurred in the Court's judgment in *Blyew v. United States,* a year before the *Slaughter-House* decision, that a federal court had no jurisdiction to hear an action resulting from a racially inspired murder. Field consistently dissented from decisions that upheld discrimination claims under the Fifteenth Amendment. He also disputed the notion that Congress had power under the Fifteenth Amendment to protect voting rights against racially motivated abridgment. Although expounding an expansive vision of the Fourteenth Amendment, it was selective and not necessarily sympathetic toward the interests that even Bradley had acknowledged were the provision's "primary cause."

Field's Preview of Economic Rights Doctrine

In dissenting from the *Slaughter-House* majority, Field maintained that the Fourteenth Amendment protected the right to ply a trade without state interference. From his perspective, the amendment had achieved a transfer of interests so that "[t]he fundamental rights, privileges and immunities which belong . . . to a free man and a free citizen" derived from national rather than state citizenship. Field thus challenged the majority's understanding of the Fourteenth Amendment as having limited redistributive consequences.

The question presented is, therefore, one of the gravest importance, not merely to the parties here, but to the whole country. It is nothing less than the question whether the recent amendments to the Federal Constitution protect the citizens of the United States against the deprivation of their common rights by State legislation. In my judgment the fourteenth amendment does afford such protection, and was so intended by the Congress which framed and the States which adopted it. . . .

The amendment does not attempt to confer any new privileges or immunities upon citizens, or to enumerate or define those already existing. It assumes that there are such privileges and immunities which belong of right to citizens as such, and ordains that they shall not be abridged by State legislation. If this inhibition has no reference to privileges and immunities of this character, but only refers, as held by the majority of the court in their opinion, to such privileges and immunities as were before its adoption specially designated in the Constitution or necessarily implied as belonging to citizens of the United States, it was a vain and idle enactment, which accomplished nothing, and most unnecessarily excited Congress and the people on its passage. With privileges and immunities thus designated or implied no State could ever have interfered by its laws, and no new constitutional provision was required to inhibit such interference. The supremacy of the Constitution and the laws of the United States always controlled any State legislation of that character. But if the amendment refers to the natural and inalienable rights which belong to all citizens, the inhibition has a profound significance and consequence.

Field's point was that the privileges and immunities clause had effected a more dramatic change in federal and state interests than the majority acknowledged. Jurisprudence and commentary since have concurred with Field's sense that the Court had reduced the clause to a dead letter. Comparing the two privileges and immunities clauses of the Constitution, an early twentieth century observer noted that "Article IV, Section 2, is held to declare that *some* state created rights, if created at all and conferred upon citizens of the state, may not be withheld from the citizens of other states; Amendment XIV declares that a state shall not abridge nation created rights. [T]his narrower construction of the privileges and immunities passage . . . [renders] it an idle provision, in that it only declares a principle already more amply and simply expressed in the constitution."

From Field's perspective, the Fourteenth Amendment's primary achievement was to redirect basic incidents of citizenship from state to federal concern. As described previously, the significance of that rerouting was diminished by the majority's narrow depiction of federal privileges and immunities. Field's analysis yielded a contrary result, as he concluded that the Fourteenth Amendment disabled the states from interfering with a broad spectrum of interests established as the incidents of national citizenship.

What, then, are the privileges and immunities which are secured against abridgment by State legislation?

In the first section of the Civil Rights Act Congress has given its interpretation to these terms, or at least has stated some of the rights which, in its judgment, these terms include; it has there declared that they include the right "to make and enforce contracts, to sue, be parties and give evidence, to inherit, purchase, lease, sell, hold, and convey real and personal property, and to full and equal benefit of all laws and proceedings for the security of person and property." That act, it is true, was passed before the fourteenth amendment, but the amendment was adopted, as I have already said, to obviate objections to the act, or, speaking more accurately, I should say, to obviate objections to legislation of a similar character, extending the protection of the National government over the common rights of all citizens of the United States. Accordingly, after its ratification, Congress re-enacted the act under the belief that whatever doubts may have previously existed of its validity, they were removed by the amendment.

The terms "privileges and immunities" are not new in the amendment; they were in the Constitution before the amendment was adopted. They are found in the second section of the fourth article, which declares that "the citizens of each State shall be entitled to all privileges and immunities of citizens in the several States," and they have been the subject of frequent consideration in judicial decisions. In *Corfield v. Coryell,* Mr. Justice Washington said he had "no hesitation in confining these expressions to those privileges and immunities which were, in their nature, fundamental; which belong of right to citizens of all free governments, and which have at all times been enjoyed by the citizens of the several States which compose the Union, from the time of their becoming free, independent, and sovereign"; and, in considering what those fundamental privileges were, he said that perhaps it would be more tedious than difficult to enumerate them, but that they might be "all comprehended under the following general heads: protection by the government; the enjoyment of life and liberty, with the right to acquire and possess property of every kind, and to pursue and obtain happiness and safety, subject, nevertheless, to such restraints as the government may justly prescribe for the general good of the whole." This appears to me to be a sound construction of the clause in question. The privileges and immunities designated are those *which of right belong to the citizens of all free governments.* Clearly among these must be placed the right to pursue a lawful employment in a lawful manner, without other restraint than such as equally affects all persons. . . .

The privileges and immunities designated in the second section of the fourth article of the Constitution are, then, according to the decision cited, those which of right belong to the citizens of all free governments, and they can be enjoyed under that clause by the citizens of each State in the several States upon the same terms and conditions as they are enjoyed by the citizens of the latter States. No discrimination can be made by one State against the citizens of other States in their enjoyment, nor can any greater imposition be levied than such as is laid upon its own citizens. It is a clause which insures equality in the enjoyment of these rights between citizens of the several States whilst in the same State. . . .

Now, what the clause in question does for the protection of citizens of one State against the creation of monopolies in favor of citizens of other States, the fourteenth amendment does for the protection of every citizen of the United States against the creation of any monopoly whatever. The privileges and immunities of citizens of the United States, of every one of them, is secured against abridgment in any form by any State. The fourteenth amendment places them under the guardianship of the National authority.

Field's vision of the Fourteenth Amendment, as the basis for economic rights not specified by the Constitution but incidental to national citizenship, did not prevail immediately. His views were endorsed by influential legal scholars such as Thomas Cooley, however, who contemporaneously urged interpretation of the Fourteenth Amendment to account for general economic freedom. The eventual success of such doctrine, as political and judicial interest in reconstruction diminished, was not incongruent with the ideology and priorities of the nineteenth century's final quarter. The period was characterized not only by the formal end of reconstruction, but also by heightened attention to industrial development and economic growth. As manufacturing, transportation and communications processes grew and expanded, various states enacted regulation to control rates, practices and other economic and social consequences. Not unlike the antebellum re-action of the South to challenges of slavery, affected business interests turned to the Constitution in an effort to identify a source of ultimate protection. Particularly influential on the development of such doctrine was Cooley's constitutional scholarship, which included a treatise advocat-ing the notion of due process as a check on legislative power. The tug of economic rights theory, repudiated when first presented by Field, was felt increasingly as Fourteenth Amendment jurisprudence progressed toward the end of the nineteenth century.

The selective focus of Field's Fourteenth Amendment perspective was disclosed in the immediate wake of his dissent. In a decision announced one day after the *Slaughter-House* ruling, Field joined a judgment and opinion upholding a state's refusal to admit a woman to the practice of law. The case of *Bradwell v. Illinois* presented Field with an opportunity to reiterate economic rights doctrine, as the challenged action denied the claimant an opportunity to pursue a "lawful industrial pursuit." His failure to reaffirm the premise, articulated when economic freedom was compromised in *Slaughter-House,* seems to have reflected a common assumption that women were not fit for such work. Field joined Justice Bradley in a concurring opinion to the effect that "[t]he paramount destiny and mission of woman are to fulfill the noble and benign offices of wife and mother." In *Minor v. Happersett,* Field subscribed to the Court's opinion that women were citizens under the Fourteenth Amendment, but a state was not prevented from denying them the right to vote. Such rulings reinforced the initial interpretive sense that the Fourteenth Amendment was concerned primar-ily with racially significant action.

Road to Substantive Due Process

Even as the Court reiterated constitutional terms of limitation, indica-tions of an eventual accounting for economic rights were manifested. In *Loan Association v. City of Topeka,* the Court struck down a local law that set a preferential tax rate for businesses relocating to the community. Justice Miller, who spoke for the majority in *Slaughter-House,* authored an opinion for the Court that did not identify a specific constitutional basis for invalidating the law. Miller found that the tax did not have a "public character, but was purely in aid of private or personal objects beyond the legislative power and an unauthorized invasion of private right." The Court then referenced its decision to rights that were not specified by the Constitution, but "implied."

The theory of our governments, State and National, is opposed to the deposit of unlimited power anywhere. The executive, the legislative, and the judicial branches of these governments are all of limited and defined powers.

There are limitations on such power which grow out of the essential nature of all free governments. Implied reservations of individual rights, without which the social compact could not exist, and which are respected by all governments entitled to the name. No court, for instance, would hesitate to declare void a statute which enacted that A. and B., who were husband and wife to each other should be so no longer, but that A. should thereafter be the husband of C., and B. the wife of D. Or which should enact that the homestead now owned by A. should no longer be his, but should henceforth be the property of B.

Without a specific constitutional reference point for invalidating the law, the Court's decision translated into a statement of natural justice. Such analysis is fundamentally indistinguishable from the substantive due process review it rejected in *Slaughter-House.* In either instance, fundamental rights were grafted onto the Constitution for purposes of checking legislative power. Whether the Court should discern or develop fundamental rights not enumerated by the document itself is a question that, as discussed in the introduction, has been debated for two centuries. As post–*Slaughter-House* case law has disclosed, the Court within several years began moving inexorably toward embracing Field's economic rights doctrine.

A significant step toward recognition of the Fourteenth Amendment as a source of economic rights was taken four years after the *Slaughter-House* decision. In *Munn v. Illinois,* the Court intimated that the due process guarantee might operate as a restriction on state regulatory power. At issue was a state law governing grain elevator rates. For purposes of its holding, the Court rejected the due process argument and did not consider whether the state-controlled rates were reasonable. The way in which the Court refused to consider the reasonableness of the regulation suggested that the actual result in *Munn* might be an exception rather than the norm. Emphasizing that it was deferring to legislative judgment because the regulated activity was clothed with "a public interest," the Court noted that "in mere private contracts, relating to matters in which the public has no interest, what is reasonable must be judicially ascertained." The opinion, authored by Justice Miller, who had delimited the due process clause's significance in the *Slaughter-House Cases,* established a premise for close judicial scrutiny of legislation interfering with alleged economic rights.

Despite generally deferring to legislative action over the next decade, the Court increasingly referred to the due process clause as a limit on state police power. In the *Railroad Commission Cases,* decided in 1886, it upheld state regulation of railroad rates. Although affirming the exercise of state power, the Court expanded the grounds for reviewing legislative policy. It stressed that a state could not govern rates in a way that "amounts to a taking of private property for use without just compensation, or without due process of law."

A year later, in *Mugler v. Kansas,* the Court evidenced further warming to substantive due process theory. The *Mugler* case presented a Fourteenth Amendment challenge to a state law prohibiting the sale of liquor. Although acknowledging legislative authority to determine and regulate what "will injuriously affect the public," it asserted that "[t]here are, of necessity, limits beyond which state police powers cannot rightfully go." Emphasizing that it "must obey the Constitution rather than the law-making department of government," the Court determined that it had a

solemn duty—to look at the substance of things, whenever they enter upon the inquiry whether the legislature has transcended the limits of its authority. If, therefore, a statute purporting to have been enacted to protect the public health, the public morals, or the public safety, has no real or substantial relation to those objects, or is a palpable invasion of rights secured by the fundamental law, it is the duty of the courts to so adjudge, and thereby give effect to the Constitution.

In *Mugler,* the Court indicated that it was prepared to determine not only whether a state had authority to regulate an activity, but also whether the means of governance appropriately and meaningfully advanced its objective. As subsequent case law demonstrated, it was a formula that enabled the judiciary to oversee and displace the output of representative governance without reference to a specifically enumerated constitutional right or freedom.

From Dissenting Principle to Mainstream Doctrine

A general blueprint for development of the Fourteenth Amendment, making due process a significant barrier to economic regulation during the first few decades of the twentieth century, was etched by the Court in *Allgeyer v. Louisiana.* At issue in *Allgeyer* was whether a state could prohibit certain insurance contracts written by out-of-state companies. After determining that the state was without power to regulate such activity, the Court discoursed further on the meaning of due process. It described the provision as guaranteeing a person the liberty to use "all his faculties . . . in all lawful ways." What it secured specifically against state interference, according to the Court, was "liberty of contract."

The *Allgeyer* decision represented the ultimate triumph of ideology that regarded the Fourteenth Amendment as a bulwark for economic rights. The interests that Justice Field had urged accounting for by means of the privileges and immunities clause thus were secured by means of the due process clause. Adoption of Fourteenth Amendment priorities, as originally ordered by Field, manifested itself both in standards of review and in results. In rejecting economic rights theory a quarter of a century before, the *Slaughter-House* Court had emphasized the Fourteenth Amendment's essential concern with "the freedom of the slave race." The *Allgeyer* decision indicated that the use of state police powers to regulate economic activity was subject to rigorous constitutional review. At the same time, the Court allowed that its review of state classifications on the basis of race would be relatively relaxed. In *Plessy v. Ferguson,* decided a year before *Allgeyer,* the Court invested in the separate but equal doctrine and deferred to official segregation as a reasonable exercise of state police power that was well grounded in custom and practice. Taken together, *Allgeyer* and *Plessy* demonstrated that what was once marginal to Fourteenth Amendment purposes had become central, and what was once at its core had become peripheral. The *Plessy* principle remained functional through the middle of this century. Although not as enduring, economic rights doctrine had an extended run into the late 1930s. Constitutional priorities and principles by the beginning of the twentieth century thus had been substantially reordered. As the first few decades of the century evolved, substantive due process concepts established significant impediments to the exercise of legislative power. The Fourteenth Amendment that had originated as a major factor in resolving one crisis of the union eventually became part of another constitutional emergency.

Bibliography

Cases

Allgeyer v. Louisiana, 165 U.S. 578 (1897).
Blylew v. United States, 80 U.S. 581 (1872).
Bradwell v. Illinois, 83 U.S. 130 (1873).
Civil Rights Cases, 109 U.S. 3 (1883).
Corfield v. Coryell, 6 F. Cas. 546 (C.C.D. Pa. 1823).
Loan Association v. City of Topeka, 87 U.S. 655 (1874).
Minor v. Happersett, 88 U.S. 162 (1874).
Mugler v. Kansas, 123 U.S. 623 (1887).

Munn v. Illinois, 94 U.S. 113 (1876).
Plessy v. Ferguson, 163 U.S. 537 (1896).
Railroad Commission Cases, 116 U.S. 307 (1886).
Slaughter-House Cases, 83 U.S. 36 (1873).

Books and Articles

Berger, R., Government by Judiciary: The Transformation of the Fourteenth Amendment (1977).

Black, C., Structure and Relationship in Constitutional Law (1969).

Cooley T., Constitutional Limitations (1868).

Fairman, C., VII History of the Supreme Court of the United States, Reconstruction and Reunion (1971) (1987).

Hyman, H., A More Perfect Union (1973).

Hyman, H., & Wiecek, W., Equal Justice under the Law (1982).

Kaczorowski, R., The Politics of Judicial Interpretation: The Federal Courts, Department of Justice and Civil Rights, 1866–1876 (1985).

Karst, K., Belonging to America (1989).

Kettner, J., The Development of American Citizenship, 1608–1870 (1978).

McGovney, *Privileges or Immunities Clause, Fourteenth Amendment*, 4 Iowa L. Bull. 219 (1918).

Sandalow, T., *Constitutional Interpretation*, 79 Mich. L. Rev. 1033 (1981).

Chapter 4

THE RISE, DEMISE AND RESURRECTION OF SUBSTANTIVE DUE PROCESS

The concept of substantive due process, as originally propounded with respect to the Fourteenth Amendment, consumed only three paragraphs of the Supreme Court's attention. Summary rejection of the due process clause as a source of fundamental rights that restricted state legislative power, in the *Slaughter-House Cases,* may have reflected accurately the limited expectations of the provision's framers. Except for Chief Justice Taney's reference to due process as a bar to congressional regulation of slavery, the Court traditionally had regarded the principle as a guarantee of procedural fairness. By negating the significance of the privileges and immunities clause, the *Slaughter-House* Court eliminated what may have been a more logical predicate for identifying and developing fundamental rights. As Justice Field saw it, economic rights were among the privileges and immunities of national citizenship. The Court's initial refusal to develop fundamental rights, either by means of the privileges and immunities clause or the due process clause, was short-lived. The *Slaughter-House* Court miscalculated the long-term appeal of the Fourteenth Amendment, and the due process clause in particular, as a check on the legislative process. Even though a continuing source of controversy, and despite the uncertain life span of rights that are glossed on the Constitution, substantive due process has endured as a significant aspect of twentieth-century constitutional jurisprudence.

Nature, Concerns and Criticism of Substantive Due Process Review

As development of fundamental rights through the due process clause has become a judicial function over the past century, without any specific guidance by the Constitution itself, it is not surprising that variances have materialized with respect to what is off limits to the legislature. Due process analysis as it evolved over the first few decades of this century is remembered primarily for its emphasis on marketplace liberty. At the peak of the economic rights era, the Court's opinions read as if scripted by Justice Field. The period is notable, however, for its development of personal liberty across a broad spectrum. As the Court observed, in *Meyer v. Nebraska,* the scope of liberty protected by the Fourteenth Amendment included

freedom from bodily restraint . . . the right of the individual to contract, to engage in any of the common occupations of life, to acquire useful knowledge, to marry, to establish a home and bring up children, to worship God according to the dictates of conscience, and generally to enjoy those privileges long recognized at common law as essential to the orderly pursuit of happiness by free men.

The Court, in the late 1930s, disclaimed substantive due process review and indicated that it would closely monitor the exercise of legislative power only when a constitutionally specified freedom was implicated. By the 1960s, it became apparent that the Court had abandoned an accounting for economic rights but not substantive due process review altogether. Fundamental rights analysis was resurrected, not for purposes of securing marketplace liberty, but to account for what was identified as the right to privacy. In both of its incarnations, substantive due process review has set certain activities or interests beyond legislative reach and generated controversy with respect to whether the judiciary has exceeded the scope of its authority and functioned anti-democratically.

The touchstone of substantive due process analysis is an independent judicial inquiry into the premises and viability of legislative policy. Once a court has discerned that regulation implicates a fundamental but unenumerated right, review involves determining whether the power to regulate exists and whether legislative methodology meaningfully relates to its objective. Identification of a fundamental right alone is not necessarily fatal to a law, therefore, if review determines that the legislature has a valid basis and persuasive reason for regulating and the means of governance are sufficiently connected toward their aim. Such review in a formal sense is reducible to assessing whether (1) a challenged regulation is within the legislature's scope of power; (2) the reason for regulatory intervention is substantial or compelling; (3) a meaningful nexus exists between regulatory methodology and objectives and (4) alternatives exist that promote the governmental objective as effectively but less injuriously to the discerned right.

Substantive due process review has resulted in variances over the course of time with respect to what is perceived and declared to be fundamental. Insofar as the judiciary has augmented constitutionally specified rights and liberties by its development of the due process clause, criticism has been predictable and persistent. The principal objection, sounded in response to emphasis on economic rights earlier in this century and on privacy rights more recently, is that the judiciary usurps legislative power and functions anti-democratically. When the judiciary identifies and develops fundamental rights, the concern is that the choice may reflect the idiosyncratic moral preferences of the Court. Determination of whether a valid legislative purpose exists, if not referenced to an enumerated check on governmental power, may be influenced by ideology that is personally rather than textually ordained. Given their often debated premises, contrasted with the documental basis of enumerated rights and liberties, fundamental freedoms grafted onto the Constitution may have an inherently ephemeral nature.

Economic Rights

Neither contractual liberty nor privacy rights are established by the text of the Constitution. In different jurisprudential generations, each has been recognized as a fundamental interest protected by the due process clause. During the early part of this century, a majority of the Court regularly invalidated legislation concerning conditions of employment and other economic circumstances. Such regulation typically ran afoul of the due process clause, which at the time was interpreted as a safeguard of freedom to contract and of property rights. Attention to marketplace liberty was mandated not by the Constitution itself but by a debatable ideology that inspired the Fourteenth Amendment's meaning at the time. Once established as a fundamental freedom under the due process clause, contractual liberty significantly cramped legislative authority to regulate economic activity. Acknowledgment of a legitimate governmental purpose did not necessarily mean that regulation was allowable. Whether accounting for economic freedom then or privacy now, analysis has focused further on whether regulatory means are sufficiently related to governmental aims. Consideration of whether legislative policy is reasonably, substantially or necessarily adapted to achieving its stated goals, like determining whether the state has exceeded the scope of its regulatory power, may be an essentially subjective enterprise.

Lochner v. New York

The quintessential substantive due process decision, at least with respect to economic rights doctrine, is *Lochner v. New York*. The *Lochner* ruling is so noteworthy, and for critics so notorious, that Lochnerism for many has become synonymous with the vicissitudes of substantive due process. In *Lochner*, the Court identified liberty of contract as a fundamental freedom that trumped a state's power to regulate conditions of employment. From *Lochner*, which amplified and hardened constitutional terms and standards identified in *Allgeyer v. Louisiana*, evolved three decades of judicially developed rights and liberties that negated a multitude of social and economic initiatives by the political process.

At issue in *Lochner* was a state law establishing maximum hours of work for bakers. Several years before *Lochner*, the Court upheld maximum-hour regulations in the mining industry despite their impact on contractual liberty. Given the dangerous working conditions of miners, it concluded in *Holden v. Hardy* that the state had reasonably exercised its power to regulate health and safety. The *Lochner* Court determined that legislation limiting bakers to sixty working hours per week or ten hours a day was neither a legitimate health or safety regulation nor a reasonable condition on "the freedom of master and employee to contract with each other in relation to this employment."

Immediately fatal to the law was the Court's sense that conditions of employment were not even a legitimate state interest. The Court acknowledged no connection with health and safety and depicted the law as labor legislation "pure and simple." Depiction of the state's concern in singular and exclusive terms, when it actually was amenable to various characterizations including that of a health or safety measure, suggested the possibility of ideologically influenced and result-oriented review. The Court attempted to defeat any impression of subjectivity, emphasizing that it was not "substituting [its] judgment for that of the legislature." The image of ideological neutrality was betrayed, however, by the observation that "[w]e do not believe in the soundness of the views which uphold the law." Displacement of regulation emanating from the representative process, on grounds of disagreement with the policy itself, is the hallmark of a super-legislature. For critics then and now, a primary concern with substantive due process review is that results are a function of policy disagreement rather than true constitutional imperative.

After *Lochner* demonstrated the vitality of economic rights doctrine, introduced by Justice Field in the *Slaughter-House Cases*, subsequent case law revealed its durability. Through the mid-1930s, the Courts frequently struck down an array of social and economic legislation on grounds that it abridged contractual liberty or property rights. The toll of such review at both the federal and the state level included collective bargaining laws, price controls and minimum wage and maximum hour legislation. Insofar as the federal government attempted to account for such interests, the Court discerned both violations of the Fifth Amendment's due process clause and an absence of power under the commerce clause. In finding Congress without authority to regulate economic activity unless it directly affected commerce, and distinguishing between manufacturing and transportation processes, the Court emphasized that such power was reserved to the states under the Tenth Amendment. As the results of contemporaneous substantive due process analysis disclosed, however, the Court also denied the legitimacy of state authority that interfered with marketplace liberty.

To establish that economic regulation was reasonable, in the *Lochner* era, it became necessary to present detailed and persuasive evidence of a clear health or safety interest. Pursuant to extensive documentation of such concerns for women, the Court in *Muller v. Oregon* upheld maximum hour legislation for women. Despite the possibility of convincing the Court that the state regulatory purpose was legitimate, case law emphasized that "freedom of contract is . . . nevertheless the general rule and restraint the exception." So profound was the Court's commitment to economic rights during the *Lochner* era that one of the few deviations from the separate but equal doctrine, which limited constitutional attention to claims of racial discrimination, was grounded in the interest of protecting economic liberty. A city ordinance restricting real estate transactions on the basis of race was struck down, in *Buchanan v. Warley,* not as discriminatory legislation violating the equal protection clause but as a deprivation of property rights.

Dissenting Opinions in *Lochner*

The *Lochner* era of substantive due process review was the logical extension of a Court shaped by late nineteenth and early twentieth-century presidents, who selected nominees based in significant part upon their commitment to preserving economic liberty. Competing against such doctrinal fidelity in the *Lochner* case itself were competing models of judicial review advanced by Justices Harlan and Holmes. Harlan, whose background is discussed in the next chapter, disagreed with the Court's depiction of the challenged law. Based on evidence to the effect that health standards for bakers were deficient, Harlan was satisfied that the enactment responded to a legitimate state concern. Like the majority, Harlan examined the record to determine if a genuine health interest existed. Even if the basis for a regulatory concern was only arguable, he favored deferring to legislatively chosen policy. Harlan's difference with the majority thus related to the level of proof required to establish a valid state concern and a different perception of whether the regulatory means were reasonable.

Oliver W. Holmes, Jr.

Justice Holmes's dissent sharply criticized a right he considered to be a mere ideological fabrication. Of the many jurists who have influenced the development of constitutional law, Holmes is among the most eminent. Holmes was nominated to the Court by Theodore Roosevelt and confirmed in 1902, after a career as a practitioner, scholar and state supreme court justice. His reputation as "the great dissenter" was not a particular badge of honor for Holmes. As he put it, "I regret being called a dissenting Judge in the papers for I don't like to dissent." The distinction nonetheless reflected not only the volume but also the long-term influence of his opinions, especially with respect to expressive freedom and the judicial function. Included in his legacy are enduring contributions, discussed in Chapter 6, toward First Amendment standards that were subscribed to nearly half a century after he and Justice Brandeis articulated them. Such results bear out Felix Frankfurter's observation that "some of [Holmes's] weightiest utterances are dissenting opinions—but they are dissents that record prophesy and shape history."

Holmes also was the author of some especially infamous civil rights decisions. When Southern officials refused to register black voters, early in this century, Holmes refused to order relief on claims that the state had denied the right to vote in violation of the Fifteenth Amendment. Writing for the Court, in *Giles v. Harris,* he denied a remedy on grounds that judicial relief would be "pointless." Later, in *Buck v. Bell,* he upheld a compulsory sterilization program for mentally retarded persons and observed that "three generations of imbeciles is enough." Even if the *Buck* decision upheld what generally is regarded now as morally repugnant policy, it illuminated Holmes' general sense that judicial review of constitutional questions does not allow factoring the sensibility of legislative policy. Acknowledging "the very powerful argument against the wisdom of the legislation," in *Noble State Bank v. Haskell,* Holmes stressed that "on that point we have nothing to say because it is not our concern." Disinterest in whether law was wise, dangerous or futile was a defining aspect of Holmes' judicial philosophy that he consistently stressed. An incongruous consequence of his sense of the judicial function was a reputation, as Frankfurter noted, for "economic and political reform theories that he does not necessarily [support] and of whose efficacy in action he is skeptical."

As Holmes commenced his tenure on the Court at the outset of the twentieth century, a dominant political and constitutional issue was the relation of government to business. Economic concentration had introduced what Louis Brandeis described as "a state . . . within the State . . . so powerful that the ordinary social and industrial forces existing are insufficient to cope with it." As society-defining questions concerning economic power, labor relations and like social issues generated constitutional litigation that for many presented a choice between freedom and reform, Holmes' judicial philosophy resulted in a calculated aloofness from the logic or foolishness of legislative action. Especially objectionable to him was the Court's use of the substantive due process clause to create and develop economic rights. Throughout the *Lochner* era, he consistently opposed the majority's expounding of principles that cramped legislative processes of innovation and reckoning. As he related in *Truax v. Corrigan* in 1921, "[t]there is nothing I more deprecate that the use of the Fourteenth Amendment beyond the absolute compulsion of its words to prevent the making of social experiments that an important part of the community desires." Consistent with his animus toward substantive due process review, Holmes depicted the majority's method in *Lochner* as imposing a debatable economic philosophy on the nation. Judicially induced principle that negated or narrowed legislative power, from his perspective, was an extension of personally favored ideology. As he put it:

This case is decided upon an economic theory which a large part of the country does not entertain. If it were a question whether I agreed with that theory, I should desire to study it further and long before making up my mind. But I do not conceive that to be my duty, because I strongly believe that my agreement or disagreement has nothing to do with the right of a majority to embody their opinions in law. It is settled by various decisions of this court that state constitutions and state laws may regulate life in many ways which we as legislators might think as injudicious or if you like as tyrannical as this, and which equally with this interfere with the liberty to contract. Sunday laws and usury laws are ancient examples. A more modern one is the prohibition of lotteries. The liberty of the citizen to do as he likes so long as he does not interfere with the liberty of others to do the same, which has been a shibboleth for some well-known writers, is interfered with by school laws, by the Post Office, by every state or municipal institution which takes his money for purposes thought desirable, whether he likes it or not. The Fourteenth Amendment does not enact Mr. Herbert Spencer's Social Statics. The other day we sustained the Massachusetts vaccination law. [Citation omitted.] United States and state statutes and decisions cutting down the liberty to contract by way of combination are familiar to this court. [Citation omitted.] Two years ago we upheld the prohibition of sales of stock on margins or for future delivery in the constitution of California. [Citation omitted.] The decision sustaining an eight hour law for miners is still recent. [Citation omitted.] Some of these laws embody convictions or prejudices which judges are likely to share. Some may not. But a constitution is not intended to embody a particular economic theory, whether of paternalism and the organic relation of the citizen to the State or of *laissez faire*.. It is made for people of fundamentally differing views, and the accident of our finding certain opinions natural and familiar or novel and even shocking ought not to

conclude our judgment upon the question whether statutes embodying them conflict with the Constitution of the United States.

General propositions do not decide concrete cases. The decision will depend on
a judgment or intuition more subtle than any articulate major premise. But I think
that the proposition just stated, if it is accepted, will carry us far toward the end.
Every opinion tends to become a law. I think that the word "liberty" in the Fourteenth Amendment is perverted when it is held to prevent the natural outcome of
a dominant opinion, unless it can be said that a rational and fair man necessarily
would admit that the statute proposed would infringe fundamental principles as
they have been understood by the traditions of our people and our law. It does
not need research to show that no such sweeping condemnation can be passed
upon the statute before us. A reasonable man might think it a proper measure on
the score of health. Men whom I certainly could not pronounce unreasonable
would uphold it as a first instalment of a general regulation of the hours of work.

The standard of review favored by Holmes in *Lochner* allowed no probing inquiry into legislative motivation or the need for regulatory action.
The nub of his argument was that the Court had no further interest in a
law once it ascertained that the enactment reasonably related to a legitimate state concern. Holmes, however, did not entirely foreclose the possibility of displacing legislative output. By suggesting that it would be appropriate to determine whether "a rational and fair man" would find that
legislation "infringe[d] fundamental principles" rooted in "the traditions
of our people and our law," Holmes left open a possibility that the judiciary might negate the work of the political process as a violation of the
Fourteenth Amendment. The reservation of judicial attention for laws impacting "fundamental principles" radiated a somewhat scrambled message.
Taken at face value, it suggested not that the process of developing fundamental rights was wrong, but that the *Lochner* Court had identified the
wrong interests. Modern standards of due process review, as discussed
later, borrow from Holmes' formula but also suffer from its internal tension.

The Demise of Economic Rights

The *Lochner* era of substantive due process review persisted into the
1930s over Holmes's almost unrelenting protest. His criticism evolved to
the point that it indicated nearly zero tolerance for development of fundamental rights not specified by the Constitution itself. Two decades after
Lochner, in *Tyson & Brother v. Bantom*, he reiterated that "a state legislature
can do whatever it sees fit to do unless it is restrained by some express
prohibition in the Constitution of the United States . . . and that Courts
should be careful not to extend such prohibitions beyond their obvious
meaning by reading into them conceptions of public policy that the partic-

ular Court may happen to entertain." Holmes resigned from the bench in 1932, the same year Franklin Roosevelt was elected president but before economic rights doctrine had run its course. As the nation became mired in a prolonged economic depression, the president and Congress responded with a multiplicity of initiatives and programs that enhanced the federal government's role in regulating the economy. Such policy collided at first with precedents that narrowly defined the power to regulate interstate commerce and broadly construed economic liberty. Interpretive conflict precipitated a constitutional crisis that was defused by extensive personnel turnover on the Court in the late 1930s, and a judicial climate that quickly warmed to Holmes's views.

A harbinger of future constitutional change emerged two years after Holmes retired when, in *Nebbia v. New York*, the Court upheld a state law setting minimum prices for milk. The majority opinion revisited principles first advanced in *Munn v. Illinois*, a decision which acknowledged a state's power to regulate when the public interest was implicated. Finding no specific class of business "affected with a public interest," the Court abandoned a distinction which, as discussed in Chapter 2, had been a significant step toward a constitutional accounting for economic liberty. Contrary to the description of its function in *Lochner* and closer to Holmes's dissent, the Court acknowledged that its power of review did not include authority to establish economic policy. It accordingly noted that states were "free to adopt whatever economic policy may reasonably be deemed to promote public welfare, and to enforce that policy by legislation adapted to its purpose."

The *Nebbia* decision, despite its rhetoric, did not terminate the *Lochner* era. A couple of years later, the Court invalidated a New York minimum wage law on grounds that it impaired contractual liberty. Meanwhile, Congress enacted a broad program of national economic reforms proposed by President Franklin Roosevelt. Judicial response to New Deal legislation conceived in response to an economic crisis soon begot a constitutional crisis. Roosevelt's reelection by an overwhelming margin in 1936 evidenced to him a broad public mandate for innovative policy reckoning with the nation's deep and prolonged depression. Central to New Deal policy was broad-spectrum regulation impacting industry, mining, farming and transportation. In a series of cases decided in 1935 and 1936, the Court invalidated laws that, among other things, established codes of fair competition, required pension systems for railroad employees, established farm subsidy programs and established maximum hours, minimum wages and price controls in the coal industry. Such decisions not only gutted the New Deal but also evinced an abiding commitment by the Court to compete with the elected branches of government over economic policy.

Responding to the judicially implanted impediments to political policy, Roosevelt proposed a radical reorganization of the Supreme Court. The proposal was calculated especially to negate the influence of those justices who for many years had championed economic rights doctrine. Roosevelt proposed expanding the Court by one seat for each member over the age of seventy who had served at least ten years. If adopted, the plan would have increased the Court's membership from nine to sixteen.

The Court-packing plan represented an obvious challenge to judicial authority. Although the source of much controversy, the proposal was defeated in Congress. Constitutional lore suggests that the threat of reorganization intimidated the Court to the point that it finally backed away from its assertive defense of economic rights. In *National Labor Relations Board v. Jones & Laughlin Steel Corp.,* a case decided soon after Roosevelt announced his proposal, the Court upheld the National Labor Relations Act and a National Labor Relations Board order prohibiting an employer from interfering with union activity. Justice Roberts, who had sided with the majority in earlier cases striking down New Deal legislation, voted in favor of heightened deference to legislative policy—a redirection that has been characterized as "the switch in time that saved nine." No clear proof exists to demonstrate actual linkage between Roosevelt's threats and doctrinal revision. Evidence exists, moreover, that the Court's retreat from economic rights doctrine was achieved independently rather than as a consequence of intimidation. Formal reorganization soon proved unnecessary to the emergence of a Court more hospitable to legislative initiative in the marketplace. Within a few years of his failed plan, and pursuant to the retirement or death of several justices, Roosevelt had restructured the Court with personnel more deferential toward politically induced economic reform.

Indications of lasting doctrinal change appeared in 1937 when, in *West Coast Hotel v. Parrish,* the Court upheld a state minimum wage law for women. In *Parrish,* the Court revisited legislation identical to what it had struck down in the past. Such regulation had been invalidated fourteen years earlier, in *Adkins v. Children's Hospital,* as a violation of contractual liberty. Evidencing the Court's new approach to the due process clause was its repudiation of precedent on grounds that the *Adkins* decision was "a departure from the true application of the principles governing the regulation by the State of the relation of employer and employed." The Court thus deferred to the state's interest in exercising its police power and concluded that any impact on contractual liberty was constitutionally significant.

Confirming the constitutional reorientation suggested by the *Parrish* decision was the Court's analysis in *United States v. Carolene Products Co.* In the *Carolene Products* case, the Court upheld federal legislation prohibiting the interstate carriage of adulterated milk products. In rejecting arguments that the provision violated the Fifth Amendment's due process clause, the Court determined that when legislative judgment is at issue review "must be restricted to the issue whether any state of facts either known or which could reasonably be assumed affords support for it." The Court noted that congressional findings established a rational basis for legislative action. More significant for purposes of future analysis, however, was its conclusion that

the existence of facts supporting the legislative judgment is to be presumed, for regulatory legislation affecting ordinary commercial transactions is not to be pronounced unconstitutional unless in the light of the facts made known or generally assumed it is of such a character as to preclude the assumption that it rests on some rational basis within the knowledge and experience of the legislators.

The Court thus abandoned its role as guardian of economic policy. Although reserving the possibility of stricter review when constitutionally enumerated rights were implicated or when "prejudice against discrete and insular minorities" distorted the political process, the Court downgraded the due process clause as a departure point for second-guessing legislative judgment.

The Long-Term Influence of Holmes

Post–*Carolene Products* jurisprudence largely has been an exercise in disclaiming Lochnerism and touting Holmes's wisdom. The *Carolene Products* decision left open whether discernment of a rational basis for legislation might entail judicial sifting through the record to determine whether economic regulation was justified. Even that possibility was foreclosed by subsequent case law that established standards of utmost deference. Upholding a state labor law, in *Lincoln Federal Labor Union v. Northwestern Iron & Metal Co.,* the Court emphasized that government may regulate commercial and business activity provided it does "not run afoul of some specific constitutional prohibition, or of some valid federal law." The decision, rendered a decade after *Carolene Products,* directly and specifically disclaimed *"Allgeyer-Lochner . . .* constitutional doctrine." Economic rights review was further discredited in 1955 when the Court upheld a state law prohibiting opticians from dispensing or refitting eyeglasses without a doctor's prescription. Arguments in *Williamson v. Lee Optical Co.* that the provision denied due process were rejected pursuant to an especially relaxed standard of review. The Court found it to be "enough that there is an evil at hand for correction, and that it might be thought that the particular legislative measure was a rational way to correct it." As the Court put it, "[t]he day is gone when this court uses the Due Process Clause [to] strike down state laws, regulatory of business and industrial conditions, because they may be unwise, improvident, or out of harmony with a particular school of thought." A fitting epitaph for the *Lochner* era of substantive due process review was inscribed in 1963. Justice Holmes, in *Lochner,* had complained that "[t]he Fourteenth Amendment does not enact Mr. Herbert Spencer's Social Statics." His understanding of constitutional interpretation then was that the Court was transforming a social Darwinist moral vision into fundamental law. In *Ferguson v. Skrupa,* the Court emphasized that "[w]hether the legislature takes for its textbook Adam Smith, Herbert Spencer, Lord Keynes, or some other is no concern of ours." In vindication of Holmes's views as expressed in *Lochner,* it declined "to sit as a 'superlegislature to weigh the wisdom of legislation.' "

The Court over the past several decades has minced few words in repudiating the results of the *Lochner* era. Since the *Parrish* decision, the Court in only one instance has invalidated state economic regulation as violative of the Fourteenth Amendment. In *Morey v. Doud,* the Court invalidated a law requiring some currency exchanges to satisfy requirements for a license. That decision, referenced to the Fourteenth Amendment's equal protection clause, eventually was overturned and dismissed as an aberration. In *City of New Orleans v. Dukes,* decided two decades later, the Court reiterated that it "may not sit as a superlegislature to judge the wisdom or desirability of legislative policy determinations made in areas that [do not] affect fundamental rights."

Consistent with the development of case law and as described by Justice Brennan, the basic lesson of the *Lochner* era is "that the Constitution . . . can actively intrude into . . . economic and policy matters only if . . . prepared to bear enormous institutional and social costs." For many critics, any Fourteenth Amendment analysis that identifies and asserts rights not specifically enumerated by the Constitution is Lochnerist. Justice Holmes himself left open the possibility of review that would consider whether, from the perspective of "a rational and fair man," legislation "infringe[d] fundamental principles as they have been understood by the traditions of our people and our law." Like Holmes, modern jurisprudence disclaims Lochnerism but reserves the opportunity to measure legislation against what the Court may perceive as "fundamental principle" rooted in the nation's "traditions." What has been exorcised from due process review is economic rights doctrine, therefore, but not the methodology of identifying and developing freedoms that are not enumerated by the Constitution itself. A common critical response to that reality is that modern fundamental rights analysis is no less subjectively influenced than Lochernism itself. Holmes suggested the possibility that "fundamental principles" exist that, when implicated, may require the Court's protection. Modern substantive due process review remains locked in controversy over what those fundamental interests are or if they exist.

New Directions in Substantive Due Process

Renewed attention to principles deriving from the nation's traditions and conscience was evidenced within a few years of *Carolene Products*. In *Skinner v. Oklahoma,* the Court invalidated a state law that required sterilization of habitual felons convicted of crimes involving moral turpitude. Although referencing its decision to the equal protection clause rather than to the due process clause, the Court stressed that the law compromised "[m]arriage and procreation," which were "fundamental to the very existence and survival of the race" and "one of the basic civil rights of man." Identification of a fundamental interest requires the same analytical exercise whether pursuant to due process or to equal protection principles. The *Skinner* decision thus forwarded a judicial interest in identifying and accounting for rights that although not enumerated by the Constitution still might be established as fundamental.

The Right to Privacy

Since the early 1960s, the Court has reinvigorated the due process clause in substantive terms that have accounted for rights perceived by the Court as fundamental. Especially prominent in modern due process analysis, as an unenumerated freedom and source of controversy, is the right to privacy. As developed by case law, the right to privacy comprehends freedom to marry, elect an abortion, use contraceptives, and maintain a family. Given the unpleasant memories of the *Lochner* era, attention to privacy rights has elicited especially intense and extensive debate over the due process clause's substantive revitalization.

The negative imagery of Lochnerism had a visible effect on the Court's recognition of a right to privacy. In *Griswold v. Connecticut,* the Court struck down a state law insofar as it denied married couples access to contraceptives. In a majority opinion authored by Justice Douglas, the Court specifically disclaimed *Lochner* and its progeny and emphasized that it "did not sit as a super-legislature." Referring specifically to "[o]vertones of some arguments suggest[ing] that *Lochner* . . . should be our guide," the Court "decline[d] that invitation." Although characterizing substantive due process as misconceived, it maintained that the right to privacy was not merely a resurrection of *Lochner*-style fundamental rights analysis. As Douglas described it, the right was comprehended by "penumbras" or projected by "emanations" of the First, Third, Fourth, Fifth and Ninth Amendments. Despite emphasis on the distance between *Lochner* and *Griswold,* the analytical differences essentially were reducible to form and value. The Court in *Griswold* and subsequent cases performed an exercise, suggested by Holmes's dissent in *Lochner,* in identifying fundamental principles grounded in the nation's traditions. Justice Goldberg reached the same result on grounds that marital privacy was rooted in the "traditions and conscience of our people" and thus a right that was fundamental and reserved by the Ninth Amendment. The *Griswold* decision demonstrated that substantive due process analysis had not been abandoned, but redirected.

The Critical Response: Lochnerism Revisited

Justice Black, who had helped hasten the demise of economic rights doctrine upon being appointed to the bench by President Roosevelt, accused the Court of pursuing a neo-Lochnerist line. Black found no appreciable difference between the *Griswold* and the *Lochner* Courts' methods of identifying a fundamental right. As he put it:

The Court talks about a constitutional "right of privacy" as though there is some constitutional provision or provisions forbidding any law ever to be passed which might abridge the "privacy" of individuals. But there is not. . . . I like my privacy as well as the next one, but I am nevertheless compelled to admit that government has a right to invade it unless prohibited by some specific constitutional provision. For these reasons I cannot agree with the Court's judgment and the reasons it gives for holding this Connecticut law unconstitutional.

Black criticized Douglas's reasoning as a constitutional masquerade that diverted attention from its true Lochnerist character. He also objected to alternative theories for referencing the right to privacy to the due process clause or Ninth Amendment. Responding to such concepts, which would enable the Court to invalidate laws it perceived as "arbitrary, capricious, unreasonable, or oppressive" or without a rational basis, Black warned that

If these formulas based on "natural justice," or others which mean the same thing, are to prevail, they require judges to determine what is or is not constitutional on the basis of their own appraisal of what laws are unwise or unnecessary. The power to make such decisions is of course that of a legislative body. Surely it has to be admitted that no provision of the Constitution specifically gives such blanket power to courts to exercise such a supervisory veto over the wisdom and value of legislative policies and to hold unconstitutional those laws which they believe unwise or dangerous. I readily admit that no legislative body, state or national, should pass laws that can justly be given any of the invidious labels invoked as constitutional excuses to strike down state laws. But perhaps it is not too much to say that no legislative body ever does pass laws without believing that they will accomplish a sane, rational, wise and justifiable purpose. While I completely subscribe to the holding of *Marbury v. Madison,* . . . and subsequent cases, that our Court has constitutional power to strike down statutes, state or federal, that violate commands of the Federal Constitution, I do not believe that we are granted power by the Due Process Clause or any other constitutional provision or provisions to measure constitutionality by our belief that legislation is arbitrary, capricious or unreasonable, or accomplishes no justifiable purpose, or is offensive to our own notions of "civilized standards of conduct." Such an appraisal of the wisdom of legislation is an attribute of the power to make laws, not of the power to interpret them. The use by federal courts of such a formula or doctrine or whatnot to veto federal or state laws simply takes away from Congress and States the power to make laws based on their own judgment of fairness and wisdom and transfers that power to this Court for ultimate determination—a power which was specifically denied to federal courts by the convention that framed the Constitution.

Whether principle and result were based on the Ninth Amendment or the Fourteenth Amendment was immaterial from Black's perspective. Either line of analysis, as he saw it, was grounded in the discredited case law of the past and reflected "the same natural law due process philosophy found in *Lochner v. New York.*"

Black's rejection of a fundamental right of privacy was based not on policy but on his understanding of the proper scope and use of judicial power. Although noting his personal disagreement with the wisdom of the challenged state law, he maintained that the only rights the Court could account for were those specified by the Constitution itself. With further references to *Lochner,* Black asserted that privacy was not a constitutional concern and thus not a basis for displacing legislative action.

I repeat so as not to be misunderstood that this Court does have power, which it should exercise, to hold laws unconstitutional where they are forbidden by the Federal Constitution. My point is that there is no provision of the Constitution which either expressly or impliedly vests power in this Court to sit as a supervisory agency over acts of duly constituted legislative bodies and set aside their laws because of the Court's belief that the legislative policies adopted are unreasonable, unwise, arbitrary, capricious or irrational. The adoption of such a loose, flexible, uncontrolled standard for holding laws unconstitutional, if ever it is finally achieved, will amount to a great unconstitutional shift of power to the courts which I believe and am constrained to say will be bad for the courts and worse for the country. Subjecting federal and state laws to such an unrestrained and unrestrainable judicial control as to the wisdom of legislative enactments would, I fear, jeopardize the separation of governmental powers that the Framers set up and at the same time threaten to take away much of the power of States to govern themselves which the Constitution plainly intended them to have.

I realize that many good and able men have eloquently spoken and written, sometimes in rhapsodical strains, about the duty of this Court to keep the Constitution in tune with the times. The idea is that the Constitution must be changed from time to time and that this Court is charged with a duty to make those changes. For myself, I must with all deference reject that philosophy. The Constitution makers knew the need for change and provided for it. Amendments suggested by the people's elected representatives can be submitted to the people or their selected agents for ratification. That method of change was good for our Fathers, and being somewhat old-fashioned I must add it is good enough for me. And so, I cannot rely on the Due Process Clause or the Ninth Amendment or any mysterious and uncertain natural law concept as a reason for striking down this state law. The Due Process Clause with an "arbitrary and capricious" or "shocking to the conscience" formula was liberally used by this Court to strike down economic legislation in the early decades of this century, threatening, many people thought, the tranquility and stability of the Nation. See, *e.g., Lochner v. New York.* That formula, based on subjective considerations of "natural justice," is no less dangerous when used to enforce this Court's views about personal rights than those about economic rights. I had thought that we had laid that formula, as a means for striking down state legislation, to rest once and for all in cases like *West Coast Hotel Co. v. Parrish.*.

In *Ferguson v. Skrupa,* this Court two years ago said in an opinion joined by all the Justices but one that "The doctrine that prevailed in *Lochner, . . .* and the like cases—that due process authorizes courts to hold laws unconstitutional when they believe the legislature has acted unwisely—has long since been discarded. We have returned to the original constitutional proposition that courts do not substitute their social and economic beliefs for the judgment of legislative bodies, who are elected to pass laws." . . . [The Court would] reinstate the *Lochner, . . .* line of cases, cases from which this Court recoiled after the 1930s, and which had been I thought totally discredited until now. Apparently my Brethren have less quarrel with state economic regulations than former Justices of their persuasion had. But any limitation upon their using the natural law due process philosophy to strike down any state law, dealing with any activity whatever, will obviously be only self-imposed. . . .

The late Judge Learned Hand, after emphasizing his view that judges should not use the due process formula suggested in the concurring opinions today or any other formula like it to invalidate legislation offensive to their "personal preferences," made the statement, with which I fully agree, that: "For myself it would be most irksome to be ruled by a bevy of Platonic Guardians, even if I knew how to choose them, which I assuredly do not." So far as I am concerned, Connecticut's law as applied here is not forbidden by any provision of the Federal Constitution as that Constitution was written, and I would therefore affirm.

Relating Back to Holmes

Central to Black's criticism was what he considered to be the Court's reinvestment in discredited doctrine. His comparison of the *Griswold* Court's work with the *Lochner* Court's output revealed a position that actually exceeded Holmes's views. In *Lochner,* Holmes had criticized accounting for economic rights. Quoting from another Holmes dissent, Black suggested an unequivocal resistance to fundamental rights analysis. As Holmes put it in *Baldwin v. Missouri*

I have not yet adequately expressed the more than anxiety that I feel at the ever increasing scope given to the Fourteenth Amendment in cutting down what I believe to be the constitutional rights of the States. As the decisions now stand, I see hardly any limit but the sky to the invalidating of those rights if they happen to strike a majority of this Court as for any reason undesirable. I cannot believe that the Amendment was intended to give us *carte blanche* to embody our economic or moral beliefs in its prohibitions. Yet I can think of no narrower reason that seems to me to justify the present and the earlier decisions to which I have referred. Of course the words "due process of law," if taken in their literal meaning, have no application to this case; and while it is too late to deny that they have been given a much more extended and artificial signification, still we ought to remember the great caution shown by the Constitution in limiting the power of the States, and should be slow to construe the clause in the Fourteenth Amendment as committing to the Court, with no guide but the Court's own discretion, the validity of whatever laws the States may pass.

Even in *Baldwin,* Holmes did not repudiate his concession in *Lochner* that the Court might consider whether "fundamental principles" rooted in the nation's traditions had been violated. In *Pierce v. Society of Sisters,* moreover, he joined the Court in identifying a fundamental right of educational choice to strike down a state law requiring all children to attend public schools. Black, however, pushed Holmes's premise to the point that it brooked no exception to judicial restraint barring a specifically identifiable constitutional basis.

Perhaps more consonant with Holmes's allowance for review that discerned and developed fundamental principles was the analysis of Justice Harlan. Concurring with the Court in *Griswold,* Harlan endorsed judicial identification of "basic values 'implicit in the concept of ordered liberty.' " He thus amplified notions related in dissent a few years earlier, in *Poe v. Ullman,* when the Court refused to consider a state anti-contraceptive law on grounds that review was premature. Harlan not only would have considered the merits of the case, but also would have found an intrusion on marital privacy that violated the due process clause. He observed that

Due process has not been reduced to any formula; its content cannot be determined by reference to any code. The best that can be said is that through the course of this Court's decisions it has represented the balance which our Nation, built upon postulates of respect for the liberty of the individual, has struck between that liberty and the demands of organized society. If the supplying of content to this Constitutional concept has of necessity been a rational process, it certainly has not been one where judges have felt free to roam where unguided speculation might take them. The balance of which I speak is the balance struck by this country, having regard to what history teaches are the traditions from which it developed as well as the traditions from which it broke. That tradition is a living thing. A decision of this Court which radically departs from it could not long survive, while a decision which builds on what has survived is likely to be sound. No formula could serve as a substitute, in this area, for judgment and restraint.

It is this outlook which has led the Court continuingly to perceive distinctions in the imperative character of Constitutional provisions, since that character must be discerned from a particular provision's larger context. And inasmuch as this context is one not of words, but of history and purposes, the full scope of the liberty guaranteed by the Due Process Clause cannot be found in or limited by the precise terms of the specific guarantees elsewhere provided in the Constitution. This "liberty" is not a series of isolated points pricked out in terms of the taking of property; the freedom of speech, press, and religion; the right to keep and bear arms; the freedom from unreasonable searches and seizures; and so on. It is a rational continuum which, broadly speaking, includes a freedom from all substantial arbitrary impositions and purposeless restraints, [citations omitted] and which also recognizes, what a reasonable and sensitive judgment must, that certain interests require particularly careful scrutiny of the state needs asserted to justify their abridgement. [Citations omitted.]

Each new claim to Constitutional protection must be considered against a background of Constitutional purposes, as they have been rationally perceived and historically developed. Though we exercise limited and sharply restrained judgment, yet there is no "mechanical yardstick," no "mechanical answer." The decision of an apparently novel claim must depend on grounds which follow closely on well-accepted principles and criteria. The new decision must take "its place in relation to what went before and further [cut] a channel for what is to come." [Citation omitted.] The matter was well put in *Rochin v. California:* "The vague contours of the Due Process Clause do not leave judges at large. We may not draw on our merely personal and private notions and disregard the limits that bind judges in their judicial function. Even though the concept of due process of law is not final and fixed, these limits are derived from considerations that are fused in the whole nature of our judicial process. . . . These are considerations deeply rooted in reason and in the compelling traditions of the legal profession."

Expanding the Scope of Constitutional Privacy

The opportunity to identify fundamental principles grounded in the nation's traditions is a significant legacy of Holmes's dissent in *Lochner.* Another equally profound aspect of that heritage is the tension that exists whenever the Court attempts to discern what interests are fundamental. Identifying what actually is "rooted in the Nation's traditions and conscience" is an elusive and vexing proposition. Especially illustrative of that reality is the constitutional controversy over abortion. In *Roe v. Wade,* the Court struck down a state law that prohibited abortion except when necessary to save a mother's life. The challenged law, according to the Court, compromised the right to privacy that "encompass[ed] a woman's decision whether or not to terminate her pregnancy." Abandoning the concept of penumbras, the Court determined that "[t]he right to privacy, whether it be founded in the Fourteenth Amendment's concept of personal liberty and restrictions upon state action, as we feel it is, or . . . in the Ninth Amendment's reservation of rights to the people, is broad enough to encompass a woman's decision whether or not to terminate her pregnancy."

Critics of the *Roe* decision regard it as an essentially legislative exercise that overreached the judiciary's function. In arguing the point, they note the Court's establishment of a regulatory framework allowing abortion with few restrictions during the first trimester of a pregnancy, permitting tighter controls during the second trimester, and recognizing a viable fetus with a protectible liberty interest of its own in the third trimester. Objections to the housing of abortion decisions within the Fourteenth Amendment, reminiscent of negative response to *Lochner,* have reflected the sense that the Court is "creating rights out of whole cloth that are not in the Constitution." Consistent with that perception, Justice Rehnquist in *Roe* alleged that the Court was engaging in a neo-Lochnerist pursuit. He complained that

While the Court's opinion quotes from the dissent of Mr. Justice Holmes in *Lochner v. New York,* 198 U.S. 45, 74 (1905), the result it reaches is more closely attuned to the majority opinion of Mr. Justice Peckham in that case. As in *Lochner* and similar cases applying substantive due process standards to economic and social welfare legislation, the adoption of the compelling state interest standard will inevitably require this Court to examine the legislative policies and pass on the wisdom of these policies in the very process of deciding whether a particular state interest put forward may or may not be "compelling." The decision here to break pregnancy into three distinct terms and to outline the permissible restrictions the State may impose in each one, for example, partakes more of judicial legislation than it does of a determination of the intent of the drafters of the Fourteenth Amendment.

The fact that a majority of the States reflecting, after all, the majority sentiment in those States, have had restrictions on abortions for at least a century is a strong indication, it seems to me, that the asserted right to an abortion is not "so rooted in the traditions and conscience of our people as to be ranked as fundamental" [citation omitted]. Even today, when society's views on abortion are changing, the very existence of the debate is evidence that the "right" to an abortion is not so universally accepted as the appellant would have us believe.

Recognition of a woman's liberty to elect an abortion has been a continuing source of controversy and division for the Court and the nation. In the two decades since *Roe,* the Court has reviewed persistent efforts by states to limit or control the freedom. Until the late 1980s, the Court consistently struck down procedural requirements perceived as serving no purpose other than to restrict or burden a woman's freedom of choice. By then, personnel changes, which had been a factor in the demise of substantive due process in the late 1930s, had become largely responsible for clouding the future of *Roe*. In *Webster v. Reproductive Health Services*, the Court upheld a state law that, among other things, prohibited abortions in public hospitals or by state employees and required testing for fetal viability beginning in the fifth month of pregnancy. Because the decision unsettled the trimester framework established in *Roe* and considered whether the legislative interest was legitimate rather than compelling, some anticipated the dismantling of a woman's freedom to choose. Although the Court in *Planned Parenthood v. Casey* eliminated the trimester framework, it affirmed the right to elect an abortion at least up to the point of viability and allowed regulation to the extent it does not impose an "undue burden" on the woman.

Once the Court recognized a right to privacy in *Griswold* and *Roe*, it was inevitable that other interests would work to broaden its contours and claim a share of constitutional protection. In *Zablocki v. Redhail*, the Court extended the right of privacy so that it comprehended the right to marry. A plurality, in *Moore v. City of East Cleveland*, found privacy rights broad enough to encompass the interests of extended families. Special attention to marriage and the family unit, as a imperative of constitutional law, relates directly back to the *Lochner* era. In *Meyer v. Nebraska*, decided in 1925, the Court itemized several interests secured by the Fourteenth Amendment including the right to marry, to establish a home and bring up children.

As noted previously, Holmes's dissent in *Lochner* resulted in conflicting signals regarding the development of fundamental rights that are not enumerated by the Constitution. Modern case law has inherited that uncertainty. Despite the Court's own apparent discomfort with the penumbral concept, as evidenced by its shift of privacy rights to the Fourteenth Amendment in *Roe*, the premise has not been banished altogether from constitutional analysis. The Court in *Roberts v. United States Jaycees* observed that because the Bill of Rights is designed to secure individual liberty, it must afford "certain kinds of highly personal relationships a substantial measure of sanctuary from unjustified interference by the State." Specifically referenced in support of that proposition were *Meyer v. Nebraska* and *Pierce v. Society of Sisters* which, during the height of the *Lochner* era, identified an array of liberty interests protected by the due process clause. Although innumerable types of personal relationships might claim constitutional protection, the *Roberts* Court maintained that such security is limited to "those that attend the creation and sustenance of a family— marriage . . . childbirth . . . the raising and education of children . . . and cohabitation with one's relatives." The case law of the *Lochner* and modern eras thus merged if not in precise form, then at least with respect to essential analysis and result.

Limiting the Scope of Constitutional Privacy

The type of personal relationships afforded constitutional security has not expanded significantly beyond the perimeters identified in the *Lochner* era. In *Village of Belle Terre v. Boraas,* decided in 1974, the Court upheld a zoning ordinance that prohibited unmarried couples from living together. A few years later, in *Moore v. City of East Cleveland,* it struck down another zoning restriction that allowed immediate but not extended family members to live together. The *Moore* decision appeared to trace the outer limits of personal relationships protected by the Fourteenth Amendment and perhaps of the due process clause itself with respect to its more recent incarnation. Since *Moore,* the Court has not abandoned the right to privacy but seldom has broadened its scope.

In *Bowers v. Hardwick,* the Court upheld a state sodomy law against a challenge that the enactment impaired the right to privacy. The majority opinion, authored by Justice White, expressed significant reservations with respect to judicial development of fundamental rights. The evil of Lochnerism, from White's perspective, was not that it just promoted an economic ideology, but that it transformed judicially favored values into constitutional principle to defeat the political process. Although not foreclosing the possibility of discerning fundamental rights not specified by the Constitution, the Court stressed that it "is most vulnerable and comes closest to illegitimacy when it deals with judge-made law having little or no cognizable roots in the language or design of the Constitution." What it characterized as a "fundamental right to engage in homosexual sodomy," therefore, was determined to be neither "implicit in the concept of ordered liberty" nor "rooted in the Nation's traditions and conscience."

Even in refusing to widen the ambit of the right to privacy, the *Bowers* Court demonstrated how substantive due process analysis may be influenced by subjective factors. A key difference between the position of the majority and that of the dissent was how the alleged right at issue was to be framed. The majority rejected what it characterized as a "fundamental right to engage in homosexual sodomy." In a dissenting opinion, Justice Blackmun maintained that the issue should have been framed not in terms of homosexual privacy specifically, but in terms of sexual privacy generally. From Blackmun's perspective, a "necessary corollary of giving individuals freedom to choose how to conduct their lives is acceptance of the fact that different individuals will make different choices." He criticized the limiting of the right to privacy as subjectively inspired, emphasizing that the freedom was not defined broadly enough to comprehend diverse and nontraditional variations of the protected activity. Blackmun himself would have put the question not in terms of whether a specific sex act or orientation was safeguarded, but in terms of whether intimate and consensual sexual activity between adults inheres in traditional expectations of personal privacy and autonomy. Consistent with what Blackmun described as the Court's "almost obsessive focus on homosexual activity," in reviewing a law that criminalized certain acts without respect to sexual orientation, Laurence Tribe has described the majority's opinion as an exercise in "prejudice rather than legal principle." As so characterized, the *Bowers* decision demonstrates that once substantive due process review is established, development of principles for extending or limiting an identified right is vulnerable to the risks of subjectivity that Holmes warned against but never entirely foreclosed.

The competing perspectives in *Hardwick* revealed that the choice of focusing on a specific unconventional activity or the general concept of liberty is crucial to decisional outcome. Further demonstrating the significance of how the claimed constitutional interest is identified was the Court's decision in *Michael H. v. Gerald D.* In that case, the Court held that a state could deny parental rights to the natural father of a child conceived in an extramarital affair. Justice Scalia, in a plurality opinion, suggested that determination of whether the actual father's claimed liberty interest was rooted in history, and tradition required attention to the particular circumstances. Instead of inquiring as to whether history and tradition supported the general proposition of a natural father's parental rights, Scalia considered whether they sustained the interests of "the natural father of a child conceived within and born into an extra marital union." Cast in such terms, he found no basis for the claimed parental right. Scalia's assessment of specific rather than general tradition reflected his sense that the latter "provides such imprecise guidance, [and] permits judges to dictate rather than discern the society's views." Critics of *Hardwick* and *Michael H.* maintain, however, that it is the focus on a specific non-mainstream activity or status that invites the influence of prejudice or other subjective considerations. The results and objections in both cases demonstrate the persisting tension in Holmesian grounded doctrine that objects to unenumerated rights generally but does not entirely foreclose their development.

A Continuing Legacy of Doctrinal Uncertainty

The conflicting pressures of modern Fourteenth Amendment jurisprudence are especially well evidenced by the Court's decision in *Cruzan v. Director, Missouri Department of Health.* In *Cruzan,* the Court upheld a state law against arguments that it impaired a person's right to die. The enactment required "clear and convincing evidence" of a person's intention to have a life-support system removed. The majority opinion was authored by Chief Justice Rehnquist, who persistently has criticized the right to privacy as a Lochnerist-type creation. In *Cruzan,* however, Rehnquist acknowledged that "a constitutionally protected liberty interest in refusing unwanted medical care may be inferred from our prior decisions." At least when a person's competency is not controverted, the Court found that "the Due Process Clause protects an interest in life as well as an interest in refusing life-sustaining medical treatment." With respect to the standards for discontinuing life support, it determined that they afforded safeguards against potential abuse and thereby justified the state's interest. Although the Court did not strike down the law, the process of balancing competing interests revealed the continuing vitality of substantive due process analysis. Like decisions in the *Lochner* era when the Court was convinced of a legitimate purpose, the Court in *Cruzan* independently examined rather than entirely deferred to legislative judgment. Such inquiry into the relation between legislative means and ends prompted the objection by Justice Scalia that the Court "has no authority to inject itself into every field of human activity where irrationality and oppression may theoretically occur, and if it tries to do so it will destroy itself." For Justice Scalia, as for Justice Black, the best resolution of the fundamental rights dilemma is for the Court to abandon substantive due process review altogether.

Activation of the due process clause in substantive terms and reaction to it perpetuate a debate over the role of the judiciary that is virtually as old as the Constitution. In his *Lochner* dissent, Holmes identified the dangers of value-driven development of fundamental rights but at the same time allowed for it to some extent. Modern fundamental rights review remains mired in debate over that "extent." Like Holmes, modern due process analysis disclaims any ideological imperative. Borrowing from the second Justice Harlan, the Court also has suggested that "[a]ppropriate limits" are set "from careful 'respect for the teachings of history' [and] solid recognition of the basic values that are rooted in our society." Actual results, virtually ordained by the literal terms of the Holmesian formula, would seem to indicate that repudiation of *Lochner* does not eliminate the possibility of Lochnerist results.

Bibliography

Cases

Adkins v. Children's Hospital, 261 U.S. 525 (1923).
Allgeyer v. Louisiana, 165 U.S. 578 (1897).
Baldwin v. Missouri, 281 U.S. 586 (1930).
Belle Terre, Village of, v. Boraas, 416 U.S. 1 (1974).
Bowers v. Hardwick, 478 U.S. 186 (1986).
Buchanan v. Warley, 245 U.S. 60 (1917).
Cruzan v. Director, Missouri Department of Health, 110 S.Ct. 2841 (1990).

Ferguson v. Skrupa, 372 U.S. 726 (1963).
Giles v. Harris, 189 U.S. 475 (1903).
Griswold v. Connecticut, 381 U.S. 479 (1965).
Holden v. Hardy, 169 U.S. 366 (1898).
Lincoln Federal Labor Union v. Northwestern Iron & Metal Co., 335 U.S. 525
      (1949).
Lochner v. New York, 198 U.S. 45 (1905).
Meyer v. Nebraska, 262 U.S. 390 (1923).
Michael H. v. Gerald D., 491 U.S. 110 (1989).
Moore v. City of East Cleveland, 431 U.S. 494 (1977).
Morey v. Doud, 354 U.S. 457 (1957).
Muller v. Oregon, 208 U.S. 412 (1908).
Munn v. Illinois, 94 U.S. 113 (1876).
National Labor Relations Board v. Jones & Laughlin Steel Corp., 301 U.S. 1 (1937).
Nebbia v. New York, 291 U.S. 502 (1934).
New Orleans, City of, v. Dukes, 427 U.S. 297 (1976).
Noble State Bank v. Haskell, 219 U.S. 104 (1911).
Pierce v. Society of Sisters, 268 U.S. 510 (1925).
Poe v. Ullman, 367 U.S. 497 (1961).
Roberts v. United States Jaycees, 468 U.S. 609 (1984).
Roe v. Wade, 410 U.S. 113 (1973).
Skinner v. Oklahoma, 316 U.S. 535 (1942).
Slaughter-House Cases, 83 U.S. 36 (1873).
Truax v. Corrigan, 257 U.S. 312 (1921).
Tyson & Brother v. Bantom, 273 U.S. 418 (1927).
United States v. Carolene Products Co., 304 U.S. 144 (1938).
Webster v. Reproductive Health Services, 492 U.S. 490 (1989).
West Coast Hotel v. Parrish, 300 U.S. 379 (1937).
Williamson v. Lee Optical Co., 348 U.S. 483 (1955).
Zablocki v. Redhail, 434 U.S. 374 (1978).

Books and Articles

Berger, R., Government by Judiciary: The Transformation of the Fourteenth
      Amendment (1977).
Cooley, T., Constitutional Limitations (1868).
Currie, *The Constitution in the Supreme Court: The Protection of Economic Interests,
      1889–1910,* 52 U. Chi. L. Rev. 324 (1985).
Fairman, C., VII History of the Supreme Court of the United States. Reconstruc-
      tion and Reunion (1971) (1987).
Frankfurter, F. (ed.), Mr. Justice Holmes (1931).
Karst, K., Belonging to America (1989).
McCloskey, R., The American Supreme Court (1960).
Nelson, W., The Fourteenth Amendment: From Political Principle to Judicial
      Doctrine (1988).
Tribe, L., American Constitutional Law (1988).

Chapter 5

COLOR AND THE CONSTITUTION

Jurisprudential development of the Fourteenth Amendment rather quickly extended and redirected what originally was perceived as its historical and pervading purpose. In its seminal opinion on the Fourteenth Amendment in the *Slaughter-House Cases,* the Supreme Court emphasized the provision's concern with "the freedom of the slave race, the security of and firm establishment of that freedom, and the protection of the newly-made free man and citizen from the oppression of those who had formerly exercised unlimited dominion over him." The "evil" that the equal protection clause responded to was state laws that, in the Court's words, "discriminated with gross injustice and hardship against . . . the newly emancipated negroes." Given that purpose, the Court "doubted[ed] very much whether any action of a State not directed by way of discrimination against the negroes as a class, or on account of their race, will ever be held to come within the purview of this provision." The influence of economic rights theory on the Fourteenth Amendment's meaning became discernible even before the formal end of reconstruction, as judicial review accelerated the drift beyond what the *Slaughter-House* Court had described as a "pervasive" concern with "the freedom of the slave race." Contrary to the sense of purpose and priority identified by the *Slaughter-House* Court, constitutional attention to economic rights soon heightened as it simultaneously diminished for racially significant discrimination.

Political Change and Judicial Resistance

Reduction of the Fourteenth Amendment's pertinence in responding to state-sanctioned racial burdens was previewed within a few years of its ratification. In *Blylew v. United States,* the Court concluded that a federal court had no jurisdiction of a criminal action under the Civil Rights Act of 1866. As noted in Chapter 3, the Court determined that because the victim of a racially motivated killing was deceased, she no longer was an "affected person" covered by the federal law. Insofar as states would not prosecute criminal actions by whites against blacks, the decision for practical purposes represented a license for white-on-black crime violence and brutalization.

The *Blylew* decision interpreted not the Constitution but legislation that inspired the Fourteenth Amendment. Its tone and result, notwithstanding the *Slaughter-House* Court's subsequent identification of the amendment's primary concern, accurately indicated the limited prospects of racially significant interpretive achievements. An initial racially pertinent Fourteenth Amendment case to reach the Court was *United States v. Cruikshank.* Reminiscent of *Blylew,* the central issue was whether a federal interest existed when the state afforded no remedy for white-on-black violence. The case arose when a political dispute in a Louisiana community erupted into a white-led attack on a black-defended courthouse. In what became known as the Colfax Massacre, large numbers of blacks were killed by gunshot or fire and the perpetrators were prosecuted under federal civil rights law. Although convictions were obtained in a federal trial, the Supreme Court reversed them on grounds that regulation of criminal activity was a state rather than a federal concern. Several years later, in *United States v. Harris,* a federal civil rights action was brought against state law enforcement officials who beat a black man to death. In reaching a like result, the Court cited to *Cruikshank* for the proposition that "[t]he duty of protecting all citizens in the enjoyment of equality of rights was originally assumed by the States, and it remains there." The final section of the Fourteenth Amendment empowers Congress "to enforce, by appropriate legislation, the provisions of this article." The indications of *Blylew, Cruikshank,* and *Harris* were that the federal interest in accounting for national citizenship and civil rights did not extend to criminal action even if sanctioned or allowed by the states.

The primary investment of intellectual energy for purposes of vitalizing the Fourteenth Amendment during the final quarter of the nineteenth century and the first third of the twentieth century was channeled toward development of general marketplace liberty. As the Fourteenth Amendment was waxed with economic rights doctrine, attention to its "pervading" race-dependent purpose waned. The reconstruction period had been a time of vigorous, extensive, but ultimately fleeting congressional attention to civil and political rights. The Thirteenth, Fourteenth and Fifteenth Amendments by their own terms respectively precluded slavery, secured citizenship and its incidents and prohibited race-dependent denial of voting rights. Further evidencing a redistribution of interest and power from state to federal authority was the assignment to Congress of enforcement power. Pursuant to the charge of the reconstruction amendments, Congress enacted a series of laws calculated to enforce constitutional policy. The Civil Rights Act of 1866, as mentioned previously, accounted for contractual, property and travel rights, personal security and equal standing before the law. It originally was passed as an exercise of enforcement power under the Thirteenth Amendment and several years later was reenacted pursuant to the Fourteenth Amendment. The Enforcement Act of 1870, grounded in the Fifteenth Amendment, criminalized public or private impairment of the right to vote. A year later, the Ku Klux Klan Act was passed to reach deprivations of civil rights by state agents or denials of equal protection by public or private action. The last major piece of reconstruction legislation, the Civil Rights Act of 1875, barred racial discrimination in public accommodations. Such enactments assumed and reflected the redistribution of governmental power that the reconstruction amendments supposedly achieved. The results in seminal cases such as *Blylew, Cruikshank* and *Harris,* however, suggested that significant impediments existed with respect to translating reconstruction theory into reality.

Early but Qualified Vindication of the Fourteenth Amendment

Early interpretation of the Fourteenth Amendment was not entirely unresponsive to the argument that the reformulated Constitution prohibited state-sanctioned racial discrimination. In *Strauder v. West Virginia,* the Supreme Court struck down a state law excluding black persons from juries. Commencing its inquiry into the Fourteenth Amendment's meaning, the Court observed that the provision could not "be understood without keeping in view the history of the times when [it] was adopted, and the general objects they plainly sought to accomplish." As the Court described it, the amendment's background revealed that "[t]he colored race, as a race, . . . especially needed protection against unfriendly action in the States where they were resident. It was in view of these considerations that the Fourteenth Amendment was framed and adopted." Amplifying in particular the need for and concern of the equal protection guarantee, the Court identified "the right to exemption from unfriendly legislation against them distinctively, as colored—exemption from legal discriminations, implying inferiority in civil society, lessening the security of their enjoyment of the rights which others enjoy, and discriminations which are steps toward reducing them to the condition of a subject race."

The *Strauder* case was first in a trilogy of decisions that collectively established and qualified a constitutional anti-discrimination principle. Consistent with *Strauder,* the Court in *Ex parte Virginia* determined that equal protection was denied when a judge excluded prospective jurors on the basis of race. The significance of the Court's response to state discrimination was diminished, however, in *Virginia v. Rives.* In *Rives,* the Court found no Fourteenth Amendment violation when exclusion of jurors on the basis of race was the work of a "subordinate officer" and not the function of clear official intent. It was unimpressed with arguments that no black person had ever served on a jury in the county and refused to find a constitutional violation minus the formal or high level state discrimination identified in *Strauder* and *Ex parte Virginia.* Although having acknowledged in *Ex parte Virginia* that the Thirteenth and Fourteenth Amendments "were intended to be, . . . [and] really are, limitations of the power of the States and enlargements of the power of Congress," the net result of the jury discrimination decisions was an acknowledgment of constitutional change but qualification of its impact.

The Cramping of Congressional Power:
The *Civil Rights Cases*

Subsequent jurisprudence further delimited the perimeters of federal interest and authority. In *Strauder,* the Court had observed that the Fourteenth Amendment was "to be construed liberally, to carry out the purposes of its framers." Such a result was consistent with general interpretive standards for remedial legislation. Post-*Strauder* jurisprudence at least until the middle of the twentieth century, however, was notable for its pinched reading of the reconstruction amendments. Three years after *Strauder,* the Court profoundly curtailed Congress's enforcement power under the Thirteenth and Fourteenth Amendments. The *Civil Rights Cases* presented a challenge to the last significant civil rights enactment of the reconstruction period. The Civil Rights Act of 1875 prohibited discrimination in a variety of public settings, including "accommodations, advantages, facilities, and privileges of inns, public conveyances on land or water, theaters and other places of public amusement." At issue specifically was whether the enforcement power of Congress, provided for by Section 5 of the Fourteenth Amendment, enabled it to reach private discrimination. The Court in the *Civil Rights Cases* determined that Section 5 was coextensive with Section 1. Because the first section of the amendment guaranteed privileges and immunities, due process and equal protection against *state* deprivation, the enforcement power of Congress was interpreted to reach no further than official discrimination.

The limitation of congressional power in the *Civil Rights Cases* indicated that the provision was being construed parsimoniously rather than liberally. The author of the Court's opinion was Justice Bradley, who a decade earlier had advanced an expansive vision of the Fourteenth Amendment. Bradley, in the *Slaughter-House Cases,* had argued for incorporating the Bill of Rights and natural law concepts into the Fourteenth Amendment. Such an interpretation assumed a major federal takeover of concerns traditionally reserved to the states. In the *Civil Rights Cases,* Bradley fretted about the potential of federal interests overtaking legitimate state concerns. He thus cautioned that the challenged act, if not invalidated, would "establish a code of municipal law regulative of all private rights between man and man in society. It would be to make Congress take the place of the State legislatures and to supersede them." In reality, the federal civil rights legislation at issue displaced less state authority than wholesale application of the Bill of Rights and natural law would have. Still, Bradley concluded that the enactment violated "the Tenth Amendment . . . which declares that 'powers not delegated to the United States by the Constitution, nor prohibited by it to the States, are reserved to the States respectively, or to the people.' "

The *Civil Rights Cases* decision cut off any federal interest under the Fourteenth Amendment in private discrimination. Analysis and result demonstrated a failure to reckon with the complexity of the circumstances at issue in the cases. Although the private discrimination affected access to public venues, such as theaters, hotels and trains, standards of review were unaffected by the mixed nature of the contexts. Rather, the Court emphasized that "[t]he wrongful act of an individual, unsupported by any [official] authority, is simply a private wrong, as a crime of that individual" and must "be vindicated by the laws of the State for redress." Overlooked by that depiction was the reality that even when aggrieved, blacks in many jurisdictions had little recourse to state courts or remedies. As Bradley himself had noted in *Blylew v. United States,* the right to testify, and thus to access the judicial system, was denied in many states "on account of . . . race and color."

The reduction of federal enforcement power under the Fourteenth Amendment, as noted previously, coincided with the provision's growth as a source of economic rights. Such development was consonant with dominant political and public attitudes of the postreconstruction period that were increasingly more concerned with economic growth and progress and less interested with intractable problems of race. Reflecting the nation's generally diminished commitment to civil rights was the rejection of arguments that discrimination in public accommodations was a badge or incident of slavery that Congress could prohibit pursuant to the Thirteenth Amendment. The Court maintained that "[i]t would be running the slavery argument into the ground, to make it apply to every act of discrimination which a person may see fit to make." It further observed that

When a man has emerged from slavery, and by the aid of beneficent legislation has shaken off the inseparable concomitants of that state, there must be some stage in the progress of his elevation when he takes the rank of a mere citizen, and ceases to be the special favorite of the laws, and when his rights as a citizen, or a man, are to be protected in the ordinary modes by which other men's rights are protected.

Harlan's Dissenting Opinion in the *Civil Rights Cases*

What were challenged as unlawful racial exclusions finally were passed off by the Court as "[m]ere discriminations" meriting neither constitutional nor congressional attention. The *Civil Rights Cases* offered a comprehensive assessment of the Thirteenth and Fourteenth Amendments that shrank from the potential implications of *Strauder*. Its narrow characterization of the federal interest under those amendments, wooden description of state action and reduction of the Thirteenth and Fourteenth Amendments' significance elicited a lengthy dissent by Justice Harlan. Shedding his original misgivings about the Thirteenth Amendment, he urged a broad interpretation that would have enabled Congress to regulate beyond slavery's most obvious incidents.

The Thirteenth Amendment, it is conceded, did something more than to prohibit slavery as an *institution,* resting upon distinctions of race, and upheld by positive law. My brethren admit that it established and decreed universal *civil freedom* throughout the United States. But did the freedom thus established involve nothing more than exemption from actual slavery? Was nothing more intended than to forbid one man from owning another as property? Was it the purpose of the nation simply to destroy the institution, and then remit the race, theretofore held in bondage, to the several States for such protection, in their civil rights, necessarily growing out of freedom, as those States, in their discretion, might choose to provide? Were the States against whose protest the institution was destroyed, to be left free, so far as national interference was concerned, to make or allow discriminations against that race, as such, in the enjoyment of those fundamental rights which by universal concession, inhere in a state of freedom? Had the Thirteenth Amendment stopped with the sweeping declaration, in its first section, against the existence of slavery and involuntary servitude, except for crime, Congress would have had the power, by implication, according to the doctrines of *Prigg v. Commonwealth of Pennsylvania,* repeated in *Strauder v. West Virginia,* to protect the freedom established, and consequently, to secure the enjoyment of such civil rights as were fundamental in freedom. That it can exert its authority to that extent is made clear, and was intended to be made clear, by the express grant of power contained in the second section of the Amendment.

John M. Harlan, Sr.

Given his background, Harlan may not have seemed the most likely candidate on the Supreme Court for championing civil rights. Harlan was a former slave owner whose pro-slavery views survived the Civil War. Even though he freed his own slaves, Harlan opposed both the Emancipation Proclamation and the Thirteenth Amendment. Despite being a unionist, Harlan did not join the Republican Party or support the cause of reconstruction until 1868. His help in securing the Republican presidential nomination for Rutherford Hayes in 1876 led to a Supreme Court appointment the next year. Harlan was a proponent of economic rights but unlike many of his colleagues, he had serious reservations about constitutional doctrine that the Court developed to protect them. As his dissent in *Lochner* demonstrated, Harlan was more amenable than the majority to state and federal regulation of economic activity. Harlan's service on the Court was characterized by a relatively high rate of dissent—123 dissenting opinions over 34 years. His sense of the Fourteenth Amendment, reiterated in dissents during the late nineteenth and early twentieth centuries, represented an understanding that was unique to an institution that otherwise considered official segregation to be "in the nature of things."

Before the *Civil Rights Cases,* Harlan had authored majority opinions that prohibited state exclusion of blacks respectively from trial juries and grand juries. Although his constitutional vision may have been advanced for the time, he was not without racial chauvinism. In criticizing the Court's allowance of official segregation and urging a color-blind constitution, Harlan referred to the white race as "the dominant race in this country . . . in prestige, in achievements, in education, in wealth, and in power." He also "doubt[ed] not, it will continue to be for all time," provided whites remained faithful to their heritage and the principles of constitutional liberty. A few years after dissenting from the separate-but-equal doctrine, Harlan authored a unanimous opinion upholding a school board's decision to close a black high school while continuing to operate a white high school. Despite such output, the sum of his work relative to the Fourteenth Amendment is notable primarily for its persistent casting of doubt on the assumptions and methodologies of racial supremacy.

Civil Rights and the Thirteenth Amendment

For Harlan, the venues governed by the Civil Rights Act of 1875 impressed private discrimination with a sufficiently public character to justify a federal interest under either the Thirteenth or Fourteenth Amendment. He thus favored upholding the civil rights legislation as a proper congressional means of removing incidents of slavery that were a concern of the Thirteenth Amendment.

That there are burdens and disabilities which constitute badges of slavery and ser-vitude, and that the power to enforce by appropriate legislation the Thirteenth Amendment may be exerted by legislation of a direct and primary character, for the eradication, not simply of the institution, but of its badges and incidents, are propositions which ought to be deemed indisputable. They lie at the foundation of the Civil Rights Act of 1866. Whether that act was authorized by the Thirteenth Amendment alone, without the support which it subsequently received from the Fourteenth Amendment, after the adoption of which it was re-enacted with some additions, my brethren do not consider it necessary to inquire. But I submit, with all respect to them, that its constitutionality is conclusively shown by their opinion. They admit, as I have said, that the Thirteenth Amendment established freedom; that there are burdens and disabilities, the necessary incidents of slavery, which constitute its substance and visible form; that Congress, by the act of 1866, passed in view of the Thirteenth Amendment, before the Fourteenth was adopted, un-dertook to remove certain burdens and disabilities, the necessary incidents of slav-ery, and to secure to all citizens of every race and color, and without regard to previous servitude, those fundamental rights which are the essence of civil free-dom, namely, the same right to make and enforce contracts, to sue, be parties, give evidence, and to inherit, purchase, lease, sell, and convey property as is en-joyed by white citizens; that under the Thirteenth Amendment, Congress has to do with slavery and its incidents; and that legislation, so far as necessary or proper to eradicate all forms and incidents of slavery and involuntary servitude, may be direct and primary, operating upon the acts of individuals, whether sanctioned by State legislation or not. These propositions being conceded, it is impossible, as it seems to me, to question the constitutional validity of the Civil Rights Act of 1866. I do not contend that the Thirteenth Amendment invests Congress with authority, by legislation, to define and regulate the entire body of the civil rights which citizens enjoy, or may enjoy, in the several States. But I hold that since slavery, as the court has repeatedly declared, *Slaughter-house Cases . . .* ; *Strauder v. West Virginia . . .* , was the moving or principal cause of the adoption of that amendment, and since that institution rested wholly upon the inferiority, as a race, of those held in bondage, their freedom necessarily involved immunity from, and protection against, all discrimination against them, because of their race, in respect of such civil rights as belong to freemen of other races. Congress, therefore, under its express power to enforce that amendment, by appropriate legislation, may enact laws to protect that people against the deprivation, *because of their race,* of any civil rights granted to other freemen in the same State; and such legislation may be of a direct and primary character, operating upon States, their officers and agents, and, also, upon, at least, such individuals and corporations as exercise public func-tions and wield power and authority under the State.

Civil Rights and the Fourteenth Amendment

Given the even broader federal interest established by the Fourteenth Amendment, which went beyond abolishing slavery to account for national citizenship and its incidents, Harlan found the Civil Rights Act of 1875 even more clearly connected to federal enforcement power. Unlike the majority, Harlan would have construed the amendment's assignment of congressional authority liberally and not coterminously with the amendment's substantive check on state power.

The assumption that this amendment consists wholly of prohibitions upon State laws and State proceedings in hostility to its provisions is unauthorized by its language. The first clause of the first section—"All persons born or naturalized in the United States, and subject to the jurisdiction thereof, are citizens of the United States, and of the State wherein they reside"—is of a distinctly affirmative character. In its application to the colored race, previously liberated, it created and granted as well citizenship of the United States as citizenship of the State in which they respectively resided. It introduced all of that race, whose ancestors had been imported and sold as slaves, at once, into the political community known as the "People of the United States." They became, instantly, citizens of the United States, *and* of their respective States. Further, they were brought, by this supreme act of the nation, within the direct operation of that provision of the Constitution which declares that "the citizens of each State shall be entitled to all privileges and immunities of citizens in the several States." Art. 4, § 2.

The citizenship thus acquired, by that race, in virtue of an affirmative grant from the nation, may be protected, not alone by the judicial branch of the government, but by congressional legislation of a primary direct character; this, because the power of Congress is not restricted to the enforcement of prohibitions upon State laws or State action. It is, in terms distinct and positive, to enforce "the *provisions of this article*" of amendment; not simply those of a prohibitive character, but the provisions—*all* of the provisions—affirmative and prohibitive, of the amendment. It is, therefore, a grave misconception to suppose that the fifth section of the amendment has reference exclusively to express prohibitions upon State laws or State action. If any right was created by that amendment, the grant of power, through appropriate legislation, to enforce its provisions, authorizes Congress, by means of legislation, operating throughout the entire Union, to guard, secure, and protect that right.

Harlan's Eventual Influence

Not until the middle of the twentieth century did the Court determine that the Thirteenth Amendment had the broader purview suggested by Harlan. Until then, the amendment was effective only in precluding systems of peonage found fundamentally akin to slavery. The better part of a century passed before the Court reconsidered whether the Thirteenth Amendment afforded a basis for broad civil rights legislation. In *Jones v. Alfred H. Mayer Co.,* it upheld a federal law prohibiting racial discrimination in housing as a permissible exercise of congressional power under the Thirteenth Amendment. Thereafter, in *Runyon v. McCrary* and on like grounds, the Court affirmed a federal enactment barring racial discrimi-

nation in the making and enforcing of contracts. Although belatedly securing federal interests established by the Civil Rights Act of 1866, the
decisions represented a logical extension and triumph of Harlan's view.
Modern case law also has recognized a federal interest in reaching private
discrimination. The Civil Rights Act of 1964, prohibiting discrimination
in various public venues and federal programs, was predicated on the
Fourteenth Amendment and the commerce power. The alternative premises for federal legislation reflected concern that the *Civil Rights Cases,*
and its narrow delineation of federal enforcement interest, had never been
overturned. The civil rights law survived constitutional challenge. The Court
in *Heart of Atlanta Motel, Inc. v. United States* and *Katzenbach v. McClung*
rejected a challenge to the public accommodations provision of the 1964
act and found instead a permissible exercise of congressional power to
regulate interstate commerce. In *United States v. Guest,* decided exactly
one century after passage of the Civil Rights Act of 1866, six justices
supported the proposition that the Fourteenth Amendment's enforcement
clause enables Congress to regulate regardless of whether or not state action is present. Such an interpretation advanced and even extended Harlan's interest in having the Fourteenth Amendment amount to more than
a symbolic gesture. As he put it, in the *Civil Rights Cases,*

But what was secured to colored citizens of the United States—as between them
and their respective States—by the national grant to them of State citizenship?
With what rights, privileges, or immunities did this grant invest them? There is
one, if there be no other—exemption from race discrimination in respect of any
civil right belonging to citizens of the white race in the same State. That, surely,
is their constitutional privilege when within the jurisdiction of other States. And
such must be their constitutional right, in their own State, unless the recent
amendments be splendid baubles, thrown out to delude those who deserved fair
and generous treatment at the hands of the nation. Citizenship in this country
necessarily imports at least equality of civil rights among citizens of every race in
the same State. It is fundamental in American citizenship that, in respect of such
rights, there shall be no discrimination by the State, or its officers, or by individuals or corporations exercising public functions or authority, against any citizen
because of his race or previous condition of servitude. . . .

    If, then, exemption from discrimination, in respect of civil rights, is a new con-
stitutional right, secured by the grant of State citizenship to colored citizens of the
United States—and I do not see how this can now be questioned—why may not
the nation, by means of its own legislation of a primary direct character, guard,
protect and enforce that right? It is a right and privilege which the nation conferred. It did not come from the States in which those colored citizens reside. It
has been the established doctrine of this court during all its history, accepted as
essential to the national supremacy, that Congress, in the absence of a positive
delegation of power to the State legislatures, may, by its own legislation, enforce
and protect any right derived from or created by the national Constitution.

Acknowledging a New Political Order

Unlike the majority, Harlan regarded the Fourteenth Amendment's redistribution of interests and power from state to federal government as a genuinely profound reworking of the nation's political system. He also found the Court's concern with excessive federal intrusion, as a consequence of such change, to be overblown and misplaced. As he put it

Exemption from race discrimination in respect of the civil rights which are fundamental in *citizenship* in a republican government, is, as we have seen, a new right, created by the nation, with express power in Congress, by legislation, to enforce the constitutional provision from which it is derived. If, in some sense, such race discrimination is, within the letter of the last clause of the first section, a denial of that equal protection of the laws which is secured against State denial to all persons, whether citizens or not, it cannot be possible that a mere prohibition upon such State denial, or a prohibition upon State laws abridging the privileges and immunities of citizens of the United States, takes from the nation the power which it has uniformly exercised of protecting, by direct primary legislation, those privileges and immunities which existed under the Constitution before the adoption of the Fourteenth Amendment, or have been created by that amendment in behalf of those thereby made *citizens* of their respective States.

This construction does not in any degree intrench upon the just rights of the States in the control of their domestic affairs. It simply recognizes the enlarged powers conferred by the recent amendments upon the general government. In the view which I take of those amendments, the States possess the same authority which they have always had to define and regulate the civil rights which their own people, in virtue of State citizenship, may enjoy within their respective limits; except that its exercise is now subject to the expressly granted power of Congress, by legislation, to enforce the provisions of such amendments—a power which necessarily carries with it authority, by national legislation, to protect and secure the privileges and immunities which are created by or are derived from those amendments. That exemption of citizens from discrimination based on race or color, in respect of civil rights, is one of those privileges or immunities can no longer be deemed an open question in this court.

Congressional Power and State Action

Harlan cautioned that if Congress could not enforce "the security of rights created by the national Constitution . . . then . . . we shall enter upon an era of constitutional law, when the rights of freedom and American citizenship cannot receive from the nation that efficient protection which heretofore was unhesitatingly accorded to slavery and the rights of the master." His warning was well placed, especially when measured by the lack of federal civil rights initiatives until the middle of the twentieth century. Even the Civil Rights Act of 1964, a broad-spectrum law prohibiting discrimination in employment, education, public accommodations and other venues, is supported by a legislative record indicating wariness of the *Civil Rights Cases* decision. As noted before, it was premised on the power of Congress under the Fourteenth Amendment and its authority to regulate interstate commerce. The Court since has upheld congressional enactments regulating private action when its authority under the Fourteenth Amendment was combined with other constitutionally assigned powers. To the extent that purely private conduct can now be reached by federal law that enforces Fourteenth Amendment goals, modern principles even exceed what Harlan contemplated.

From Harlan's perspective, the Fourteenth Amendment did not allow Congress to regulate mere social preferences. He accordingly "agree[d] that government has nothing to do with social, as distinguished from technically legal, rights of individuals." Harlan nonetheless stressed that any person or entity exercising "power under State authority for the public benefit or public convenience" was not immune from congressional action under the Fourteenth Amendment. Modern state action review has borrowed from Harlan's flexible model of analysis. State action has been identified, for instance, when a private party is performing a traditional state function or private and public conduct is mingled. Contemporary decisions, however, repudiate Harlan's suggestion that regulation or licensing is sufficient to establish state action.

Premonitions of a Color-Blind Constitution

Harlan's general vision of the Fourteenth Amendment remains pertinent to contemporary racial issues. Responding to the Court's characterization of black persons as "the special favorite of the laws," Harlan asserted that the civil rights law at issue was

for the benefit of citizens of every race and color. What the nation, through Congress, has sought to accomplish in reference to that race, is—what had already been done in every State of the Union for the white race—to secure and protect rights belonging to them as freemen and citizens; nothing more. It was not deemed enough "to help the feeble up, but to support him after." The one underlying purpose of congressional legislation has been to enable the black race to take the rank of mere citizens. The difficulty has been to compel a recognition of the legal right of the black race to take the rank of citizens, and to secure the enjoyment of privileges belonging, under the law, to them as a component part of the people for whose welfare and happiness government is ordained. At every step, in this direction, the nation has been confronted with class tyranny, which a contemporary English historian says is, of all tyrannies, the most intolerable, "for it is ubiquitous in its operation, and weighs, perhaps, most heavily on those whose obscurity or distance would withdraw them from the notice of a single despot." To-day, it is the colored race which is denied, by corporations and individuals wielding public authority, rights fundamental in their freedom and citizenship. At some future time, it may be that some other race will fall under the ban of race discrimination. If the constitutional amendments be enforced, according to the intent with which, as I conceive, they were adopted, there cannot be, in this republic, any class of human beings in practical subjection to another class, with power in the latter to dole out to the former just such privileges as they may choose to grant. The supreme law of the land has decreed that no authority shall be exercised in this country upon the basis of discrimination, in respect of civil rights, against freemen and citizens because of their race, color, or previous condition of servitude. To that decree—for the due enforcement of which, by appropriate legislation, Congress has been invested with express power—every one must bow, whatever may have been, or whatever now are, his individual views as to the wisdom or policy, either of the recent changes in the fundamental law, or of the legislation which has been enacted to give them effect.

The *Civil Rights Cases* was neither the first nor the last instance of judicial insensitivity to interests of racial justice. A little more than a decade after the *Civil Rights* decision, the Court upheld official segregation. The resultant separate-but-equal era has defined the meaning of equal protection for nearly half of the Fourteenth Amendment's existence. Development of such constitutional principles did not elicit disagreement within the Court, except from Harlan. Although representing neither mainstream political nor jurisprudential thought, and preceding acceptance of color-blind principles by several decades, the dissenting views of Justice Harlan made up with profundity what they lacked in popular acclaim.

Harlan's characterization of the Fourteenth Amendment as a guarantee of the rights and equality of all citizens, not merely a particular class, has been adverted to by modern critics of racially preferential policies. In *Fullilove v. Klutznick,* Justices Stewart and Rehnquist dissented from the Court's allowance of a federal set-aside program for minority contractors. Drawing on Harlan's sense of the Fourteenth Amendment as a guarantee for all citizens, they argued that

Our Constitution is color-blind, and neither knows nor tolerates classes among citizens. . . . The law regards man as man, and takes no account of his surroundings or of his color. . . ." Those words were written by a Member of this Court 84 years ago. *Plessy v. Ferguson,* . . . (Harlan, J., dissenting). His colleagues disagreed with him, and held that a statute that required the separation of people on the basis of their race was constitutionally valid because it was a "reasonable" exercise of legislative power and had been "enacted in good faith for the promotion [of] the public good. . . ." *Id.* . . . Today, the Court upholds a statute that accords a preference to citizens who are "Negroes, Spanish-speaking, Orientals, Indians, Eskimos, and Aleuts," for much the same reasons. I think today's decision is wrong for the same reason that *Plessy v. Ferguson* was wrong, and I respectfully dissent.

Separate but Equal: *Plessy v. Ferguson*

Harlan's description of the Fourteenth Amendment in terms that transcended the interests of a single race previewed the principle of constitutional color blindness, which was the basic reference point for his objection to the separate-but-equal doctrine in *Plessy v. Ferguson.* In the final years of the nineteenth century, Southern states increasingly formalized and extended what the Court in the *Civil Rights Cases* had dismissed as "[m]ere discriminations." Such laws, unlike the private preferences placed beyond Congress's reach in the *Civil Rights Cases,* established racial segregation by official prescription. Because state action was manifest, they were challenged as a direct violation of the Constitution itself. In *Plessy v. Ferguson,* the Court examined a Louisiana law requiring "equal but separate accommodations for the white and colored races" on passenger trains. In disposing of arguments that the statute violated the Thirteenth Amendment, the Court concluded that a mere "legal distinction between the white and colored race . . . has no tendency to destroy the legal equality of the two races, or reestablish a state of involuntary servitude." The constitutional prohibition against slavery, diminished in the *Civil Rights Cases,* was further reduced by the *Plessy* Court to concern with the technical existence of "a state of bondage; the ownership of mankind or a chattel, or at least the control of the labor and services of one man for the benefit of another."

Although acknowledging that the Fourteenth Amendment was intended to establish "the absolute equality of the two races before the law," the Court determined that it did not "abolish distinction based upon color, or . . . enforce social, as distinguished from political inequality, or a commingling of the two races upon terms unsatisfactory to either." Authority to segregate, according to the majority, was within the state's police power subject only to the requirement of reasonableness. From the Court's perspective, formal separation of the races was reasonable because it operated for the public good rather than "the annoyance or oppression of a particular class." It also comported with "established usages, customs, and traditions of the people" and accounted for "the promotion of their comfort, and the preservation of the public peace and good order."

Justification of official segregation required a reckoning with established precedent. In *Strauder v. West Virginia,* the Court had construed the Fourteenth Amendment as establishing an "exemption from legal discriminations, implying inferiority in civil society." Distinguishing its decision from the implications of *Strauder,* the *Plessy* Court noted that any understanding that the law connoted racial inferiority was "not by reason of anything found in the act, but solely because the colored race chooses to put that construction on it." Although stressing that neither race could be constitutionally inferior to the other if their civil and political rights are equal, it noted that "(i)f one race is inferior to the other socially, the Constitution of the United States cannot put them on the same plane." The Court, consistent with the spirit of the *Civil Rights Cases,* limited the scope of the Fourteenth Amendment by acknowledging only a relatively narrow band of federal interest. Even in those areas of federal concern, however, states retained discretion if not with respect to whether civil and political rights were distributed then at least with respect to how they were exercised.

Even in the context of a culture that largely accepted racial segregation and premises of white superiority, the Court's reasoning was evasive and disingenuous. Social distinctions were indistinguishable from civil or political differences insofar as exclusion and discrimination were formalized by law. To not have recognized segregation's true significance required avoidance or disregard of its background and foundation. Formal separation of the races was a direct descendant of previously outlawed methodologies of race management such as slavery and the Black Codes. Like its antecedents, official segregation was a radiation of white supremacist ideology. Enshrined by state law, racial segregation was understood not only by its victims but also by its creators as assuming the inherent inferiority of blacks. As described by Leonard Levy, it was the extension of "a conviction being stridently trumpeted by white supremacists from the press, the pulpit, and the platform, as well as from the legislative halls of the South." If not explicitly touting white supremacy, the *Plessy* Court at least referred to the status of the dominant race as a property interest and set a tone for future legislation and case law that accepted maintenance of racial purity as a legitimate state concern.

Harlan's Dissent in *Plessy*

Justice Harlan perceived in *Plessy* a result that would be regarded eventually "as pernicious as the decision made . . . in the *Dred Scott Case.*" Cutting through the imagery of race neutrality propounded by the majority, Harlan identified what he regarded as segregation's true premises and constitutionally unacceptable nature. What the majority characterized as a provision reasonably accounting for public peace and order was depicted by Harlan as resting on the impermissible assumption "that colored citizens are . . . inferior and degraded." He thus advanced an understanding of the Constitution allowing no racial qualification of civil freedom and equality.

In respect of civil rights, common to all citizens, the Constitution of the United States does not, I think, permit any public authority to know the race of those entitled to be protected in the enjoyment of such rights. Every true man has pride of race, and under appropriate circumstances when the rights of others, his equals before the law, are not to be affected, it is his privilege to express such pride and to take such action based upon it as to him seems proper. But I deny that any legislative body or judicial tribunal may have regard to the race of citizens when the civil rights of those citizens are involved. Indeed, such legislation, as that here in question, is inconsistent not only with that equality of rights which pertains to citizenship, National and State, but with the personal liberty enjoyed by every one within the United States.

Harlan was unimpressed with the outward symmetry of official segregation. Responding to the contention that the law did not discriminate, but established a rule "applicable alike to white and colored citizens," he maintained that

this argument does not meet the difficulty. Every one knows that the statute in question had its origin in the purpose, not so much to exclude white persons from railroad cars occupied by blacks, as to exclude colored people from coaches occupied by or assigned to white persons. Railroad corporations of Louisiana did not make discrimination among whites in the matter of accommodation for travellers. The thing to accomplish was, under the guise of giving equal accommodation for whites and blacks, to compel the latter to keep to themselves while travelling in railroad passenger coaches. No one would be so wanting in candor as to assert the contrary. The fundamental objection, therefore, to the statute is that it interferes with the personal freedom of citizens. "Personal liberty," it has been well said, "consists in the power of locomotion, of changing situation, or removing one's person to whatsoever places one's own inclination may direct, without imprisonment or restraint, unless by due course of law." [Citation omitted.] If a white man and a black man choose to occupy the same public conveyance on a public highway, it is their right to do so, and no government, proceeding alone on grounds of race, can prevent it without infringing the personal liberty of each.

Because of its implications of racial inferiority and impairment of personal liberty, the law for Harlan was constitutionally defective. Official segregation also collided with his vision of a color-blind constitution.

[I]n view of the Constitution, in the eye of the law, there is in this country no superior, dominant, ruling class of citizens. There is no caste here. Our Constitution is color-blind, and neither knows nor tolerates classes among citizens. In respect of civil rights, all citizens are equal before the law. The humblest is the peer of the most powerful. The law regards man as man, and takes no account of his surroundings or of his color when his civil rights as guaranteed by the supreme law of the land are involved. It is, therefore, to be regretted that this high tribunal, the final expositor of the fundamental law of the land, has reached the conclusion that it is competent for a State to regulate the enjoyment by citizens of their civil rights solely upon the basis of race.

What made the majority's decision akin to the discredited *Dred Scott* ruling, from Harlan's perspective, was that it accommodated a "dominant class." Referring specifically to Chief Justice Taney's characterization of "a subordinate and inferior class of beings, who . . . had no rights or privileges but such as those who held the power and the government might choose to grant," he observed that the reconstruction amendments supposedly "had eradicated these principles from our institutions." Official segregation represented to Harlan the constitutionalization of racial superiority and encouragement of further disparagement and oppression on the basis of race. He accordingly noted that

It seems that we have yet, in some of the States, a dominant race—a superior class of citizens, which assumes to regulate the enjoyment of civil rights, common to all citizens, upon the basis of race. The present decision, it may well be apprehended, will not only stimulate aggressions, more or less brutal and irritating, upon the admitted rights of colored citizens, but will encourage the belief that it is possible, by means of state enactments, to defeat the beneficent purposes which the people of the United States had in view when they adopted the recent amendments of the Constitution, by one of which the blacks of this country were made citizens of the United States and of the States in which they respectively reside, and whose privileges and immunities, as citizens, the States are forbidden to abridge. Sixty millions of whites are in no danger from the presence here of eight millions of blacks. The destinies of the two races, in this country, are indissolubly linked together, and the interests of both require that the common government of all shall not permit the seeds of race hate to be planted under the sanction of law. What can more certainly arouse race hate, what more certainly create and perpetuate a feeling of distrust between these races, than state enactments, which, in fact, proceed on the ground that colored citizens are so inferior and degraded that they cannot be allowed to sit in public coaches occupied by white citizens? That, as all will admit, is the real meaning of such legislation as was enacted in Louisiana.

Finally, Harlan challenged the premise that prescriptive separation was a reasonable exercise of state power. From his perspective, interests in public peace and order over the long run were retarded rather than facilitated by segregative methodology.

The sure guarantee of the peace and security of each race is the clear, distinct, unconditional recognition by our governments, National and State, of every right that inheres in civil freedom, and of the equality before the law of all citizens of the United States without regard to race. State enactments, regulating the enjoyment of civil rights, upon the basis of race, and cunningly devised to defeat legitimate results of the war, under the pretence of recognizing equality of rights, can have no other result than to render permanent peace impossible, and to keep alive a conflict of races, the continuance of which must do harm to all concerned. This question is not met by the suggestion that social equality cannot exist between the white and black races in this country. That argument, if it can be properly regarded as one, is scarcely worthy of consideration; for social equality no more exists between two races when travelling in a passenger coach or a public highway than when members of the same races sit by each other in a street car or in the jury box, or stand or sit with each other in a political assembly, or when they use in common the streets of a city or town, or when they are in the same room for the purpose of having their names placed on the registry of voters, or when they approach the ballot-box in order to exercise the high privilege of voting. . . .

If evils will result from the commingling of the two races upon public highways established for the benefit of all, they will be infinitely less than those that will surely come from state legislation regulating the enjoyment of civil rights upon the basis of race. We boast of the freedom enjoyed by our people above all other peoples. But it is difficult to reconcile that boast with a state of the law which, practically, puts the brand of servitude and degradation upon a large class of our fellow-citizens, our equals before the law. The thin disguise of "equal" accommodations for passengers in railroad coaches will not mislead any one, nor atone for the wrong this day done.

The Separate-but-Equal Era: An Emphasis on Separation

Progress toward Harlan's ideal of a color-blind constitution was slow, as the separate-but-equal doctrine became firmly embedded in the Fourteenth Amendment's landscape. Typifying the real meaning of the separate-but-equal doctrine was a county's closure of its only black high school. The decision, justified on grounds that the district only had funds sufficient to support a white high school and primary education for both races, was upheld in *Cumming v. Board of Education.* Consistent with practical emphasis on racial separation at the expense of equality, funding of public education was characterized by enormous disparities. Spending by South Carolina in 1915, for instance, was ten times for white schools what it was for black schools. Only when official segregation became endangered by the middle of this century did states, in the interests of maintaining racial separation, finally promise meaningful attention to equalized funding.

Until the middle of the twentieth century, official segregation was the defining feature of race relations in the United States. Reminiscent of the North's accommodation of slavery before the Civil War, the entire union deferred to regional preference by providing for segregation of various national institutions including the military. Prescriptive segregation became so comprehensive and intrusive in regulating social relations that, barely a decade after *Plessy,* the Court upheld a state law prohibiting racial mixing even in private schools. In *Berea College v. Kentucky,* the Court upheld the state's power to regulate the distribution of educational services to different racial groups. As a corporation created by the state, the college was found subject to such control. The *Berea College* decision represented a notable departure from the Court's otherwise vigorous defense of contract and property rights. Three years earlier, in *Lochner v. New York,* the Court had identified the due process clause as a constitutional barrier to state interference with contractual arrangements negotiated by private parties.

Justice Byron White has observed that the *Lochner* and *Plessy* doctrines "were nowhere more eloquently or incisively criticized than in the dissenting opinions of Justice . . . Harlan." It was Harlan's *Berea College* dissent, however, that most poignantly illuminated the incongruity if not hypocrisy of the Fourteenth Amendment's development. Although he had dissented from the Court's decision in *Lochner,* Harlan reminded the Court of its accounting for economic rights. He noted specifically that "[t]he right to impart instruction . . . is a substantial right of property—especially where the services are rendered for compensation." Citing to the Court's decisions, Harlan related "that the liberty guaranteed by the Fourteenth Amendment embraces 'the right of the citizen to be free in the enjoyment of all his facilities.' " Fourteenth Amendment review, that closely monitored legislative judgment when economic interests unrelated to race were affected but deferred to policy establishing racial classifications, struck Harlan as incongruous. The exemption from fundamental rights analysis in *Berea College* compounded the perversion. Given what he described as the "innocent purposes" of the proscribed activity, Harlan asked whether the nation had

become so inoculated with prejudice of race that an American government, professedly based on the principles of freedom, and charged with the protection of all citizens alike, can make distinctions between such citizens in the matter of their voluntary meeting for innocent purposes simply because of their respective races?

So entrenched was segregation constitutionally and practically that few significant challenges were directed at it over the next few decades. In *McCabe v. Atchison, Topeka & Santa Fe Railway Co.,* the Court affirmed the requirement of separate train accommodations even in the absence of significant non-white patronage. It refused to order relief, however, in the particular case. Because the complaining parties had never sought or been denied service themselves, the Court found them entitled to no remedy. Like the *Cumming* decision, the result in *McCabe* demonstrated how the constitutional doctrine could step down in application from a separate to nonexistent right.

A pattern of consistent deference to legislated racial classifications was broken two decades after *Plessy* in the case of *Buchanan v. Warley.* In *Buchanan,* the Court struck down a city ordinance requiring blacks and

whites to live on separate blocks. The Court described the racially determined zoning scheme as an "interference with property rights" that violated due process requirements. Realistically, property rights were no more
burdened in *Buchanan* than in *Berea College.* As decisional reasoning evidenced, however, the Court was sensitive to the reality that the burden
on property rights in *Buchanan* extended not only to blacks but to whites.

The *Buchanan* decision may have been aberrational in its limitation of
state power to segregate, but it was consistent with the Court's guardianship of economic rights. The ruling thus illuminated the odd relation between Fourteenth Amendment purpose and case law, as it was only because of attention to Lochnerist principles that the racial classification was
defeated. Barring a like coincidence of fundamental rights merged with
anti-discrimination aims, the separate-but-equal doctrine was destined to
harden. In *Gong Lum v. Rice,* decided in 1927, the constitutional ambit for
official segregation widened. In *Gong Lum,* a student of Chinese descent
challenged the school board's assignment of her to a "colored" school. A
unanimous Court found no denial of equal protection.

The Separate-but-Equal Era: Challenging Official Segregation

Not until the mid-1930s did some serious chinks begin to appear in
official segregation's armor. With the counsel of Charles Howard and
Thurgood Marshall, the National Association for the Advancement of
Colored People (NAACP) commenced a long-term challenge to the separate-but-equal doctrine. The NAACP strategy was twofold. First, it sought
equalization of gross disparities that had evolved in public schooling. Second, it aimed ultimately at undoing segregative premises by demonstrating
that separate and equal were mutually incompatible concepts. Over two
decades, the NAACP secured state and federal court judgments that required integration of graduate and professional education if separate
schooling was not provided. In *Missouri ex rel. Gaines v. Canada,* for instance, Missouri's provision of a law school for whites but not for blacks
was challenged. Although the state offered to subsidize a separate-but-
equal legal education in another state, the Court determined that Missouri
had defaulted on its equal protection responsibilities. Unless providing a
separate law school for black students, the state was obligated to provide
for admission to the law school of the state university.

The NAACP's successful inroads into the separate-but-equal doctrine
were a prelude to the principle's undoing. At the midpoint of this century,
the challenge to segregated education expanded from a focus on disparate
funding to institutional differences in prestige, faculty, facilities and con-
nections. Sensing the vulnerability of the separate-but-equal doctrine,

Southern states promised to invest unprecedented sums of money for equalization purposes. Emphasizing the intangible advantages of white graduate and professional education, in *Sweatt v. Painter,* the Court ordered integration of a state law despite equalization pledges.

New Standards of Review: A Prelude to *Brown*

Divestment of constitutional principle that "tolerates classes among citizens," as Harlan had put it, required new standards of review and a reckoning with history. In foreclosing the *Lochner* era of substantive due process review, the Court in *United States v. Carolene Products Co.* had reserved the option of determining "whether prejudice against discrete and insular minorities may be a special condition, which tends seriously to curtail the operation of those political processes ordinarily to be relied upon to protect minorities, and which may call for a correspondingly more searching judicial inquiry." Several years after *Carolene Products,* in reviewing the relocation of Japanese Americans from the West Coast during World War II, the Court advanced a more exacting standard of review for racial classifications. Although deferring to the wholesale detention of citizens on national security grounds, the Court in *Korematsu v. United States* asserted

that all legal restrictions which curtail the civil rights of a single racial group are immediately suspect. That is not to say that all such restrictions are unconstitutional. It is to say that courts must subject them to the most rigid scrutiny. Pressing public necessity may sometimes justify the existence of such restrictions, racial antagonism never can.

The Undoing of Formal Segregation: *Brown v. Board of Education*

In assessing the consummate challenge to the separate-but-equal doctrine in *Brown v. Board of Education,* the Court was armed with standards that required not deference toward but compelling justification by the state for officially segregated education. Even with criteria for closer judicial scrutiny of prescriptive segregation, a primary impediment to constitutional change was the history of the Fourteenth Amendment. The Court postponed a decision in *Brown* for a full term to hear reargument on the amendment's original intent. What the record disclosed was little evidence that the amendment's drafters and its ratifying states had contemplated racially mixed education. The Fourteenth Amendment had been adopted against a backdrop of law in many states that required racially separate public schools. The same Congress responsible for the Fourteenth

Amendment had provided for segregated education in the District of Columbia.

Despite the historical evidence, the Court determined that it could not "turn the clock back to 1868 when the Amendment was adopted, or even to 1896 when *Plessy v. Ferguson* was written." Because public education at the time of reconstruction had not evolved to the point of societal and personal significance it would later achieve, the Court refused to be bound by original provision for and accommodation of racial segregation. Recognizing that education had become a primary function of local government and was crucial to meaningful individual opportunity, the Court determined that the equal protection guarantee required appraisal from a modern perspective. What it discerned was that education had become the linchpin for citizenship and material self-development. The Court also determined that official segregation of the educational process "has a detrimental effect upon the colored children . . . [and] is usually interpreted as denoting the inferiority of the negro group."

Six decades after Harlan recognized that prescriptive racial separation assumed "that colored citizens are . . . inferior" and its harmful nature was not misapprehended by segregation's victims, the Court concurred with his perception. It accordingly concluded "that in the field of public education the doctrine of 'separate but equal' has no place. Separate educational facilities are inherently unequal." Official segregation, upheld in *Plessy* as a reasonable exercise of state police power, was defeated because it "deprived of the equal protection of the laws guaranteed by the Fourteenth Amendment." Modern jurisprudence now refers in a single breath to the *Brown* decision and Harlan dissent. As the Court observed in *Patterson v. McLean Credit Union,* they establish "a firm national policy to prohibit racial segregation and discrimination."

The desegregation mandate announced in *Brown* was quickly extended by case law to a broad spectrum of public venues. A decade later, Congress passed the Civil Rights Act of 1964, which prohibited racial and other types of discrimination in employment, public education, facilities, accommodations and federally assisted programs. Within another few years, Congress had prohibited discrimination in housing and enacted comprehensive and detailed legislation protecting against racially based deprivation of the right to vote.

The *Brown* decision, responding to the stigma of formal segregation that Harlan had perceived in 1896, translated the equal protection guarantee into a prohibition of official racial classifications. The Court also ordered the dismantling of racially identifiable schools "with all deliberate speed." Actual desegregation achievements, however, have been limited by two factors. Original Southern reaction to the *Brown* mandate was characterized to a significant extent by resistance, evasion and delay. So slow was progress toward unitary schools that by the end of the 1960s, the Court announced that "[t]he time for mere deliberate speed" in achieving deseg-regation "has run out." The *Brown* Court had counted on good faith ef-forts that would tailor policies to unique community needs but ultimately achieve desegregation. Responding to the widespread lack of accomplish-ment, the Court, in *Green v. County School Board of New Kent County,* fi-nally demanded "a plan that promises realistically to work, and promises realistically to work *now.*"

The Qualification and Devolution of *Brown*

Emphasis on immediate results more than a decade after *Brown* had a relatively short-term and ultimately limited impact. As Northern and Western communities became increasingly aware of desegregation's poten-tial relevance to them, reservations about and objections to the principle began to mount. After extensive personnel turnover in the late 1960s and early 1970s, the Court introduced standards that substantially qualified the reach of desegregation. As the first condition for a desegregation remedy, the Court in *Keyes v. School District No. 1* required proof of segregative intent. Showing such purpose had been simple enough when the law for-mally prescribed racial separation. Official intent was difficult to prove, however, insofar as it might be hidden, subtle or unconscious. The deter-mination that equal protection was not implicated, absent identification of segregative purpose, effectively exempted communities in which racially separate schools were a result of residential settlement patterns rather than official arrangement. Consistent with discriminatory motive criteria, the Court in *Milliken v. Bradley* determined that metropolitan desegregation relief was contingent on proof of segregative manipulation by communi-ties to be affected by the remedy. The requirement largely exempted new and predominantly white suburban communities that had emerged since *Brown.* In *Pasadena City Board of Education v. Spangler* the Court deter-mined that desegregation obligations were not enduring. To the extent that white flight unaided by official action results in school resegregation, therefore, such reversion is constitutionally insignificant. Finally, in *Board of Education of Oklahoma City Public Schools v. Dowell* and in *Freeman v. Pitts,* the Court which previously had insisted on eradication of segrega-tion's vestiges "root and branch" announced that it would settle for "elim-inat[ion] to the extent practicable."

Accumulated qualification of the desegregation principle has elicited ex-tensive criticism. Justice Marshall's objections were especially strident. As he saw it, the guarantee of equal protection had been redefined to the point that it afforded "no remedy at all . . . guaranteeing that Negro chil-dren . . . will receive the same separate and inherently unequal education in the future as they have been unconstitutionally afforded in the past."

Constitutional Color Blindness and Modern Problems

Predicting how Harlan would have responded to what the Court regards as constitutionally insignificant *de facto* segregation is subject to the uncertainties of projecting any principle uttered in one era to another. The sum of his dissents in the *Civil Rights Cases, Plessy* and *Berea College* suggests a respect for private decision-making but intolerance for public policy that prescribes, allows or acquiesces in overt classifications on the basis of race. Given those tendencies, the development of desegregation principles in the post-*Brown* era probably squares well with Harlan's vision.

How Harlan might have responded to modern affirmative action controversies may be less clear. Although criticizing color-conscious distinctions, his objections reflected disapproval of a methodology that served and maintained a "dominant class of citizens." If Harlan's exclusive or primary concern was with the purpose of a racial classification, the possibility exists that he may have allowed for distinctions based on actual aims. Racially preferential policies, calculated to repair past discrimination or achieve the benefits of diversification, at least arguably are distinguishable from the racist output condemned by Harlan in *Plessy*. Although many have urged such a distinction, it is uncertain whether Harlan would have made it himself. Assuming that he would not have, and referencing his description of the Fourteenth Amendment as a provision "for the benefit of citizens of every race and color," modern critics of affirmative action have cited to Harlan's dissents. In *Metro Broadcasting, Inc. v. Federal Communications Commission,* Justices Kennedy and Scalia criticized the Court's validation of Federal Communications Commission policies establishing racial preferences in the broadcast licensing process. They noted that although

The racial composition of this Nation is far more diverse than the first Justice Harlan foresaw, his warning in dissent is now all the more apposite: "The destinies of the two races, in this country, are indissolubly linked together, and the interests of both require that the common government of all shall not permit the seeds of race hate to be planted under the sanction of law." *Plessy, . . .* (dissenting opinion). Perhaps the Court can succeed in its assumed role of case-by-case arbiter of when it is desirable and benign for the Government to disfavor some citizens and favor others based on the color of their skin. Perhaps the tolerance and decency to which our people aspire will let the disfavored rise above hostility and the favored escape condescension. But history suggests much peril in this enterprise, and so the Constitution forbids us to undertake it. I regret that after a century of judicial opinions we interpret the Constitution to do no more than move us from "separate but equal" to "unequal but benign."

The triumph of Harlan's dissenting views was a protracted rather than sudden process. Nearly three quarters of a century elapsed between his dissent in the *Civil Rights Cases* and the decision in *Brown* that repudiated the letter of *Plessy* and the spirit of *Dred Scott.* Modern constitutional interpretation essentially has embraced the concept of a color-blind constitution. Controversy survives with respect to whether allowance should be made for policies that promote diversification of the workplace, schoolplace and other contexts. Justice Blackmun, although stressing that "[w]e cannot . . . let the Equal Protection Clause perpetrate racial supremacy" in *Regents of the University of California v. Bakke,* nonetheless observed that "[i]n order to get beyond racism, we must first take account of race." Over the latter half of this century, constitutional law has evolved toward the racially neutral ends that Harlan favored. Abiding controversy over the requirements of equal protection reveal a challenge still in accounting for the full dimensions and implications of a color-blind constitution.

Bibliography

Cases

Allgeyer v. Louisiana, 165 U.S. 575 (1897).
Berea College v. Kentucky, 211 U.S. 45 (1908).
Blylew v. United States, 80 U.S. 581 (1872).
Brown v. Board of Education, 347 U.S. 483 (1954).
Buchanan v. Warley, 245 U.S. 60 (1917).
Civil Rights Cases, 109 U.S. 3 (1883).
Cumming v. Board of Education, 175 U.S. 528 (1899).
Dred Scott v. Sandford, 60 U.S. 393 (1857).
Freeman v. Pitts, 112 S.Ct. 1430 (1992).
Fullilove v. Klutznick, 448 U.S. 448 (1980).
Giles v. Harris, 189 U.S., 475 (1903).
Gong Lum v. Rice, 275 U.S. 78 (1927).
Green v. County School Board of New Kent County, 391 U.S. 430 (1968).
Heart of Atlanta Motel, Inc. v. United States, 379 U.S. 241 (1964).
Jones v. Alfred H. Mayer Co., 392 U.S. 409 (1968).
Katzenbach v. McClung, 379 U.S. 294 (1964).
Keyes v. School District No. 1, 413 U.S. 189 (1973).
Korematsu v. United States, 323 U.S. 414 (1944).
Lochner v. New York, 198 U.S. 45 (1905).
McCabe v. Atchison, Topeka & Santa Fe Railway Co., 235 U.S. 151 (1908).
Metro Broadcasting, Inc. v. Federal Communications Commission, 110 S.Ct. 2997 (1990).
Milliken v. Bradley, 418 U.S. 717 (1974).
Missouri ex rel. Gaines v. Canada, 305 U.S. 337 (1938).
Pasadena City Board of Education v. Spangler, 427 U.S. 424 (1976).
Patterson v. McLean Credit Union, 491 U.S. 164 (1989).
Plessy v. Ferguson, 163 U.S. 537 (1896).
Regents of the University of California v. Bakke, 438 U.S. 265 (1978).

Runyon v. McCrary, 427 U.S. 160 (1976).
Slaughter-House Cases, 83 U.S. 36 (1873).
Strauder v. West Virginia, 100 U.S. 303 (1880).
Sweatt v. Painter, 339 U.S. 629 (1950).
United States v. Carolene Products Co., 304 U.S. 144 (1938).
United States v. Cruikshank, 92 U.S. 542 (1876).
United States v. Guest, 383 U.S. 745 (1966).
United States v. Harris, 106 U.S. 629 (1883).
Virginia, Ex parte, 100 U.S. 373 (1880).
Virginia v. Rives, 100 U.S. 339 (1880).

Books and Articles

Fairman, C., VII History of the Supreme Court of the United States, Reconstruction and Reunion (1971) (1987).
Kluger, R., Simple Justice (1976).
Levy, L., *Plessy v. Ferguson,* in Civil Rights and Equality (K. Karst, ed., 1989).
Lewis, A., Portrait of a Decade: The Second American Revolution (1964).
Marshall, T., *An Evaluation of Recent Efforts to Achieve Racial Integration in Education through Resort to the Courts,* 21 J. Negro Educ. 316 (1952).
Ripple, K., Constitutional Litigation (1984).
Schmidt, B., *Principle and Prejudice: The Supreme Court and Race in the Progressive Era, Part 1: The Heyday of Jim Crow,* 82 Col. L. Rev. 444 (1982).

Chapter 6

FREEDOM OF SPEECH: THE "INDISPENSABLE" LIBERTY

Freedom of expression has been described in various ways and at various times as the most essential constitutional guarantee. Typifying its special esteem in the constitutional order is the Supreme Court's characterization of freedom of speech, in *Palko v. Connecticut,* as "the matrix, the indispensable condition of every other form of freedom." Recognition of the nexus between freedom and general liberty predated the First Amendment. John Milton, in 1644, wrote that "the liberty to know, to utter, and to argue freely according to conscience, [is] above all liberties." The natural law theories of John Locke, which were especially influential in the development of the Declaration of Independence, also emphasized freedom of expression as a crucial liberty that facilitated the enjoyment of other rights.

The First Amendment: Background and Early History

Unlike the Fourteenth Amendment, freedom of speech and the press was not an immediate subject of litigation and interpretation. Not until the twentieth century, as expressive freedom was included within the meaning of liberty secured by the Fourteenth Amendment, did the Court seriously probe its significance, develop pertinent principles and amplify its content. Belated jurisprudential attention to the First Amendment did not indicate a record free of official speech management and control. Suppression of expression is a tradition that evolved coextensively with methodologies for efficient reproduction and mass dissemination of printed information. English licensing laws, which governed the printing industry until 1694, afforded the Crown unfettered discretion to determine what was published and by whom. Even when formal licensing was abandoned, other methodologies of restraint emerged. Techniques of suppression in the American colonies during the eighteenth century included systems of taxation and censorship and the law of defamation.

Official control of expression eventually became a contributing factor to the American Revolution. A legacy of negative and subversive reaction to official speech control began to evolve as the colonial press began to mature. The trial of John Peter Zenger represented a particularly notable conflict between the interests of speech freedom and control. Zenger was a New York printer who published political tracts that criticized the governor. Claiming that his reputation had been injured, the governor brought an action for libel. As the law then existed, truth was not a defense to but an aggravation of a libelous statement. Despite the absence of any real dispute over the content and impact of the expression, the jury found in Zenger's favor. Although establishing no formal precedent, the Zenger experience inspired subsequent challenges to colonial controls and became a visible achievement of libertarian ideology.

As originally proposed for ratification, the Constitution contained no itemization of personal rights or liberties. The Bill of Rights, which includes the First Amendment, was introduced to rescue the entire Constitution from mounting anti-ratification sentiment. Although appended as somewhat of an afterthought, the significance of the First Amendment should not be diminished by the strategic imperatives accounting for its introduction. Antifederalists who championed the Bill of Rights saw it as an essential safeguard against the risk of overreaching and abuse of power by a newly created central government. Even those who did not consider the Bill of Rights a necessary condition for ratification were not antagonistic to its content. For Federalist participants in the Constitution's conception, the existence of such freedoms was so obvious that enumeration of them was unnecessary. Differences existed, therefore, not with respect to the existence but to the form of accounting for basic rights and liberties.

Thomas Emerson has observed that the concept of freedom of expression "does not come naturally to the ordinary citizen but needs to be learned. It must be restated and reiterated not only for each generation, but for each situation." Evidence of the challenge that the First Amendment presents to its beneficiaries is related by political developments in the nation's formative years. By its terms, the amendment provides that "Congress shall make no law . . . abridging the freedom of speech, or of the press." Seven years after the provision's ratification, Congress enacted a law manifestly grounded in political intolerance. Passage of the Sedition Act represented a culmination of ideological rivalry between the Federalist and Democratic-Republican Parties. Political friction, attributable to competing perspectives concerning how the nation should develop, related back to the formation of the union. The Sedition Act represented a calculated strategy by Federalist-dominated executive and legislative branches to silence their Republican critics. The law specifically criminalized "false, scandalous and malicious writing" against the "federal" government or "either house of Congress . . . or the President . . . with intent to defame . . . or to bring them . . . into contempt or disrepute." Violation of the law incurred the risk of up to two years in prison and a fine.

Although clearly implicating the First Amendment, the enactment never became the subject of direct judicial review. Rather, it became an early casualty of political change as the presidency and Congress fell into Republican hands. The Sedition Act was repealed within a few years of its passage. Even if short-lived, the act and its contradictory relation to the First Amendment have been an enduring source of attention. Despite never having tested the enactment itself, the Supreme Court has observed that "the attack upon its validity has carried the day in the court of history." In *New York Times Co. v. Sullivan,* the Court thus related how Congress and the president had repudiated the Sedition Act and contributed to "a broad consensus that the Act, because of the restraint it imposed upon criticism of government and public officials, was inconsistent with the First Amendment."

The Sedition Act reflected intolerance of political diversity that was neither isolated nor unique in the nation's history. Freedom of expression for critics of the American Revolution, for instance, was denied by acts of mob violence and intimidation. The emergence of the abolitionist movement during the early 1830s prompted Southern states to enact laws prohibiting the dissemination of anti-slavery literature in their respective jurisdictions. Overt abolitionist sentiment largely was purged from the South, as the last abolitionist organizations disappeared by the late 1830s. Although abridging expressive freedom, state prohibition of abolitionist expression presented no grounds for a First Amendment claim at the time. Not until the twentieth century was freedom of speech and of the press incorporated into the meaning of liberty under the Fourteenth Amendment. Pending that development, the First Amendment was a check only on the exercise of congressional power.

The sum of nineteenth-century constitutional jurisprudence includes only marginal references to freedom of speech and of the press. In *Dred Scott v. Sandford,* for instance, the Court adverted to the First Amendment in exemplifying the existence of specified constitutional restrictions on the exercise of congressional power in U.S. territories. The majority opinion in the *Slaughter-House Cases,* in itemizing privileges of national citizenship, referred to the "right to peaceably assemble and petition for redress of grievances." Typical of nineteenth-century constitutional development, neither *Dred Scott* nor *Slaughter-House* expounded on or even directly considered the meaning of freedom of speech and of the press.

Initial Questions of Coverage

As the twentieth century unfolded, speech and press liberties became objects of forthright and extensive attention. In a case not directly implicating the First Amendment—*Patterson v. Colorado*—Justice Holmes observed that the "main purpose" of the freedom of the press clause was " 'to prevent all such *previous restraints* upon publications as had been practiced by other governments,' [but not to] prevent the subsequent punishment of such as may be deemed contrary to the public welfare." A strong presumption against prior restraint remains a prominent feature in First Amendment jurisprudence. It does not, however, exclusively define the significance of freedom of speech and of the press. Nor, as developments soon after *Patterson* indicated, was the rule against prior restraint indefeasible. As methodologies for processing and disseminating information enhanced the capacity and influence of mass media, many states responded with regulatory initiatives. The advent of motion pictures, for instance, resulted in the creation of censorship boards that determined what films were fit for public consumption. In *Mutual Film Corp. v. Industrial Commission of Ohio,* the Court upheld such a system of prior restraint against challenges that it abridged liberty of the press. Although a First Amendment claim was dropped in favor of a state constitutional claim, during the appeals process, the Court revealed its sense of the scope of press liberty. It characterized "the exhibition of moving pictures [a]s a part of the press of the country." Given the medium's "capability and power" for "evil," accentuated by the presence of children in the audience, however, the Court found a reasonable exercise of a legitimate state regulatory power in controlling it.

Early Freedom of Speech Cases: A Search for Standards

Seminal development of principles relating to freedom of expression became the responsibility of the Court at the same time it was heavily invested in substantive due process theory. The *Lochner* era of fundamental rights development is primarily notable for the Court's vigorous championing of economic freedom. Marketplace liberty, however, was a prominent but not exclusive aspect of a Fourteenth Amendment legacy that generated and attended to an array of individual liberties. Consistent with the Court's understanding of the Fourteenth Amendment at the time, protection of expression from state abridgment was achieved by defining freedom of speech and of the press as a liberty within the meaning of the due process clause.

Early First Amendment principles were characterized by substantial deference toward governmental regulation of expression. Undemanding standards of review, deferring to what were perceived as reasonable exercises of state police power, contrasted with the exacting review that contemporaneously denied or narrowed regulatory authority when economic rights were implicated. Early interpretation of the First Amendment generated results that may have seemed more consistent with the deferential model of review propounded by Justice Holmes in his *Lochner* dissent. In reality, the Court independently examined legislation burdening expressive liberty, but unlike its response to much economic regulation agreed with regulatory means and ends. As the author of the Court's seminal opinions on free speech, Holmes had a significant influence on the formative meaning of the First Amendment. It was his opinions with Justice Brandeis objecting to the Court's early allowance of speech control and sanctions, however, that have had an enduring influence on the development of expressive freedom.

In the modern order of First Amendment priorities, political speech is most valued by the Court and thus the most protected form of expression. Such status reflects the sense of theorists such as Alexander Meiklejohn that speech pertaining to informed self-governance is at the core of the First Amendment's concern. Reflecting that premise are standards that make it more difficult for public officials to prevail in defamation claims. As Justice Brennan observed in *New York Times Co. v. Sullivan,* such a case implicates "the profound national commitment to the principle that debate on public issues should be uninhibited, robust, and wide-open, and that it may include vehement, caustic, and sometimes unpleasantly sharp attacks on government." At issue in the Supreme Court's earliest freedom of speech decision was the Espionage Act of 1917, which criminalized expression intended to interfere with the war effort, cause insubordination or disloyalty or interfere with recruiting or enlistment. In *Schenck v. United States,* the Court upheld convictions for conspiracy to distribute antidraft literature that was "calculated to cause . . . insubordination and obstruction." Among other things, the material asserted that the draft violated the Thirteenth Amendment, urged recipients to "Assert Your Rights" and criticized the war as a "monstrous wrong" for the benefit of a "chosen few."

Responding to the argument that the expression was protected by the First Amendment, Holmes acknowledged "that in many places and in many times the defendants in saying all that was said in the circular would have been within their constitutional rights." Given the nation's involvement in war and the special security interests associated with it, however, he stressed that "the character of every act depends upon the circumstances in which it is done." He thus related that

The most stringent protection of free speech would not protect a man in falsely shouting fire in a theatre and causing a panic. It does not even protect a man from an injunction against uttering words that may have all the effect of force. [Citation omitted.] The question in every case is whether the words used are used in such circumstances and are of such a nature as to create a clear and present danger that they will bring about the substantive evils that Congress has a right to prevent. It is a question of proximity and degree. When a nation is at war many things that might be said in time of peace are such a hindrance to its effort that their utterance will not be endured so long as men fight and that no Court could regard them as protected by any constitutional right. It seems to be admitted that if an actual obstruction of the recruiting service were proved, liability for words that produced that effect might be enforced.

In *Schenck,* the interests of speech control prevailed over those of speech freedom. What now would be protected political dissent—part of the broad spectrum of expression essential to informed self-government—then was the basis for serious sanctions including imprisonment. The *Schenck* decision was significant not just for its immediate result, but for its contribution of principle for the longer term. Holmes's introduction of the clear-and-present-danger concept was not well amplified beyond the observation that it was "a question of proximity and degree." Subsequent case law eventually defined, with mixed results for several decades, how immediate and profound the risk of harm had to be for speech to be regulated. As originally presented, clear-and-present-danger criteria did not steer toward results that were favorable to expressive diversity.

The *Schenck* opinion was one of three opinions that Holmes authored in 1919 that reached similar results. The Court, in *Frohwerk v. United States,* upheld Espionage Act convictions for obstruction of military recruiting. The expression, contained in newspaper articles criticizing American participation in the war, praising Germany and protesting the draft, was described by Holmes as "words of persuasion." Without even mentioning clear and present danger principles, he concluded that the Constitution did not "give immunity for every possible use of language." In *Debs v. United States,* the Court upheld the Espionage Act conviction of a prominent socialist politician for a speech that expressed opposition to the war. While incarcerated, Eugene Debs received nearly 1 million votes as a presidential candidate in 1920. Harry Kalven, Jr., described Debs's conviction as comparable to putting "George McGovern . . . in prison for his criticism of the [Vietnam] War" when he ran for president in 1972. The *Frohwerk* opinion, in the words of Samuel Konefsky, suggested that "the author of the clear and present danger doctrine completely ignored his own brain-child."

Toward a More Speech-Protective Theory

The Court's initial expoundments on the First Amendment were notable for their deference to legislative judgment and general unresponsive-

ness to the interests of expressive pluralism. The early results indicated
no institutional sense of an especially profound interest necessitating close
attention and even raise doubt as to whether Holmes fully appreciated the
significance of his clear and present danger formula. Holmes's correspondence soon after the initial free speech decisions indicates a perception on
his part that regulation of expressive liberty merited no special consideration. More than a decade before *Schenck,* the Court had determined that a
compulsory immunization plan violated no constitutionally protected liberty interest. As he wrote in the aftermath of *Schenck,* liberty of expression
"stands no differently than freedom of vaccination." Holmes's original position thus squared with his general philosophy, manifested especially well
in the substantive due process cases, of judicial to lerance for legislative
choices.

Minus occasion for further reflection and development, "clear and present danger" may have been, as Justice Frankfurter described it, no more
than a "felicitous" phrase. As originally applied, clear and present danger
standards offered little indication of their future vitality as a speech-
protective doctrine. In the same year that *Schenck, Frohwerk* and *Debs* were
decided, however, Holmes penned an impassioned defense of free expression values that endures as a First Amendment classic. In *Abrams v. United
States,* the Court upheld Espionage Act convictions for the printing of cir-
culars intended to encourage resistance to the war against Germany and
cripple or hinder the war effort. Although the leafleteer's point actually
was to discourage American interference with the Russian Revolution, the
Court found a specific intent to hinder the war with Germany. Without
any reference to the clear and present danger terminology of *Schenck,* the
Court suggested that speech could be regulated speech to the extent that
it had a harmful tendency.

Responding to the majority in a dissenting opinion joined by Justice
Brandeis, Holmes emphasized the need for standards that accounted more
sensitively for expressive freedom. Expanding on the clear and present
danger principles he introduced in *Schenck,* Holmes urged the distinction
between words intended to produce the prohibited end proximately and
those with more remote consequences. For Holmes, it was necessary to
distinguish between the possibility of immediate and distant consequences
to avoid "absurd" results. He thus observed that "[a] patriot might think
that we were wasting money on aeroplanes, or making more cannon of a
certain kind than we needed, and might advocate curtailment with success,
yet . . . none would hold such a conduct a crime." Holmes's dissent added
substance to a clear-and-present-danger theory that in *Schenck* was at best
a skeletal concept, but in *Abrams* advanced a philosophy of expressive tolerance.

I do not doubt for a moment that by the same reasoning that would justify pun-
ishing persuasion to murder, the United States constitutionally may punish speech

that produces or is intended to produce a clear and imminent danger that it will bring about forthwith certain substantive evils that the United States constitutionally may seek to prevent. The power undoubtedly is greater in time of war than in time of peace because war opens dangers that do not exist at other times.

But as against dangers peculiar to war, as against others, the principle of the right to free speech is always the same. It is only the present danger of immediate evil or an intent to bring it about that warrants Congress in setting a limit to the expression of opinion where private rights are not concerned. Congress certainly cannot forbid all effort to change the mind of the country. Now nobody can suppose that the surreptitious publishing of a silly leaflet by an unknown man, without more, would present any immediate danger that its opinions would hinder the success of the government arms or have any appreciable tendency to do so. Publishing those opinions for the very purpose of obstructing, however, might indicate a greater danger and at any rate would have the quality of an attempt. So I assume that the second leaflet if published for the purposes alleged in the fourth count might be punishable. But it seems pretty clear to me that nothing less than that would bring these papers within the scope of this law. An actual intent in the sense that I have explained is necessary to constitute an attempt, where a further act of the same individual is required to complete the substantive crime. . . . It is necessary where the success of the attempt depends upon others because if that intent is not present the actor's aim may be accomplished without bringing about the evils sought to be checked. An intent to prevent interference with the revolution in Russia might have been satisfied without any hindrance to carrying on the war in which we were engaged.

Holmes objected not only to the majority's standard of review, but also to the harsh sentences that were upheld. The defendants in *Abrams* were sentenced to twenty years in prison for publishing two leaflets that he "believe[d] the defendants had as much right to publish as the Government has to publish the Constitution of the United States now vainly invoked by them." As he described them, heavy sanctions reflected an interest in punishment "not for what the indictment alleges but for the creed they avow." Such consequences were troubling to Holmes, who saw a dangerous potential in such regulation. Because truth is elusive and even mutable over the course of time, he expressed concern with official controls that presumed to establish thought as settled. History demonstrated and the Constitution assumed, from Holmes's perspective, the need for open and uninhibited public discourse. With that premise, he introduced his marketplace of ideas theory that for many represents a First Amendment gospel.

Persecution for the expression of opinions seems to me perfectly logical. If you have no doubt of your premises or your power and want a certain result with all your heart you naturally express your wishes in law and sweep away all opposition. To allow opposition by speech seems to indicate that you think the speech impotent, as when a man says that he has squared the circle, or that you do not care whole-heartedly for the result, or that you doubt either your power or your premises. But when men have realized that time has upset many fighting faiths, they may come to believe even more than they believe the very foundations of their own conduct that the ultimate good desired is better reached by free trade in ideas—that the best test of truth is the power of the thought to get itself accepted in the competition of the market, and that truth is the only ground upon which their wishes safely can be carried out. That at any rate is the theory of our Constitution. It is an experiment, as all life is an experiment. Every year if not every day we have to wager our salvation upon some prophecy based upon imperfect knowledge. While that experiment is part of our system I thing that we should be eternally vigilant against attempts to check the expression of opinions that we loathe and believe to be fraught with death, unless they so imminently threaten immediate interference with the lawful and pressing purposes of the law that an immediate check is required to save the country. I wholly disagree with the argument of the Government that the First Amendment left the common law as to seditious libel in force. History seems to me against the notion. I had conceived that the United States through many years had shown its repentance for the Sedition Act of 1798, by repaying fines that it imposed. Only the emergency that makes it immediately dangerous to leave the correction of evil counsels to time warrants making any exception to the sweeping command, "Congress shall make no law . . . abridging the freedom of speech." Of course I am speaking only of expressions of opinion and exhortations, which were all that were uttered here, but I regret that I cannot put into more impressive words my belief that in their conviction upon this indictment the defendants were deprived of their rights under the Constitution of the United States.

The tone and content of Holmes's dissent in *Abrams,* as noted previously, reflected a major redirection of thought in the short time since *Schenck, Frohwerk* and *Debs.* Some observers credit the transformation to the influence of Judge Learned Hand. In correspondence between the two jurists after the first set of Espionage Act cases. Hand emphasized that interests of democracy and truth required special latitude for dissent. He also warned about standards of review that required speculation on the future consequences of expression. Hand himself, in a district court opinion preceding *Schenck, Frohwerk* and *Debs,* advanced a standard of review that required attention to "the gravity of the evil discounted by its improbability." Describing words as "triggers of action" in *Masses Publishing Co. v. Patten,* Hand denied constitutional protection to expression "which ha[s] no purport but to counsel the violation of law." Even if sensitized by his dialogue with Hand, Holmes did not borrow the *Masses* test or follow its inattention to whether an alleged harm, even if serious or probable, was imminent. In practical operation, therefore, Hand's formula was open to translation into whether speech had a harmful tendency. Holmes's fortified clear-and-present-danger test, therefore, offered an alternative to analytical models that were susceptible to speculation of harm and overreaction to remote threats. The theme of direct incitement and imminent harm, missing from Holmes's original formulations of the clear-and-present-danger test, the Court's standards and the *Masses* formula, was a distinctive aspect of his dissent in *Abrams*.

Louis D. Brandeis

Holmes's dissent, as noted previously, was joined by Louis Brandeis. In the decade following *Abrams*, Holmes and Brandeis combined to generate several opinions that, although not commanding a majority, helped to establish a foundation for future First Amendment doctrine. Louis Brandeis's nomination to the Supreme Court by President Wilson in 1916 was a shock to the legal system. At a time when the Court was a guardian of contractual and property rights, and prohibited government from responding to accumulations of industrial power or their social fall-out, Brandeis had earned a reputation for his contributions to social and economic reform. Wilson himself introduced him as "the people's advocate when public interests called for an effective champion." Brandeis had abandoned a lucrative business practice at the turn of the century and turned his attention to community service, a career change prompted by capitalistic excesses that he regarded as a threat to democratic traditions. For Brandeis, law was a tool of societal development and the Court was obligated to nurture change. Before his appointment, Brandeis had won a notable victory by demonstrating to the Court that a wage and hour law for women was a legitimate exercise of a state's police power. The decision, in *Muller v. Oregon,* crossed the constitutional currents of the *Lochner* era. The written arguments he presented in *Muller,* heavily laden with facts and statistics, became a model for demonstrating that a state's interest in exercising its police power was legitimate. The "Brandeis brief" was a document crammed with social and economic data that its author considered as relevant as legal precedent in reviewing social legislation. The litigative innovation, as described by Felix Frankfurter, was "epoch-making . . . because of the authoritative recognition by the Supreme Court that the way in which Mr. Brandeis presented the case . . . laid down a new technique for counsel [in] arguing such constitutional questions, and an obligation upon courts to insist upon such method of argument." Such style and substance also previewed the nature of Brandeis' opinions that likewise were weighted with extensive detail and represented what A. T. Mason described as an effort "to explore and illumine not only the law but also the relations which law governs." Particularly in dissent, they were designed to offer "a persuasive demonstration of what the law ought to be in terms of social justice." Brandeis' contributions to the law's development were a function of his assumption that "a lawyer who has not studied economics and sociology is very apt to become a public enemy." His nomination to the Supreme Court elicited significant opposition, some of which had anti-Semitic overtones. Brandeis' legacy is especially notable for principles that account for personal liberty, reckon with abuse of official and private power and enable modern government to innovate and experiment in regulating social and economic problems.

A Foundation for the Future: The *Gitlow* and *Whitney* Dissents

In *Schenck,* the Court had indicated that freedom of speech standards would vary according to whether the nation was at war or at peace. Case law in the decade after *Schenck* demonstrated that even if war no longer was a factor in the Court's analysis, results were no more accommodating toward political dissent. During the Red Scare that followed World War I, many states prosecuted radical dissenters under laws that prohibited expression advocating violent overthrow of the government. In *Gitlow v. New York,* the Court reinvested in the harmful tendency criteria of its *Abrams* opinion. At issue in *Gitlow* were convictions under a criminal anarchy law for publishing and disseminating a document urging political strikes. Although the *Gitlow* majority did not respond sympathetically to the constitutional claim, it nonetheless contributed to some progress in First Amendment principle. For the first time, the Court specifically acknowledged that freedom of speech was part of the liberty protected by the due process clause of the Fourteenth Amendment. To the extent a state enacted a law prohibiting a specified form of expression, the Court concluded that legislative judgment was "not open for consideration." Clear-and-present-danger criteria, the Court noted, applied only "in those cases where the statute merely prohibits certain acts involving the danger of substantive evil, without any reference to language itself, and it is sought to apply its provisions to language used by the defendant for the purpose of bringing out the prohibited results."

Again joined by Justice Brandeis, Holmes dissented from the Court's judgment and opinion. Noting that any idea may be an incitement, he stressed the need for attention to whether the expression was intended to cause an imminent peril to government. Minus doctrinal attention to the proximity of speech to evil, competition among ideologies and viewpoints was unfair and the function of reason was pinched.

If what I think the correct test is applied, it is manifest that there was no present danger of an attempt to overthrow the government by force on the part of the admittedly small minority who shared the defendant's views. It is said that this manifesto was more than a theory, that it was an incitement. Every idea is an incitement. It offers itself for belief and if believed it is acted on unless some other belief outweights it or some failure of energy stifles the movement at its birth. The only difference between the expression of an opinion and an incitement in the narrower sense is the speaker's enthusiasm for the result. Eloquence may set fire to reason. But whatever may be thought of the redundant discourse before us it had no chance of starting a present conflagration. If in the long run the beliefs expressed in proletarian dictatorship are destined to be accepted by the dominant forces of the community, the only meaning of free speech is that they should be given their chance and have their way.

If the publication of this document had been laid as an attempt to induce an uprising against government at once and not at some indefinite time in the future it would have presented a different question. The object would have been one with which the law might deal, subject to the doubt whether there was any danger that the publication could produce any result, or in other words, whether it was not futile and too remote from possible consequences.

Differences underlying the Court's deferential review and the more probing inquiry of Holmes and Brandeis were aired again two years after *Gitlow.* In *Whitney v. California,* the Court upheld the conviction of a woman charged with violating a criminal syndicalism law. As defined by the enactment, criminal syndicalism consisted of "advocating, teaching or aiding and abetting . . . crime, sabotage . . . or unlawful acts of force or violence" as a means of effecting political or economic change. The defendant had been convicted under the law for assisting in the organization of a communist group. At an organizing convention, where a majority supported violent insurrection, she had spoken in favor of peaceful change through the democratic process. Although claiming no knowledge of the group's illegal purpose when helping to organize it, she was convicted on the basis of being at the convention. Because the defendant had not raised a clear-and-present danger defense, and could not challenge on appeal the facts used to convict her, Holmes and Brandeis did not "inquire into the errors now alleged" and concurred in the Court's judgment. Their opinion challenged the majority's reasoning in dissent-like terms, however, as Brandeis joined by Holmes demonstrated that the activity would have have been lawful under clear and present danger criteria. In the process, they offered an especially compelling perspective on the value of free expression and perils of official overreaction.

This Court has not yet fixed the standard by which to determine when a danger shall be deemed clear; how remote the danger may be and yet be deemed present; and what degree of evil shall be deemed sufficiently substantial to justify resort to abridgment of free speech and assembly as the means of protection. To reach sound conclusions on these matters, we must bear in mind why a State is, ordinarily, denied the power to prohibit dissemination of social, economic and political doctrine which a vast majority of its citizens believes to be false and fraught with evil consequence.

Those who won our independence believed that the final end of the State was to make men free to develop their faculties; and that in its government the deliberative forces should prevail over the arbitrary. They valued liberty both as an end and as a means. They believed liberty to be the secret of happiness and courage to be the secret of liberty. They believed that freedom to think as you will and to speak as you think are means indispensable to the discovery and spread of political truth; that without free speech and assembly discussion would be futile; that with them, discussion affords ordinarily adequate protection against the dissemination of noxious doctrine; that the greatest menace to freedom is an inert people; that public discussion is a political duty; and that this should be a fundamental principle of the American government. They recognized the risks to which all human institutions are subject. But they knew that order cannot be secured merely through fear of punishment for its infraction; that it is hazardous to discourage thought, hope and imagination; that fear breeds repression; that repression breeds hate; that hate menaces stable government; that the path of safety lies in the opportunity to discuss freely supposed grievances and proposed remedies; and that the fitting remedy for evil counsels is good ones. Believing in the power of reason as applied through public discussion, they eschewed silence coerced by law—the argument of force in its worst form. Recognizing the occasional tyrannies of governing majorities, they amended the Constitution so that free speech and assembly should be guaranteed.

Fear of serious injury cannot alone justify suppression of free speech and assembly. Men feared witches and burnt women. It is the function of speech to free men from the bondage of irrational fears. To justify suppression of free speech there must be reasonable ground to fear that serious evil will result if free speech is practiced. There must be reasonable ground to believe that the danger apprehended is imminent. There must be reasonable ground to believe that the evil to be prevented is a serious one. Every denunciation of existing law tends in some measure to increase the probability that there will be violation of it. Condonation of a breach enhances the probability. Expressions of approval add to the probability. Propagation of the criminal state of mind by teaching syndicalism increases it. Advocacy of law-breaking heightens it still further. But even advocacy of violation, however reprehensible morally, is not a justification for denying free speech where the advocacy falls short of incitement and there is nothing to indicate that the advocacy would be immediately acted on. The wide difference between advocacy and incitement, between preparation and attempt, between assembling and conspiracy, must be borne in mind. In order to support a finding of clear and present danger it must be shown either that immediate serious violence was to be expected or was advocated, or that the past conduct furnished reason to believe that such advocacy was then contemplated.

Those who won our independence by revolution were not cowards. They did not fear political change. They did not exalt order at the cost of liberty. To courageous, self-reliant men, with confidence in the power of free and fearless reasoning applied through the processes of popular government, no danger flowing from speech can be deemed clear and present, unless the incidence of the evil apprehended is so imminent that it may befall before there is opportunity for full discussion. If there be time to expose through discussion the falsehood and fallacies, to avert the evil by the processes of education, the remedy to be applied is more speech, not enforced silence. Only an emergency can justify repression. Such must be the rule if authority is to be reconciled with freedom. Such, in my opinion, is the command of the Constitution. It is therefore always open to Americans to challenge a law abridging free speech and assembly by showing that there was no emergency justifying it.

Moreover, even imminent danger cannot justify resort to prohibition of these functions essential to effective democracy, unless the evil apprehended is relatively serious. Prohibition of free speech and assembly is a measure so stringent that it would be inappropriate as the means for averting a relatively trivial harm to society. A police measure may be unconstitutional merely because the remedy, although effective as means of protection, is unduly harsh or oppressive. Thus, a State might, in the exercise of its police power, make any trespass upon the land of another a crime, regardless of the results or of the intent or purpose of the trespasser. It might, also, punish an attempt, a conspiracy, or an incitement to commit the trespass. But it is hardly conceivable that this Court would hold constitutional a statute which punished as a felony the mere voluntary assembly with a society formed to teach that pedestrians had the moral right to cross unenclosed, unposted, waste lands and to advocate their doing so, even if there was imminent danger that advocacy would lead to a trespass. The fact that speech is likely to result in some violence or in destruction of property is not enough to justify its suppression. There must be the probability of serious injury to the State. Among free men, the deterrents ordinarily to be applied to prevent crime are education and punishment for violations of the law, not abridgment of the rights of free speech and assembly. . . . I am unable to assent to the suggestion in the opinion of the Court that assemblying with a political party, formed to advocate the desirability of a proletarian revolution by mass action at some date necessarily far in the future, is not a right within the protection of the Fourteenth Amendment.

Decisions in the decade after *Whitney* represented initial instances in which convictions were reversed in free speech cases. In *Fiske v. Kansas,* decided on the same day as *Whitney,* the Court reversed a criminal syndicalism conviction based on reference to class struggle in the preamble to a labor organization's constitution. The decision reflected a sense that "[n]o substantial inference can . . . be drawn from the language of this preamble, that the organization taught, advocated, or suggested the duty, necessity, propriety, or expediency of . . . unlawful acts or methods." A few years later, in *Stromberg v. California,* the Court struck down a state law prohibiting the display of red flags as a symbol "of opposition to organized government." The statute was found unconstitutionally vague, as it had the potential to chill red-flag displays for legitimate purposes. The *Fiske* and *Stromberg* decisions did not represent significant doctrinal change. To the extent their outcomes may have reflected a reduction of national paranoia that had peaked during the early 1920s, they indicated further how applicable standards were subject to variable perceptions of risk and harm.

Doctrinal Inroads: Early Usage of Clear-and-Present-Danger Standards

As the Court commenced a retreat from economic rights doctrine during the late 1930s, it simultaneously demonstrated enhanced attention to First Amendment interests. The Court's abandonment of substantive due process review, in *United States v. Carolene Products Co.*, reserved the possibility of closely reviewing legislative action that burdened constitutionally enumerated rights and liberties. A year before *Carolene Products*, the First Amendment logic of Holmes and Brandeis seemed to have a discernible effect on the Court's analytical direction. In *De Jonge v. Oregon*, the Court determined that rights of "speech or press or assembly" could not be abridged absent "incite[ment] to violence and crime." For the first time, the Court reversed a conviction on grounds that it directly violated the First Amendment. The influence of Holmes and Brandeis was even more palpable in *Herndon v. Lowry*. The *Herndon* case concerned a conviction under Georgia law for attempting "to incite insurrection" and had significant racial overtones. The petitioner was a black organizer for the Communist Party who was convicted for inciting insurrection by promoting "equal rights for the Negroes and self-determination of the Black Belt." Rejecting arguments by the state that *Gitlow* was dispositive, the Court found "an unwarranted invasion of the right of freedom of speech." It specifically dismissed the proposition that "a law general in its description of the mischief to be remedied" could establish a standard of guilt based on the "dangerous tendency of the words." Even when the legislature specified the speech it was prohibiting, the Court determined that regulation was permissible only to the extent "justifi[ed] in a reasonable apprehension of danger to organized government."

The standard of review in *Herndon* indicated that freedom of speech could not be curbed without taking into account the probability that a prohibited harm would occur. Analysis thus was severed from the premises of *Abrams* and *Gitlow* and redirected toward the Holmes-Brandeis model. Significant progress in fastening First Amendment law to clear-and-present-danger standards was achieved a few years later in *Bridges v. California*. The *Bridges* decision represented a major triumph of Holmes-Brandeis doctrine. At issue was a contempt of court citation in response to public criticism of a judicial proceeding. Such a sanction traditionally had been justified on grounds that critical expression impaired the administration of justice. In an opinion punctuated with frequent references to Brandeis and Holmes's concurring opinion in *Whitney*, the Court related that "[w]hat finally emerges from the 'clear and present danger' cases is a working principle that the substantive evil must be extremely serious and the degree of imminence extremely high before utterances can be punished." The terms of analysis, emphasizing magnitude and imminence of danger, evidenced further evolution of Holmes-Brandeis logic into mainstream principle.

Limits of Clear and Present Danger

Although clear-and-present-danger criteria were used in *Bridges* to evaluate criticism of the government, they were not established as a general purpose standard of review. One year after *Bridges,* the Court in *Chaplinsky v. New Hampshire* determined that certain forms of expression were not even entitled to First Amendment protection. The *Chaplinsky* case concerned the conviction of a religious leafleteer who, while being removed from a public sidewalk, called a police officer a "God damned racketeer and a damned fascist." The Court characterized the expression as "fighting words," which "by their very utterance inflict injury or tend to incite an immediate breach of the peace." From the Court's perspective, the speech was "no essential part of any exposition of ideas, and [was] of such slight social value as a step toward the truth that any benefit that may be derived from [it] is clearly outweighted by the social interest in order and morality." Fighting words as a category thus were excluded from the First Amendment's protective ambit.

The *Chaplinsky* decision was significant, apart from its immediate result, because it introduced an analytical process that substantially narrows the First Amendment's reach. The Court's opinion represented an early exercise in speech classification that, on a wholesale basis, determines whether a category of expression merits constitutional attention. As indicated by the *Chaplinsky* decision, exclusion of speech from First Amendment protection was not unique to fighting words. The Court noted that obscene or defamatory expression also had "slight social value" and thus categorically was unprotected. In the same year that *Chaplinsky* was decided, the Court in *Valentine v. Chrestensen* indicated that commercial speech also was outside the First Amendment's purview. Since *Chaplinsky,* fighting words have been defined as an especially narrow category of expression that nonetheless remains constitutionally insignificant. The law of obscenity has evolved with consistent emphasis on a lack of social value and consequent impertinence of the First Amendment. Exceptions to the unprotected status of defamation eventually evolved as a sensed need to protect vigorous criticism of government resulted in special standards of proof in actions by public officials and public figures. Commercial expression also acquired constitutional security, at least to the extent that it was not false or misleading, government had no substantial interest in regulating it, or less restrictive means of control were available.

The classification process, excluding some expression entirely from First

Amendment consideration and resulting in specialized standards for other types of speech, limited the potential operation of clear-and-present-danger principles. The most significant impact of Holmes-Brandeis logic has been in the political context, from which it sprung. In the 1950s, the cold war and national security concerns presented a challenge to First Amendment values and standards reminiscent of what Holmes and Brandeis had witnessed a few decades before. Government policy in both contexts focused on organizations and activities considered politically subversive. In a series of cases concerning federal law prohibiting the Communist Party and membership therein, the Court revisited issues that had engaged the attention of Holmes and Brandeis.

Doctrinal Regression and Drift

The first significant constitutional test of federal anti-subversive legislation occurred in *Dennis v. United States.* The decision, which upheld convictions under the Smith Act for conspiring to organize the Communist Party, created analytical confusion rather than order. A plurality opinion authored by Chief Justice Vinson indicated that the challenged regulation should be assessed pursuant to clear-and-present-danger principles. As applied by Vinson, the standard was a departure from the Brandeis-Holmes formulation related in *Whitney.* The key focus of the plurality was on "whether the gravity of the 'evil,' discounted by its improbability, justifies such invasion of free speech as is necessary to avoid the danger." Lost in the translation of clear-and-present-danger standards was consideration of the probability and imminence of danger. As emphasized by Holmes and Brandeis in their *Abrams, Gitlow* and *Whitney* opinions, such reference points were crucial to accommodation of political dissent. The plurality bypassed attention to the probability or proximity of harm, however, reasoning that the government did not have to wait until the *"putsch* is about to be executed." The Vinson opinion, instead of applying clear-and-present danger principles developed by Holmes and Brandeis, actually borrowed the Learned Hand formula that they had rejected in 1919. Failing also to distinguish between actual incitement and persuasive expression "counseling the violation of the law," analysis seemed to revert toward a harmful tendency model.

A resurgence of principles advanced by Holmes and Brandeis evidenced itself in post-*Dennis* decisions. In *Yates v. United States,* the Court refused to affirm the convictions of several persons who had been charged with advocating and teaching violent insurrection. It also asserted that the *Dennis* decision had not "obliterated the traditional dividing line between advocacy of abstract doctrine and advocacy of action." The distinction was important in clarifying that espousal of principle untied to action was constitutionally protected.

The *Yates* decision did not represent unqualified investment in the Holmes-Brandeis model of clear-and-present-danger analysis. In *Scales v. United States,* the Court upheld a conviction based on membership in the Communist Party. For the *Scales* Court, it was sufficient that the petitioner knew of the organization's illegal objectives and intended to help advance them when "circumstances would permit." The Court pointedly disclaimed any imminence requirement, which was the linchpin of the Holmes-Brandeis clear-and-present-danger formula. It accordingly interpreted *Dennis* and *Yates* as putting "to rest any doubt that present advocacy of *future* action for violent overthrow satisfies . . . constitutional requirements equally with advocacy of *immediate* action to that end."

Beyond Clear and Present Danger: The First Amendment as an Absolute

The Court's judgment and opinion were not without dissent. Justice Douglas objected on grounds that punishment was based merely on belief. Similarly, Justice Black maintained that the "Petitioner is being sent to jail for the express reason that he has associated with people who have entertained unlawful ideas and said unlawful things and that of course is a *direct* abridgment of his freedoms of speech and assembly." Both expressed concern with a balancing test that Black described as "capable of being used to justify almost any action Government may wish to take to suppress First Amendment freedom." Perceptions of a departure from "traditional concepts of First Amendment rights," as Douglas put it, contributed to a proposed model of speech protection exceeding even what Holmes and Brandeis had contemplated. In *Konigsberg v. State Bar of California,* decided little more than a month before *Scales,* Justice Black characterized the First Amendment as an absolute bar to government regulation of speech. The *Konigsberg* case concerned a denial of admission to the bar, because the applicant had refused to answer questions concerning Communist Party membership. As Black saw it, in an opinion joined by Douglas and Chief Justice Warren, balancing of constitutional and regulatory interests presented unacceptable risks to liberty of expression. The factoring and weighing of competing considerations, essential even in clear-and-present-danger analysis, resulted in rights being " 'balanced' away whenever a majority of this Court thinks that a state might have interest sufficient to justify abridgment of these freedoms." Although having used a balancing analysis himself in authoring the *Bridges* opinion that implemented clear-and-present-danger standards, Black eventually repudiated them. In *Konigsberg,* he expressed his "belie[f] that the unequivocal command that there shall be no abridgment of the rights of free speech and assembly shows that the men who drafted our Bill of Rights did all the 'balancing' that was to be done in this field."

Black's absolutist view of the First Amendment never commanded majority support and was specifically rejected by the majority in *Konigsberg*. The disagreement over standards suggested continuing uncertainty with respect to how criteria pertaining to political expression eventually would evolve. In *Bond v. Floyd*, decided in 1966, the Court considered a legislature's refusal to seat an elected member. The state house had voted against administering an oath of office or seating the representative because of his criticism of the Vietnam War. The legislature specifically equated his support of draft protesters with advocacy of refusing military induction. Pursuant to its decision in *Yates*, the Court held that the lawmaker's statements had not constituted an incitement of illegal conduct. The Court drew a like distinction between incitement and protected speech three years later when it reversed a conviction under a federal law prohibiting threats against the president's life. Given the context and response to the speech, showing that it was taken humorously, the Court in *Watts v. United States* found "political hyperbole" rather than a true incitement of violent action.

Holmes and Brandeis's Legacy: The Modern Clear-and-Present-Danger Test

The Court's emphasis on actual incitement as a condition for speech regulation or sanction reflected the abiding but still not consummated influence of Holmes and Brandeis. The case of *Brandenburg v. Ohio*, decided in the same year as *Watts*, represented wholesale investment in their half-century old doctrine. At issue in *Brandenburg* was the conviction of a Ku Klux Klan official under a state criminal syndicalism law. The pertinent statute was indistinguishable from the law upheld in *Whitney*. The speech, which resulted in prosecution, consisted of the following comments:

This is an organizers' meeting. We have had quite a few members here today which are—we have hundreds, hundreds of members throughout the State of Ohio. I can quote from a newspaper clipping from the Columbus, Ohio Dispatch, five weeks ago Sunday morning. The Klan has more members in the State of Ohio than does any other organization. We're not a revenge organization, but if our President, our Congress, our Supreme Court, continues to suppress the white, Caucasian race, it's possible that there might have to be some revengeance taken.

We are marching on Congress July the Fourth, four hundred thousand strong. From there we are dividing into two groups, one group to march on St. Augustine, Florida, the other group to march into Mississippi. Thank you.

Crowd reaction to the speech included such remarks as:

How far is the nigger going to—yeah.

This is what we are going to do to the niggers.

A dirty nigger.

Send the Jews back to Israel.

Let's give them back to the dark garden.

Save America.

Let's go back to constitutional betterment.

Bury the niggers.

We intend to do our part.

Give us our state rights.

Freedom for the whites.

Nigger will have to fight for every inch he gets from now on.

Although the expression was provocative, the Court specifically over-ruled *Whitney* and implemented the reasoning advanced by Holmes and Brandeis in that case.

The Ohio Criminal Syndicalism Statute was enacted in 1919. From 1917 to 1920, identical or quite similar laws were adopted by 20 States and two territories. [Citation omitted.] In 1927, this Court sustained the constitutionality of California's Criminal Syndicalism Act, . . . the text of which is quite similar to that of the laws of Ohio. *Whitney v. California,* . . . The Court upheld the statute on the ground that, without more, "advocating" violent means to effect political and economic change involves such danger to the security of the State that the State may outlaw it. Cf. *Fiske v. Kansas.* . . . But *Whitney* has been thoroughly discredited by later decisions. See *Dennis v. United States.* . . . These later decisions have fashioned the principle that the constitutional guarantees of free speech and free press do not permit a State to forbid or proscribe advocacy of the use of force or of law violation except where such advocacy is directed to inciting or producing imminent lawless action and is likely to incite or produce such action. As we said in *Noto v. United States,* . . . "the mere abstract teaching . . . of the moral propriety or even moral necessity for a resort to force and violence, is not the same as preparing a group for violent action and steering it to such action." See also *Herndon v. Lowry . . . ; Bond v. Floyd.* . . . A statute which fails to draw this distinction impermissibly intrudes upon the freedoms guaranteed by the First and Fourteenth Amendments. It sweeps within its condemnation speech which our Constitution has immunized from governmental control. [Citations omitted.]

Measured by this test, Ohio's Criminal Syndicalism Act cannot be sustained. The Act punishes persons who "advocate or teach the duty, necessity, or propriety" of violence "as a means of accomplishing industrial or political reform"; or who publish or circulate or display any book or paper containing such advocacy; or who "justify" the commission of violent acts "with intent to exemplify, spread or advocate the propriety of the doctrines of criminal syndicalism"; or who "voluntarily assemble" with a group formed "to teach or advocate the doctrines of criminal syndicalism." Neither the indictment nor the trial judge's instructions to the jury in any way refined the statute's bald definition of the crime in terms of mere advocacy not distinguished from incitement to imminent lawless action.

Accordingly, we are here confronted with a statute which, by its own words and as applied, purports to punish mere advocacy and to forbid, on pain of criminal punishment, assembly with others merely to advocate the described type of action. Such a statute falls within the condemnation of the First and Fourteenth Amendments. The contrary teaching of *Whitney v. California* . . . cannot be supported, and that decisoin is therefore overruled.

First Amendment standards in *Brandenburg* conclusively displaced an unqualified focus on expression's harmful tendencies. Speech as a consequence may not be regulated unless it is calculated and likely to incite or produce imminent violation of the law. The improbability of imminent consequences, seldom a fatal factor before *Brandenburg,* has been a dispositive concern since. Consistent with the clear-and-present-danger principles adopted in *Brandenburg,* the Court reversed a disorderly conduct conviction based on the exclamation during an antiwar protest that "we'll take the fucking street later." In *Hess v. Indiana,* it found that the defendant "did not appear to be exhorting the crowd to go back into the street" and the statement "at worst, . . . amounted to nothing more than advocacy of illegal actions at some indefinite future time." Because the speech had no real nexus to imminent and unlawful results, the First Amendment barred a disorderly conduct conviction.

Although established precedent since the late 1960s, the clear-and-present-danger test as inspired by Holmes and Brandeis is not without criticism. Based on their experience during the 1950s, when First Amendment standards were substantially diluted, Justices Black and Douglas in *Brandenburg* asserted that any system of balancing was susceptible to manipulation. At least in theory, modern clear-and-present-danger standards afford more latitude to politically unorthodox expression than was provided during the 1920s and 1950s. The acid test for standards of review are circumstances akin to what perverted First Amendment results at those times. Popular hostility toward incidents of flag-burning in the late 1980s prompted legislative prohibitions of such activity, and Supreme Court decisions that narrowly defeated those laws. The flag-burning cases demonstrate that even in relatively stable times, political perceptions and processes are an ever-present threat to the means and scope of political dissent. Barring interpretation of the First Amendment in absolute terms, an abiding concern is not whether but to what extent intolerance may influence analytical outcome. The emergence of speech protective criteria, in the context of a controversial and divisive war during the late 1960s, suggests that official overreaching can be minimized by careful and sensitive review. As constitutional history also discloses, the future vitality of Holmes and Brandeis's First Amendment vision depends not on continuing recitation of the principles they identified but on appreciation of and fidelity toward the values underlying the system of free expression they contemplated.

Bibliography

Cases

Abrams v. United States, 250 U.S. 616 (1919).
Bond v. Floyd, 385 U.S. 110 (1966).
Brandenburg v. Ohio, 395 U.S. 444 (1969).
Bridges v. California, 314 U.S. 252 (1941).
Chaplinsky v. New Hampshire, 315 U.S. 568 (1942).
Debs v. United States, 249 U.S. 211 (1919).
Dennis v. United States, 341 U.S. 494 (1951).
Dred Scott v. Sandford, 60 U.S. 393 (1857).
Fiske v. Kansas, 274 U.S. 380 (1927).
Frohwerk v. United States, 249 U.S. 204 (1919).
Gitlow v. New York, 268 U.S. 652 (1925).
Herndon v. Lowry, 301 U.S. 242 (1937).
Hess v. Indiana, 414 U.S.105 (1973).
Konigsberg v. State Bar of California, 366 U.S. 36 (1961).
Lochner v. New York, 198 U.S. 45 (1905).
Masses Publishing Co. v. Patten, 244 F. 535 (S.D.N.Y.), rev'd, 246 F. 24 (2d Cir.
    1917).
Muller v. Oregon, 208 U.S. 412 (1908).
Mutual Film Corp. v. Industrial Commission of Ohio, 236 U.S. 230 (1915).
New York Times Co. v. Sullivan, 376 U.S. 254 (1964).
Palko v. Connecticut, 302 U.S. 319 (1937).
Patterson v. Colorado, 205 U.S. 454 (1907).
Scales v. United States, 367 U.S. 203 (1961).
Schenck v. United States, 249 U.S. 47 (1919).
Slaughter-House Cases, 83 U.S. 36 (1873).
Stromberg v. California, 283 U.S. 359 (1931).
United States v. Carolene Products Co., 304 U.S. 144 (1938).
Valentine v. Chrestensen, 316 U.S. 52 (1942).
Watts v. United States, 394 U.S. 705 (1969).
Whitney v. California, 274 U.S. 357 (1927).
Yates v. United States, 354 U.S. 298 (1957).

Books and Articles

Brandeis, L., The Curse of Bigness (1934).
Chafee, Z., Free Speech in the United States (1941).
Emerson, T., The System of Freedom of Expression (1970).

Emery, E., The Press and America (1971).

Kalven, H., *Ernst Freund and the First American Tradition,* 40 U. Chi. L. Rev. 235 (1973).

Konefsky, S., The Legacy of Holmes and Brandeis (1956).

Levy, L., Legacy of Suppression: Freedom of Speech and Press in Early American History (1960).

Meiklejohn, A., Free Speech and Its Relation to Self-Government (1948).

Meiklejohn, A., *The First Amendment Is an Absolute,* 1961 Sup. Ct. Rev. 245 (1961).

Milton, J., Areopagitica: A Speech for the Liberty of Unlicensed Printing to the Parliament of England (1644).

Chapter 7

THE RIGHT TO BE LET ALONE

The right of privacy, like economic liberty, is not specified by the Constitution. Unlike marketplace freedom, which was abandoned as a constitutional concern earlier this century, privacy has evolved and endured as a fundamental right secured by the Fourteenth Amendment. In *Lochner v. New York,* Justice Holmes expressed his opposition to the constitutionalization of contractual liberty. For the rest of his career, as discussed in Chapter 4, he strenuously objected to recognition of economic rights as an incident of due process. Criticism of modern privacy rights, by detractors such as Justice Black in *Griswold v. Connecticut* and Justices White and Rehnquist in *Roe v. Wade* and other decisions, reflects a sense akin to Holmes' that the Court has forgotten its limited range and the Constitution's spaciousness. Despite such protest, the right of privacy has evolved to a level of acceptance never achieved by economic liberty. Even if its source and scope are debated, the basic right seems reasonably settled. For all the controversy generated by its development, it is notable that only one justice dissented from the Court's acknowledgment in 1990 of a fundamental privacy interest broad enough to include the liberty to refuse life-supporting medical care.

Origins of the Right of Privacy

Before its constitutional dimensions were established, privacy traditionally had been a concern of tort law. By common law and statute, states traditionally have afforded rights of action against unreasonable intrusion into personal zones of privacy, disclosure of intimate personal details, portrayal of a person in a false light and commercial exploitation of name, likeness or image. Elevation of privacy interests to constitutional status is a relatively recent phenomenon of the twentieth century. In its constitutional sense, privacy transcends common law definitions and concerns. As described by Justice Stevens, it includes the "individual interest in avoiding disclosure of personal matters [and] . . . in independence in making certain kinds of important decisions." The right of privacy for constitutional purposes thus establishes some personal safe harbors and reserves certain question for self-determination. As Laurence Tribe has described it, "privacy is nothing less than society's limiting principle."

Brandeis's Early Privacy Concerns

The origins of a right to privacy, as it has evolved in a constitutional sense, relate back to late-nineteenth-century legal scholarship. In 1890, Louis Brandeis coauthored a law review article suggesting the existence of a right to privacy. As touted by Brandeis, the right responded to the nature and influence of mass media as they had evolved by the end of the nineteenth century. As he saw it, the press in the nation's first century had become increasingly intrusive and overly concerned with sensationalism, banality and indecency. At a time when newspapers and magazines were acquiring photojournalistic capabilities and becoming an increasingly pervasive phenomenon, Brandeis's theory of a right to privacy responded in significant part to the changing nature and growing influence of the media.

That the individual shall have full protection in person and in property is a principle as old as the common law; but it has been found necessary from time to time to define anew the exact nature and extent of such protection. Political, social, and economic changes entail the recognition of new rights, and the common law, in its eternal youth, grows to meet the demands of society. Thus, in very early times, the law gave a remedy only for physical interference with life and property, for trespasses *vi et armis.* Then the "right to life" served only to protect the subject from battery in its various forms; liberty meant freedom from actual restraint; and the right to property secured to the individual his lands and his cattle. Later, there came a recognition of man's spiritual nature, of his feelings and his intellect. Gradually the scope of these legal rights broadened; and now the right to life has come to mean the right to enjoy life,—the right to be let alone; the right to liberty secures the exercise of extensive civil privileges; and the term "property" has grown to comprise every form of possession—intangible, as well as tangible. . . .

Recent inventions and business methods call attention to the next step which must be taken for the protection of the person, and for securing to the individual what Judge Cooley calls the right "to be let alone." Instantaneous photographs and newspaper enterprise have invaded the sacred precincts of private and domestic life; and numerous mechanical devices threaten to make good the prediction that "what is whispered in the closet shall be proclaimed from the housetops." For years there has been a feeling that the law must afford some remedy for the unauthorized circulation of portraits of private persons; and the evil of the invasion of privacy by the newspapers, long keenly felt, has been but recently discussed by an able writer. The alleged facts of a somewhat notorious case brought before an inferior tribunal in New York a few months ago, directly involved the consideration of the right of circulating portraits; and the question whether our law will recognize and protect the right to privacy in this and in other respects must soon come before our courts for consideration.

Of the desirability—indeed of the necessity—of some such protection, there can, it is believed, be no doubt. The press is overstepping in every direction the obvious bounds of propriety and of decency. Gossip is no longer the resource of the idle and of the vicious, but has become a trade, which is pursued with industry as well as effrontery. To satisfy a prurient taste the details of sexual relations are spread broadcast in the columns of the daily papers. To occupy the indolent, column upon column is filled with idle gossip, which can only be procured by intrusion upon the domestic circle. The intensity and complexity of life, attendant upon advancing civilization, have rendered necessary some retreat from the world, and man, under the refining influence of culture, has become more sensitive to publicity, so that solitude and privacy have become more essential to the individual; but modern enterprise and invention have, through invasions upon his privacy, subjected him to mental pain and distress, far greater than could be inflicted by mere bodily injury. Nor is the harm wrought by such invasions confined to the suffering of those who may be made the subjects of journalistic or other enterprise. In this, as in other branches of commerce, the supply creates the demand. Each crop of unseemly gossip, thus harvested, becomes the seed of more, and, in direct proportion to its circulation, results in a lowering of social standards and of morality. Even gossip apparently harmless, when widely and persistently circulated, is potent for evil. It both belittles and perverts. It belittles by inverting the relative importance of things, thus dwarfing the thoughts and aspirations of a people. When personal gossip attains the dignity of print, and crowds the space available for matters of real interest to the community, what wonder that the ignorant and thoughtless mistake its relative importance. Easy of comprehension, appealing to that weak side of human nature which is never wholly cast down by the misfortunes and frailties of our neighbors, no one can be surprised that it usurps the place of interest in brains capable of other things. Triviality destroys at once robustness of thought and delicacy of feeling. No enthusiasm can flourish, no generous impulse can survive under its blighting influence.

In describing the need to protect "thoughts, sentiments, and emotions" from the impact "of writing or of the arts," Brandeis characterized regulation "so far as it consists in preventing publication, [a]s merely an instance of the enforcement of the more general right of the individual to be let alone." What was depicted as the "right to be let alone" acquired constitutional currency during the twentieth century, as it eventually was introduced into case law by Brandeis and developed by him and other jurists. As initially described, the right to privacy was like the right not to be assaulted or beaten, the right not to be imprisoned, the right not to be maliciously prosecuted, the right not to be defamed. In each of these rights, as indeed in all other rights recognized by the law, there inheres the quality of being owned or possessed—and (as that is the distinguishing attribute of property) there may be some propriety in speaking of those rights as property. But, obviously, they bear little resemblance to what is ordinarily comprehended under that term. The principle which protects personal writings and all other personal productions, not against theft and physical appropriation, but against publication in any form, is in reality not the principle of private property, but that of an inviolate personality. . . .

We must therefore conclude that the rights, so protected, whatever their exact nature, are not rights arising from contract or from special trust, but are rights as against the world; and, as above stated, the principle which has been applied to protect these rights is in reality not the principle of private property, unless that word be used in an extended and unusual sense. The principle which protects personal writings and any other productions of the intellect or of the emotions, is the right to privacy, and the law has no new principle to formulate when it extends this protection to the personal appearance, sayings, acts, and to personal relation, domestic or otherwise.

Doctrinal Opportunity and Denial

The *Lochner* era of substantive due process review, as discussed in Chapter 4, was notable for its emphasis on economic liberty. While Holmes was disturbed by the judicial erosion of state powers achieved by fundamental rights analysis, Brandeis was opposed to due process review that precluded legislative attention to economic and social problems. Even thought both usually reached the same Fourteenth Amendment results, Holmes did so by virtue of a philosophy favoring legislative discretion even if he thought the policy dubious. Brandeis's work, on the other hand, is characterized by an interest in the wisdom and necessity of governmental power to control private abuses and promote public welfare. As described by Harold Laski, "Holmes was a liberal by negation [and Brandeis] was a liberal by affirmation." How their divergent priorities and styles led to similar results was well evidenced by their dissents from the Court's affirmance of an injunction against a union boycott in *Truax v. Corrigan*. Holmes stressed that "[t]here is nothing more I deprecate than the use of the Fourteenth Amendment" to stifle popularly enacted social experiments, even if he found them "futile" or "noxious." Brandeis also championed the interests of social experimentation but favored careful attention to "the contemporary conditions, social, industrial and political of the community" in determining the legality of state law. As he put it, "[a] state is free since the adoption of the Fourteenth Amendment, as it was before, not only to determine what system of law shall prevail in it, but, also, by what processes legal rights shall be asserted, and in what courts they may be enforced." Objecting particularly to the Court's prioritization of capitalistic interests, in a way that cramped policy choices in response to private concentrations of power and their social consequences, Brandeis suggested that "[r]ights of property and the liberty of the individual must be remolded, from time to time, to meet the changing needs of society."

At the same time that the Court was emphasizing marketplace rights, it also was expanding and developing the concept of liberty in ways that eventually helped to "remold" personal freedom and rights. Two cases in particular provided ground for future cultivation of privacy concepts. The decisions, *Meyer v. Nebraska* and *Pierce v. Society of Sisters,* suggested limits on governmental power to "standardize" or "homogen[ize]" the populace. In *Meyer,* the Court struck down a state law requiring all grade school instruction to be in English. Its ruling in *Pierce* invalidated state legislation requiring all students to attend public schools. Both decisions found a deprivation of liberty in violation of the Fourteenth Amendment's due process clause and emphasized interests of parents, children and teachers in personal choice. The *Meyer* Court described liberty in an especially broad sense that included

not merely freedom from bodily restraint but also the right of the individual to contract, to engage in any of the common occupations of life, to acquire useful knowledge, to marry, to establish a home and bring up children, to worship God according to the dictates of conscience, and generally to enjoy those privileges long recognized at common law as essential to the orderly pursuit of happiness by free men.

In foreclosing the *Lochner* era of substantive due process review, the Court in *United States v. Carolene Products Co.* maintained the possibility of exacting judicial review when legislation falls "within a specific prohibition of the Constitution, such as those of the first ten amendments." The *Meyer* decision in particular reflected a model of review regularly criticized by Holmes, although he joined the Court's judgment and opinion in *Pierce.* Even if acknowledging that the law in *Meyer* might be unwise, he saw a proper interest in having all citizens "speak a common tongue" and a question of methodology on which "men might reasonably differ." His failure to make the same point in *Pierce* evidenced flexibility, uncertainty and a basis for legislative monitoring even in Holmes's otherwise spartan sense of the judicial function. Modern case law has cited approvingly to both decisions in establishing and extending the right of privacy in its constitutional sense.

Ironically, *Meyer* and *Pierce* proved more influential over the long run in accounting for personal autonomy and choice than when first enunciated at the height of the *Lochner* era. In *Buck v. Bell,* decided in 1927, the Court upheld a compulsory sterilization requirement for "mental defectives" or "feebleminded" people. The state law at issue provided for the measurement of mental deficiency by standards that half of the nation's adult white male population would have failed. Justice Holmes, who authored the opinion for the Court, stressed that it was the legislature that was best qualified to determine the need for such procedures. The result was consistent with his general reluctance to develop the Fourteenth Amendment in terms that cramped legislative authority. The style of the *Buck* decision was reminiscent less of the deference to legislative discretion usually associated with Holmes and more of the affirmative support for legislative aims typical of a Brandeis opinion. Holmes thus observed that "[i]t is better for all the world, if instead of waiting to execute degenerate offspring for crime, or to let them starve for their imbecility, society can prevent those who are manifestly unfit from continuing their kind." The *Meyer* and *Pierce* decisions, despite their eventual contribution to principle securing personal control and autonomy, afforded no defense against involuntary sterilization in *Buck*. Despite his reputation as "the people's advocate," Brandeis did not dissent from the Court's judgment and opinion in *Buck*. Although he had joined the majority in *Meyer* to strike down the state language law, his position in *Buck* was faithful to an attitude disfavoring development of the Fourteenth Amendment in a way that would impair legislative innovation. For Brandeis, a general right to privacy housed in the Fourteenth Amendment may have conflicted with his own objections to the Court's methods of animating the due process clause. Brandeis himself never suggested that a right to privacy was secured by the Fourteenth Amendment. Insofar as he intimated the existence of a fundamental interest not specified by the Constitution, however, his idea of a right to privacy, like economic liberty, was an extension of value.

Privacy and the Fourth Amendment: Brandeis's Dissent in *Olmstead v. United States*

Brandeis's expoundment on the constitutional dimensions of privacy arose in connection with a passage in the document most obviously concerned with privacy. By its terms, the Fourth Amendment establishes a constitutional interest in personal privacy relative to official processes of investigation. Specifically, it establishes a right of personal security against unreasonable searches and seizures and a general standard for issuing search warrants. The amendment itself provides that

The right of the people to be secure in their persons, houses, papers and effects, against unreasonable searches and seizures, shall not be violated, and no Warrants shall issue, but upon probable cause, supported by Oath or affirmation, and particularly describing the place to be searched, and the persons or things to be seized.

Over the course of the Fourth Amendment's existence, police surveillance methodologies have become increasingly sophisticated and intrusive. In *Olmstead v. United States,* the Court was asked to account constitutionally for evolving capabilities of investigative technology. At issue in *Olmstead* was whether electronic eavesdropping on telephone conversations implicated the Fourth Amendment. Law enforcement techniques and consequences had progressed dramatically beyond what was available and even foreseeable when the Constitution was framed and ratified. The Court in *Olmstead* determined that wiretapping did not constitute a search and seizure because no "place" was physically entered and no "things" were seized. Consistent with his sense that the law must be as dynamic as the society it governs, and that the Court should help adapt it to new realities, Justice Brandeis dissented. In so doing, he argued that the Fourth Amendment was interested in official invasion of personal privacy, regardless of the methodology used.

Time works changes, brings into existence new conditions and purposes. Therefore a principle to be vital must be capable of wider application than the mischief which gave it birth. This is peculiarly true of constitutions. They are not ephemeral enactments, designed to meet passing occasions. They are, to use the words of Chief Justice Marshall "designed to approach immortality as nearly as human institutions can approach it." The future is their care and provision for events of good and bad tendencies of which no prophecy can be made. In the application of a constitution, therefore, our contemplation cannot be only of what has been but of what may be. Under any other rule a constitution would indeed be as easy of application as it would be deficient in efficacy and power. Its general principles would have little value and be converted by precedent into impotent and lifeless formulas. Rights declared in words might be lost in reality.

When the Fourth and Fifth Amendments were adopted, "the form that evil had theretofore taken," had been necessarily simple. Force and violence were then the only means known to man by which a Government could directly effect self-incrimination. It could compel the individual to testify—a compulsion effected, if need be, by torture. It could secure possession of his papers and other articles incident to his private life—a seizure effected, if need be, by breaking and entry. Protection against such invasion of "the sanctities of a man's home and the privacies of life" was provided in the Fourth and Fifth Amendments by specific language. [Citation omitted] . . . But "time works changes, brings into existence new conditions and purposes." Subtler and more far-reaching means of invading privacy have become available to the Government. Discovery and invention have made it possible for the Government, by means far more effective than stretching upon the rack, to obtain disclosure in court of what is whispered in the closet.

In addition to concern with existing law enforcement capability, Brandeis warned about the potential of further technological progress. In terms directly pertinent to development of the Fourth and Fifth Amendments, he stressed the need for constitutional development that was responsive to change and its consequences.

"We must never forget," said Mr. Chief Justice Marshall in *McCulloch v. Maryland* . . . "that it is a constitution we are expounding." Since then, this Court has repeatedly sustained the exercise of power by Congress, under various clauses of that instrument, over objects of which the Fathers could not have dreamed. . . .

Moreover, "in the application of a constitution, our contemplation cannot be only of what has been but of what may be." The progress of science in furnishing the Government with means of espionage is not likely to stop with wire-tapping. Ways may some day be developed by which the Government, without removing papers from secret drawers, can reproduce them in court, and by which it will be enabled to expose to a jury the most intimate occurrences of the home. Advances in the psychic and related sciences may bring means of exploring unexpressed beliefs, thoughts and emotions. "That places the liberty of every man in the hands of every petty officer" was said by James Otis of much lesser intrusions than these. To Lord Camden, a far slighter intrusion seemed "subversive of all the comforts of society." Can it be that the Constitution affords no protection against such invasions of individual security?

A sufficient answer is found in *Boyd v. United States,* . . . a case that will be remembered as long as civil liberty lives in the United States. This Court there reviewed the history that lay behind the Fourth and Fifth Amendments. We said with reference to [an English decision] that "The principles laid down in this opinion affect the very essence of constitutional liberty and security. They reach farther than the concrete form of the case there before the court, with its adventitious circumstances; they apply to all invasions on the part of the Government and its employes of the sanctities of a man's home and the privacies of life. It is not the breaking of his doors, and the rummaging of his drawers, that constitutes the essence of the offence; but it is the invasion of his indefeasible right of personal security, personal liberty and private property, where that right has never been forfeited by his conviction of some public offence,—it is the invasion of this sacred right which underlies and constitutes the essence of Lord Camden's judgment. Breaking into a house and opening boxes and drawers are circumstances of aggravation; but any forcible and compulsory extortion of a man's own testimony or of his private papers to be used as evidence of a crime or to forfeit his goods, is within the condemnation of that judgment. In this regard the Fourth and Fifth Amendments run almost into each other. . . ."

Decency, security and liberty alike demand that government officials shall be subjected to the same rules of conduct that are commands to the citizen. In a government of laws, existence of the government will be imperilled if it fails to observe the law scrupulously. Our Government is the potent, the omnipresent teacher. For good or for ill, it teaches the whole people by its example. Crime is contagious. If the Government becomes a lawbreaker, it breeds contempt for law; it invites every man to become a law unto himself; it invites anarchy. To declare that in the administration of the criminal law the end justifies the means—to declare that the Government may commit crimes in order to secure the conviction of a private criminal—would bring terrible retribution. Against that pernicious doctrine this Court should resolutely set its face.

Brandeis's View Triumphant

The emphasis on the imperatives of personal privacy, although focused primarily on Fourth Amendment circumstance, had potentially broader implications. Brandeis himself appeared to understand that possibility in noting that the interest secured by the Fourth and Fifth Amendments had transcendent significance.

The protection guaranteed by the Amendments is much broader in scope. The makers of our Constitution undertook to secure conditions favorable to the pursuit of happiness. They recognized the significance of man's spiritual nature, of his feelings and of his intellect. They knew that only a part of the pain, pleasure and satisfactions of life are to be found in material things. They sought to protect Americans in their beliefs, their thoughts, their emotions and their sensations. They conferred, as against the Government, the right to be let alone—the most comprehensive of rights and the right most valued by civilized men.

The potential for and reality of official intrusion and abuse, which Brandeis identified in the *Olmstead* case, was recognized sooner by Congress and later by the Court. Several years after *Olmstead*, the Communications Act of 1934 prohibited electronic interception of telephone communications. Such legislative protection did not guard against increasingly sophisticated electronic surveillance techniques that used neither telephone nor wire. Constitutional case law, for a few more decades, turned primarily on *Olmstead* notions of whether a physical intrusion had occurred into a protected place. In *Katz v. United States,* decided in 1967, the Court rejected an interpretation of the Fourth Amendment that would have "translated into a general constitutional 'right of privacy.' " It also abandoned the reasoning of the *Olmstead* majority, however, and concluded "that the Fourth Amendment protects people—and not simply 'areas.' " In a significant concurring opinion, Justice Harlan suggested that the Fourth Amendment precluded searches and seizures that invaded a "reasonable expectation of privacy." Regardless of context—which in *Katz* was a telephone booth— the Fourth Amendment's focus was adjusted from trespass concepts to whether investigative procedures breached "the privacy upon which [a person] justifiably relied upon" or which "society is prepared to recognize as 'reasonable.' " The Court thus concluded that "[w]herever a man may be, he is entitled to know that he will be free from unreasonable searches and seizures."

Seeds of Expansion

The *Katz* decision represented a triumph of logic expressed by Brandeis's dissent in *Olmstead*. Recent decisions of the Rehnquist Court have reduced search and seizure standards to a highly deferential standard of reasonableness. Even before *Katz,* and despite subsequent dilution of standards in the criminal justice context, the idea of a legitimate expectation of privacy had extended to other settings. In *Packer Corp. v. Utah,* decided in 1931, the Court upheld the regulation of display advertising by means of billboards, street car signs and placards. Especially significant in Brandeis's majority opinion was his emphasis on the intrusive nature of such methodologies.

Advertisements of this sort are constantly before the eyes of observers on the streets and in street cars to be seen without the exercise of choice or volition on their part. Other forms of advertising are ordinarily seen as a matter of choice on the part of the observer. The young people as well as the adults have the message of the billboard thrust upon them by all the arts and devices that skill can produce. In the case of newspapers and magazines, there must be some seeking by the one who is to see and read the advertisement. The radio can be turned off, but not so the billboard or street car placard. These distinctions clearly place this kind of advertisement in a position to be classified so that regulations or prohibitions may be imposed upon all within the class.

Forwarding and Extending Brandeis's Concepts: Zones of Privacy

The primary torchbearer of a right to privacy after Brandeis's passage from the Court in 1939 was Justice Douglas, who filled the vacancy created by Brandeis's resignation. Douglas's opinions pointed toward recognition of "the right to be let alone" as an essential aspect of liberty protected by the Fifth and Fourteenth Amendments. In *Public Utilities Commission v. Pollak,* Douglas amplified a privacy right that comprehended not only security against official intrusion, but also respect for personal autonomy and insularity. At issue in *Pollak* was whether piped-in radio programming on city buses compromised "constitutional rights of privacy of the passengers." A majority of the Court rejected the privacy argument on grounds that it "wrongly assume[d] that the Fifth Amendment secures to each passenger on a public vehicle regulated by the Federal Government a right of privacy substantially equal to the privacy to which he is entitled in his own home." The decision elicited a dissent from Justice Douglas, who forwarded and expanded arguments presented by Brandeis.

Douglas described privacy as a cornerstone of all other liberties and suggested a constitutional basis for it that transcended any enumerated guarantee.

The case comes down to the meaning of "liberty" as used in the Fifth Amendment. Liberty in the constitutional sense must mean more than freedom from unlawful governmental restraint; it must include privacy as well, if it is to be a repository of freedom. The right to be let alone is indeed the beginning of all freedom. Part of our claim to privacy is in the prohibition of the Fourth Amendment against unreasonable searches and seizures. It gives the guarantee that a man's home is his castle beyond invasion either by inquisitive or by officious people. A man loses that privacy of course when he goes upon the streets or enters public places. But even in his activities outside the home he has immunities from controls bearing on privacy. He may not be compelled against his will to attend a religious service; he may not be forced to make an affirmation or observe a ritual that violates his scruples; he may not be made to accept one religious, political, or philosophical creed as against another. Freedom of religion and freedom of speech guaranteed by the First Amendment give more than the privilege to worship, to write, to speak as one chooses; they give freedom not to do nor to act as the government chooses. The First Amendment in its respect for the conscience of the individual honors the sanctity of thought and belief. To think as one chooses, to believe what one wishes are important aspects of the right to be let alone. . . .

When we force people to listen to another's ideas, we give the propagandist a powerful weapon. Today it is a business enterprise working out a radio program under the auspices of government. Tomorrow it may be a dominant political or religious group. Today the purpose is benign; there is no invidious cast to the programs. But the vice is inherent in the system. Once privacy is invaded, privacy is gone. Once a man is forced to submit to one type of radio program, he can be forced to submit to another. It may be but a short step from a cultural program to a political program.

If liberty is to flourish, government should never be allowed to force people to listen to any radio program. The right of privacy should include the right to pick and choose from competing entertainments, competing propaganda, competing political philosophies. If people are let alone in those choices, the right of privacy will pay dividends in character and integrity. The strength of our system is in the dignity, the resourcefulness, and the independence of our people. Our confidence is in their ability as individuals to make the wisest choice. That system cannot flourish if regimentation takes hold. The right of privacy, today violated, is a powerful deterrent to any one who would control men's minds.

Douglas thus embellished Brandeis's "right to be let alone" in terms that further referenced it to the Constitution. The notion of a zone of individual existence exempt from official control derived from Brandeis's emphasis in *Olmstead* on "the sanctities of a man's home and the privacies of life." It was a concept that, by the 1960s, also acquired broader currency. State law prohibiting the distribution and use of birth control devices, in *Gris-*

wold v. Connecticut, implicated "the sacred precincts of marital bedrooms" and was struck down. In *Stanley v. Georgia,* the Court reversed an obscenity conviction based on possession of prohibited materials. Although obscenity is not protected by the First Amendment, and thus may be criminalized, the Court established a zone of privacy for possession of obscenity in the privacy of the home. Citing directly to and quoting from Brandeis's dissent in *Olmstead,* the Court found that "fundamental . . . is the right to be free, except in very limited circumstances, from unwarranted government intrusion into one's privacy."

Limiting the Zone of Privacy

A few years later, the Court refused to draw an arguably logical extension from *Stanley.* In *Paris Adult Theatre I v. Slaton,* it "declined to equate the privacy of the home relied on in *Stanley* with a 'zone' of 'privacy' that follows a distributor or a consumer of obscene materials wherever he goes." The Court thus upheld the obscenity conviction of a theater owner despite the fact that he had allowed access only to consenting adults. The *Stanley* principle was narrowed further when the Court, in *Bowers v. Hardwick,* refused to use it as a precedent for recognizing what was characterized as "a fundamental right to engage in homosexual sodomy" in the privacy of one's home. Four justices, in a dissenting opinion authored by Justice Blackmun, maintained that the issue was "no more about 'a fundamental right to engage in homosexual sodomy' . . . than *Stanley v. Georgia* was about a fundamental right to watch obscene movies, or *Katz v. United States* was about a fundamental right to place interstate bets from a telephone booth." Quoting from Brandeis's opinion in *Olmstead,* Blackmun stressed that this case concerned "the most comprehensive rights and right most valued by civilized men, namely, the right to be let alone."

The *Paris Adult Theatre* and *Bowers* decisions indicated that, like any other fundamental guarantee, privacy rights are not absolute or limitless. Both rulings deferred to regulatory interests and endorsed the underlying moral judgments of the state. In *Paris Adult Theatre,* the Court related that "civilized societies, legislators and judges" even if acting on an "unprovable assumption" may determine that obscenity has "a tendency to exert a corrupting and debasing impact leading to antisocial behavior[.]" The state was allowed to "conclude that a sensitive, key relationship of human existence, central to family life, community welfare, and the development of human personality, can be debased by crass commercial exploitation of sex." Rejecting any interest of personal autonomy in the matter, the Court observed that "modern societies [do not] leave disposal of garbage and sewage up to the individual 'free will.' " It accordingly approved the qualification of private choice "to protect *'the social interest in order and*

morality.' " Ample regulatory latitude is a normal consequence when unprotected expression, such as obscenity, is at issue. In *Hardwick,* morally
inspired qualification of privacy was allowable even though a bedroom ar-
rest implicated the same Fourth Amendment concerns that inspired Brandeis's dissent in *Olmstead.* The *Hardwick* Court referred to what it characterized as "proscriptions against . . . conduct hav[ing] ancient roots" and
what Chief Justice Burger depicted as a "millennia of moral teaching" pertinent to "an heinous act 'the very mention of which is a disgrace to the
human race.' " Such reasoning has elicited criticism of a failure to comprehend why privacy is constitutionally revered and, in Blackmun's words,
that a "necessary corollary of giving individuals freedom to choose how to
conduct their lives is acceptance of the fact that different individuals will
make different choices."

Privacy Versus the First Amendment

When not vying against dominant moral standards, privacy concepts have
competed effectively to the point of even outranking textually explicit
constitutional interests. In *Lehman v. City of Shaker Heights,* decided in
1974, the Court upheld prohibition of political advertising inside public
transit cars. Although no opinion commanded a majority in *Lehman,* five
justices referred to privacy themes identified by Brandeis in *Packer* and
Douglas in *Pollak.* In his plurality opinion, Justice Blackmun stressed that
the circumstances examined in those cases and at issue in *Lehman* were
"different from the traditional settings where First Amendment values in-
alterably prevail." Douglas himself wrote a concurring opinion restating
his position in *Pollak* and reiterating his agreement with Brandeis.

In asking us to force the system to accept his message as a vindication of his
constitutional rights, the petitioner overlooks the constitutional rights of the commuters. While petitioner clearly has a right to express his views to those who wish
to listen, he has no right to force his message upon an audience incapable of
declining to receive it. In my view the right of the commuters to be free from
forced intrusions on their privacy precludes the city from transforming its vehicles
of public transportation into forums for the dissemination of ideas upon this captive audience. . . .
I agree with Mr. Justice Brandeis who, quoting from a Utah State Court decision, said that the visual message in streetcars is no different, for "[a]dvertisements
of this sort are constantly before the eyes of observers on the streets and in street
cars to be seen without the exercise of choice or volition on their part. Other
forms of advertising are ordinarily seen as a matter of choice on the part of the
observer. . . . In the case of newspapers and magazines, there must be some
seeking by the one who is to see and read the advertisement. The radio can be
turned off, but not so the billboard or street car placard." *Packer Corp. v. Utah.* . . .

Since I do not believe that petitioner has any constitutional right to spread his message before this captive audience, I concur in the Court's judgment.

The idea of a personal safe harbor that is constitutionally secured from "invasion either by inquisitive or by officious people," as depicted by Justice Douglas, comported with and extended the premise of Brandeis's dissent in *Olmstead*. Privacy considerations, as discussed later, have supported content regulation of modern media and consequently limited freedom of the press. The result resolves a conflict between privacy and expressive freedom that concerned Brandeis long before commencing his career as a jurist.

Modern Dimensions of Privacy: Personal Autonomy

The "right to be let alone," by its terms of introduction, had obvious potential for development beyond its immediate Fourth Amendment context. Since established, the challenge has been to identify logical and principled implications and extensions of it. Although presented by Brandeis as a safeguard against unreasonable intrusion, a logical dimension of "the right to be let alone" is the freedom to make highly personal decisions with respect to one's life. As Charles Fried has described it, the concept of privacy comprehends the "moral fact that a person belongs to himself and not others nor to society as a whole." Defining the perimeters of personal autonomy has been both a convoluted and debatable enterprise.

Procreation

Although not resulting in specific support for a right of privacy, compulsory sterilization cases earlier this century offered a breeding ground for such doctrine. In *Buck v. Bell,* as noted previously, the Court upheld a sterilization requirement for mentally defective or feebleminded people, denied any relevance of the Fourteenth Amendment and espoused no concern for a "right to be let alone." The Court's decision in *Skinner v. Oklahoma,* in 1942, reached a different conclusion. In *Skinner,* the Court determined that compulsory sterilization of habitual felons implicated marriage and procreation. As the Court saw it, those interests were among "the basic civil rights of man" that "are fundamental to the very existence and survival of the race." Those sterilized were "forever denied of a basic liberty." The premise that "[t]here is no redemption for the individual whom the law touches" eventually was developed into a principle that accounted for personal control over one's reproductive destiny.

Use of Contraceptives

A fundamental right of privacy emerged more clearly but somewhat un-
certainly in the 1960s. As noted in Chapter 4, Justice Harlan's dissenting
opinion in *Poe v. Ullman* proposed a right of marital privacy grounded in
the due process clause. In *Griswold v. Connecticut,* the Court recognized
such a right but suggested a different constitutional source for it. At issue
in *Griswold* was a state law that prohibited the use or distribution of contraceptives. The Court responded to the regulation's impact on reproductive decisions in the context of marriage, which implicated "a right of privacy older than the Bill of Rights itself." Before examining the merits of
the claim, it disclaimed any ties to Lochnerist analysis and stressed that it
did "not sit as a super-legislature to determine the wisdom, need, and
propriety of laws that touch economic problems, business affairs, or social
conditions." Although diverting analysis from the Fourteenth Amendment
as an independent source of privacy rights, the Court nonetheless reached
beyond specific textual commands of the Constitution and considered the
law's impact "on an intimate relation of husband and wife." Writing for a
majority of the Court, Justice Douglas ventured "that specific guarantees
have penumbras, formed by emanations from those guarantees that help
give them life and substance." Those "guarantees," Douglas wrote, "create
zones of privacy" and include

The right of association contained in the penumbra of the First Amendment. . . .
The Third Amendment in its prohibition against the quartering of soldiers "in any
house" in time of peace without the consent of the owner is another facet of that
privacy. The Fourth Amendment explicitly affirms the "right of the people to be
secure in their persons, houses, papers, and effects, against unreasonable searches
and seizures." The Fifth Amendment in its Self-Incrimination Clause enables the
citizen to create a zone of privacy which government may not force him to surren-
der to his detriment. The Ninth Amendment provides: "The enumeration in the
Constitution, of certain rights, shall not be construed to deny or disparage others
retained by the people."

Referring to past decisions, including *Skinner,* the Court emphasized that
such "cases bear witness that the right of privacy which presses for recognition here is a legitimate one."

The *Griswold* decision constitutionalized a significant new dimension of
privacy. Douglas's rhetorical question as to whether "we [would] allow the
police to search the sacred precincts of marital bedrooms for telltale signs
of the use of contraceptives" could not be answered negatively by a mere
focus on place. A bedroom, like any other locus, is not immune from
search and seizure. From the Court's perspective, the law was "repulsive

to the notions of privacy surrounding the marriage relationship." The regulation failed because of its "destructive impact upon that relationship."

In a concurring opinion, joined by Chief Justice Warren and Justice Brennan, Justice Goldberg suggested that both "the marital relation and the marital home" were constitutionally protected. Goldberg suggested that the right to privacy was supported "by the language and history of the Ninth Amendment," which reserves to the people rights not specifically enumerated by the Constitution. In agreeing that the right to privacy emanates from the totality of the constitutional scheme, he referenced Brandeis's dissent in *Olmstead* as "comprehensively summarizing the principles underlying the Constitution's guarantees of privacy."

Also influenced by Brandeis was Justice Harlan, whose *Griswold* concurrence referenced his detailed dissent in *Poe v. Ullman*. Harlan in *Poe* characterized the *Olmstead* dissent as "the most comprehensive statement of the principle of liberty underlying these aspects of the Constitution." Although noting that case law had developed in support of constitutionally protecting the privacy of the home against unreasonable invasion of any nature, Harlan emphasized that "[w]e would indeed be straining at a gnat and swallowing a camel were we to show concern for the niceties of property law . . . yet fail at least to see any substantial claim [here]." For Harlan, marital privacy was fundamental among rights belonging to "the citizens of all free governments" and within the "full scope of the liberty guaranteed by the Due Process Clause."

Distinctions with respect to the specific source of privacy as a fundamental right were less significant than the general agreement that it was constitutionally rooted. Only Justices Black and Stewart dissented from its recognition. Noting that the "right to privacy" had initially gained currency from the law review article Brandeis had coauthored in the late nineteenth century, Black joined by Stewart criticized "exalting a phrase which . . . Brandeis used in discussing grounds for tort relief, to the level of a constitutional rule which prevents state legislatures from passing any law defined by this Court to interfere with 'privacy.'"

Having established constitutional grounding for a right of privacy in *Griswold,* the Court soon was asked to consider its scope. In *Eisenstadt v. Baird,* the Court invalidated a state restriction on contraceptives for unmarried couples. Because it was unable to distinguish rationally between married and unmarried persons under the circumstances, the Court found a denial of equal protection. In his opinion for the majority, Justice Brennan related that "[i]f right of privacy means anything, it is the right of the *individual,* married or single, to be free from unwanted intrusion into matters so fundamentally affecting a person as the decision whether to bear or beget a child."

Abortion

The notion of constitutional penumbras, even if designed to avoid criticism of extraconstitutional, subjective or natural law analysis, did not succeed in dispelling the imagery of Lochnerism. In further developing the right of privacy, the Court reconstituted its basis in terms accepted by Justice Stewart as consistent with "a long line of . . . cases decided under the doctrine of substantive due process." Stewart's observation responded to the Court's invalidation of abortion restrictions in *Roe v. Wade.* In *Roe,* the Court determined that a state law prohibiting abortion except when the mother's life was at risk was unconstitutional. Justice Blackmun, who authored the majority opinion, found specifically that the "right of privacy . . . is broad enough to encompass a woman's decision whether or not to terminate her pregnancy." What Douglas had found as an emanation from several constitutional sources, and Goldberg had suggested was reserved by the Ninth Amendment, in *Roe* was anchored in the due process clause of the Fourteenth Amendment. Although acknowledging that "[t]he Constitution does not explicitly mention any right of privacy," Blackmun related that

the Court has recognized that a right of personal privacy, or a guarantee of certain areas or zones of privacy, does exist under the Constitution. In varying contexts, the Court or individual Justices have, indeed, found at least the roots of that right in the First Amendment, *Stanley v. Georgia,* . . . in the Fourth and Fifth Amendments, *Terry v. Ohio,* . . . *Katz v. United States,* . . . *Boyd v. United States,* . . . see *Olmstead v. United States,* . . . (Brandeis, J., dissenting); in the penumbras of the Bill of Rights, *Griswold v. Connecticut,* . . . in the Ninth Amendment, *id.,* . . . (Goldberg, J., concurring); or in the concept of liberty guaranteed by the first section of the Fourteenth Amendment, see *Meyer v. Nebraska.* . . . These decisions make it clear that only personal rights that can be deemed "fundamental" or "implicit in the concept of ordered liberty," *Palko v. Connecticut,* . . . are included in this guarantee of personal privacy. They also make it clear that the right has some extension to activities relating to marriage, . . . procreation, . . . contraception, . . . family relationships, . . . and child rearing and education. [Citations omitted.]

This right of privacy, whether it be founded in the Fourteenth Amendment's concept of personal liberty and restrictions upon state action, as we feel it is, or, as the District Court determined, in the Ninth Amendment's reservation of rights to the people, is broad enough to encompass a woman's decision whether or not to terminate her pregnancy. The detriment that the State would impose upon the pregnant woman by denying this choice altogether is apparent. Specific and direct harm medically diagnosable even in early pregnancy may be involved. Maternity, or additional offspring, may force upon the woman a distressful life and future. Psychological harm may be imminent. Mental and physical health may be taxed by child care. There is also the distress, for all concerned, associated with the unwanted child, and there is the problem of bringing a child into a family already unable, psychologically and otherwise, to care for it. In other cases, as in this one, the additional difficulties and continuing stigma of unwed motherhood may be involved. All these are factors the woman and her responsible physician necessarily will consider in consultation.

Doctrinal Backlash Against *Roe v. Wade*

As subsequent case law and political developments have evidenced, the Court's decision in *Roe* was as effective in conclusively resolving the abortion debate as the *Dred Scott* ruling was in terminating the slavery controversy. The *Roe* decision prompted immediate dissenting views to the effect that the Court had perverted the concept of privacy. Justice Rehnquist expressed

difficulty in concluding, as the Court does, that the right of "privacy" is involved in this case. Texas, by the statute here challenged, bars the performance of a medical abortion by a licensed physician on a plaintiff such as Roe. A transaction resulting in an operation such as this is not "private" in the ordinary usage of that word. Nor is the "privacy" that the Court finds here even a distant relative of the freedom from searches and seizures protected by the Fourth Amendment to the Constitution, which the Court has referred to as embodying a right to privacy.

Justice White complained that the result and principle in *Roe* were mandated by the Court but not by the Constitution.

I find nothing in the language or history of the Constitution to support the Court's judgment. The Court simply fashions and announces a new constitutional right for pregnant mothers and, with scarcely any reason or authority for its action, invests that right with sufficient substance to override most existing state abortion statutes. The upshot is that the people and the legislatures of the 50 States are constitutionally disentitled to weigh the relative importance of the continued existence and development of the fetus, on the one hand, against a spectrum of possible impacts on the mother, on the other hand. As an exercise of raw judicial power, the Court perhaps has authority to do what it does today; but in my view its judgment is an improvident and extravagant exercise of the power of judicial review that the Constitution extends to this Court.

The Court apparently values the convenience of the pregnant mother more than the continued existence and development of the life or potential life that she carries. Whether or not I might agree with that marshaling of values, I can in no event join the Court's judgment because I find no constitutional warrant for imposing such an order of priorities on the people and legislatures of the States. In a sensitive area such as this, involving as it does issues over which reasonable men may easily and heatedly differ, I cannot accept the Court's exercise of its clear power of choice by interposing a constitutional barrier to state efforts to protect human life and by investing mothers and doctors with the constitutionally protected right to exterminate it. This issue, for the most part, should be left with the people and to the political processes the people have devised to govern their affairs.

White's criticism of *Roe* reflected a general sense, expressed in *Bowers v. Hardwick* more than a decade later, that "[t]he Court is most vulnerable and comes nearest to illegitimacy when it deals with judge-made constitutional law having little or no cognizable roots in the language or design of the Constitution."

Implicit in Rehnquist's argument, that the right of privacy in *Roe* was unconnected to the Fourth Amendment, was the notion that the Court had exceeded the outer limits of Brandeis's premise in *Olmstead.* The primary objection to securing the choice of abortion as a constitutionally endowed prerogative is reflected by Robert Bork's characterization of *Roe* as "an exercise in moral and political philosophy," and thus an "assumption of illegitimate judicial power and a usurpation of the democratic authority of the American people." The very nature of the inquiry pursued in *Griswold, Roe* and their progeny continues to animate critics who pick up where Justice Black finished. Central to the development of modern privacy rights is an inquiry into what is "implicit in the concept of ordered liberty" or what is "deeply rooted in this Nation's history and tradition." Bork has described such criteria as "pretty vaporous stuff," which he contrasts with textually specified rights that itemize liberties and ensure that any "line-drawing [that] must be done starts from a solid-base."

The Outer Limits of Constitutional Privacy

Despite such concerns, the scope of constitutional privacy interests has been amplified to account for other aspects of personal choice. In *Moore v. City of East Cleveland,* the Court struck down a zoning ordinance that effectively prohibited extended families from sharing the same dwelling. Writing for a plurality, Justice Powell emphasized "that the Constitution protects the sanctity of the family," an interest that is "deeply rooted in . . . history and tradition." The Court, in *Zablocki v. Redhail,* found the right to marry "part of the fundamental right to privacy implicit in the fourteenth amendment's due process clause." The *Zablocki* case was decided in 1978 and negated a state law prohibiting marriage by persons who could prove neither compliance with child support obligations nor that their children would avoid becoming "public charges." Justice Rehnquist, although acknowledging that restriction of marital opportunity for indigents might be irrational and thus unenforceable, reiterated his sense that a constitutional right was not implicated.

The *Moore* and *Zablocki* decisions represented an apex in the development of privacy as a fundamental right. The Court in *Bowers v. Hardwick* in 1986, delimited the right of privacy so that it did not comprehend "a fundamental right to engage in homosexual sodomy." In *Michael H. v. Gerald D.*, the Court refused to extend "the sanctity of the family" to protect a natural parent's interest in visiting a child born from an adulterous affair. In *Cruzan v. Director, Missouri Department of Health*, the Court acknowledged "a constitutionally protected liberty interest in refusing unwanted medical care." Despite suggesting a new dimension of choice, it found the liberty interest outweighed by state regulatory concerns. With respect to abortion itself, the Court for several years after *Roe* refused to allow a woman's choice to be compromised by various restrictions that among other things would have regulated abortion procedures, required testing for fetal viability or required parental or spousal consent. In *Webster v. Reproductive Health Services,* however, the Court upheld fetal viability testing after twenty weeks of pregnancy. By so doing, it destabilized the trimester framework of *Roe* and relaxed previously exacting standards of review. The Court, in *Planned Parenthood v. Casey,* focused on viability as a cut-off point for relatively unimpaired personal choice. It thus scuttled the trimester regime and allowed for state regulation that did not result in an "undue burden on the woman." Provisions of a state law requiring disclosure of abortion alternatives and information on fetal development, a 24-hour waiting period and publicly accessible records of each abortion performed were upheld. Struck down as an "undue burden" was an obligation for a married woman to inform her spouse of a decision to seek an abortion.

A Collision of Privacy Interests

The development of privacy doctrine that accounts for protected places and protected choices has engendered a collision of underlying values and principles. The clash was especially well evidenced in *Federal Communications Commission v. Pacifica Foundation,* which necessitated an ordering of privacy interests. In the *Pacifica* case, the Court upheld the Federal Communications Commission's (FCC's) regulation of indecent expression in broadcasting. Central to the FCC's justification and Court's reasoning was the interest of privacy. As Justice Stevens put it, "indecent material presented over airwaves confronts the citizen, not only in public, but also in the privacy of the home, where the individual's right to be let alone plainly outweighs the First Amendment rights of an intruder." The *Pacifica* decision prioritized a specific privacy concern over freedom of the press. It also set one privacy interest against another. The privacy of the home affords a basis not only for regulation of an invasive activity, as illustrated by *Pacifica*, but for proscription of official monitoring or meddling. When the interest of personal choice is factored into the constitutional equation, the ordering of competing interests actually may tilt against the result arrived at in *Pacifica*.

The *Pacifica* decision inverted priorities established in *Cohen v. California*, when the Court reversed the conviction of a draft protester for displaying an obscene slogan on his jacket while in a public place. In a majority opinion, Justice Harlan observed that the privacy interest was not strong enough for "the State to cleanse public debate to the point where it is grammatically palatable to the most squeamish of it." As noted by the Court in another case concerning exposure to offensive conduct, *Erznoznik v. City of Jacksonville*, a person can "avoid further bombardment of his sensibilities by averting his eyes." In *Pacifica*, Justice Brennan expressed his "wholehearted agreement with my Brethren that an individual's right 'to be let alone' when engaged in private activity within the confines of his own home is encompassed within the 'substantial privacy interests' to which Harlan referred in *Cohen*, and is entitled to the greatest solicitude." For Brennan, the privacy interest stressed by the Court was diminished by (1) the public nature of the medium, (2) the voluntary decision to allow it into the home, and (3) the control that the person retained to switch off unwanted programming. Further outweighing the privacy concern identified by the Court was what Brennan considered to be the more profound interest of the public in exercising autonomy in what it wished to hear.

The *Pacifica* Court determined that when the FCC "finds that a pig has entered the parlor, the exercise of its regulatory power does not depend on proof that the regulation is obscene." In his seminal work on privacy, Brandeis endorsed regulation of expression that exceeded "the obvious bounds of decency." In advocating a right of privacy, it is unlikely that he could have foreseen its full doctrinal potential and problems. The *Pacifica* case concerned not only offensive expression, but also speech with a satirical edge that may have catered to Brandeis's simultaneously articulated priority of "robustness of thought." He also might have distinguished, as in *Packer Corp. v. Utah*, between a message that is "thrust upon" people and "radio [that] can be turned off." Robert Bork has described a decision like *Cohen* as an exercise in "moral relativism." Noting specifically Harlan's observation that if "one man's vulgarity is another's lyric," he has argued that "[i]f the statement . . . were taken seriously, it would be impossible to see how law on any subject could be permitted to exist. After all, one man's larceny is another's just distribution of goods." Harlan's point, however, reflected his understanding of an enumerated constitutional guarantee that "leaves matters of taste and style . . . largely to the individual." It suggests also that when privacy is in conflict with itself and with expressive freedom, an especially sensitive accounting is required. As Laurence Tribe has observed, *"the necessary premise of all such rights is that being forced by the sovereign to conform is more intrusive than being forced by the individual to avert one's gaze.*

A Fundamental but Uncertain Right

When a constitutional seed is planted, it is uncertain when, how or even if it will grow. The history of the right of privacy aptly illustrates the uncertainties of constitutional development. If left to Justice Black, a general right of privacy never would have been acknowledged as fundamental. Despite his objections and persistent criticism by others, it remains rooted in the Fourteenth Amendment. Although constitutionally secured, its limits and even its existence continue to be debated. Viewed in a broader historical context, modern privacy concepts further a legacy of fundamental rights development that includes Taney's use of due process to support slavery and the *Lochner* Court's emphasis on it to protect economic freedom. In its contemporary context, privacy also is a concept that is at war with itself. Whether a principle flourishes as a fundamental right or withers as a failed theory is a function of constitutional choice and prioritization. Although established by precedent, the right of privacy is not immunized by constitutional text from pressures to eliminate or reduce it. Its nature and durability depend ultimately on the continuing viability and influence of the values that generated and have maintained it.

Bibliography

Cases

Bowers v. Hardwick, 478 U.S. 186 (1986).
Buck v. Bell, 274 U.S. 200 (1927).
Cohen v. California, 403 U.S. 15 (1971).
Cruzan v. Director, Missouri Department of Health, 110 S.Ct. 2841 (1990).
Eisenstadt v. Baird, 405 U.S. 438 (1972).
Erznoznik v. City of Jacksonville, 422 U.S. 205 (1975).
Federal Communications Commission v. Pacifica Foundation, 438 U.S. 726 (1978).
Griswold v. Connecticut, 381 U.S. 479 (1965).
Katz v. United States, 389 U.S. 347 (1967).
Lehman v. City of Shaker Heights, 418 U.S. 298 (1974).
Meyer v. Nebraska, 262 U.S. 390 (1923).
Michael H. v. Gerald D., 491 U.S. 110 (1989).
Moore v. City of East Cleveland, 431 U.S. 494 (1977).
Olmstead v. United States, 277 U.S. 438 (1928).
Packer Corp. v. Utah, 285 U.S. 106 (1932).
Paris Adult Theatre I v. Slaton, 413 U.S. 49 (1973).

Pierce v. Society of Sisters, 268 U.S. 510 (1925).
Poe v. Ullman, 367 U.S. 497 (1961).
Public Utilities Commission v. Pollak, 343 U.S. 451 (1952).
Roe v. Wade, 410 U.S. 113 (1973).
Skinner v. Oklahoma, 316 U.S. 535 (1942).
Stanley v. Georgia, 394 U.S. 557 (1969).
Terry v. Ohio, 392 U.S. 1 (1968).
Truax v. Corrigan, 257 U.S. 312 (1921).
United States v. Carolene Products Co., 304 U.S. 144 (1938).
Webster v. Reproductive Health Systems, Inc., 492 U.S. 490 (1989).
Whalen v. Roe, 429 U.S. 589 (1977).
Zablocki v. Redhail, 434 U.S. 374 (1978).

Books and Articles

Bork, R., The Tempting of America (1990).
Brandeis, L., & Warren, S., *The Right to Privacy,* 4 Harv. L. Rev. 193 (1890).
Brest, P., *The Fundamental Rights Controversy: The Essential Contradictions of Normative Constitutional Scholarship,* 90 Yale L. J. 1063 (1981).
Fried, C., *Correspondence,* 6 Phil. & Pub. Aff. 288 (1977).
Karst, K., Belonging to America (1989).
Laski, H., *Mr. Justice Brandeis,* Harper's, Jan. 1934, at 209.
Tribe, L., American Constitutional Law (1988).

AFTERWORD

Justice Blackmun, dissenting from the majority's opinion in *Bowers v. Hardwick,* expressed a hope that the Court eventually would understand "that depriving individuals of the right to choose for themselves how to conduct their intimate relations poses a far greater threat to the values most deeply rooted in our nation's history than tolerance of nonconformity could ever do." Blackmun's lament, although responsive to the Court's restrictive charting of the perimeters of privacy, reflects a tone that is not uncommon among dissenting opinions that sense misplaced understanding. In a dissent authored by Justice Sutherland in *West Coast Hotel v. Parrish,* it was argued that the Fourteenth Amendment's accounting for "freedom of contract is so well settled as to be no longer open to question." Sutherland's assumption that "liberty of contract is the general rule" and was not "questioned by the present decision" seemed especially plaintive as the Court proceeded to dismantle precisely that premise.

Commenting on Blackmun's reaction in *Hardwick,* Laurence Tribe suggested that "[b]efore that hope is too readily dismissed as a dissenter's wishful thinking, we should recall that Justice Brandeis' formulation of the right of privacy as the 'right to be let alone'—the most frequently quoted words in the jurist's privacy lexicon—was also penned in dissent." The observation is relevant not only for critics who, like Tribe, assert that *Hardwick* "probably was not decided on principled grounds." It also illuminates a significant truth about constitutional development in general. Simply put, a point ventured may be eventually accepted even if immediately rejected, and what comes half circle may travel full circle.

The history of fundamental rights analysis exemplifies both possibilities. Substantive due process review originally was rejected, later embraced, thereafter repudiated, subsequently revived and even now is controverted. Constitutional redirection also may be a function more of form than of substance. Incorporation of the Bill of Rights and development of fundamental rights through the privileges and immunities clause of the Fourteenth Amendment were rejected at the earliest stage of interpretation. Over the course of the twentieth century, most of the Bill of Rights have been incorporated into and fundamental rights have been glossed onto the amendment's due process clause. Regardless of how achieved, the net result is a recasting of constitutional meaning that checks political authority in conformance with what at first were dissenting notions. The potential resiliency and maneuverability of doctrine, even when disclaimed, manifests itself in modern arguments for renewed judicial attention to economic rights. Emphasis on contractual liberty and property rights created a legacy from which the modern Court still works to distance itself. Even so, it has expressed fresh interest in regulation diminishing the use or value of land as a violation of the Fifth Amendment command that no "private property [shall] be taken for public use, without just compensation."

Two centuries of constitutional jurisprudence discloses more doctrinal origination points than absolute termination points. Such a reality, even if at odds with interests of certainty and predictability, is inherent in a system that in significant part is open-ended. The truth is that resolution of constitutional questions, even in rejecting a premise in a particular case, seldom forecloses doctrinal possibilities over the long run. As evidenced by the Thirteenth Amendment's termination of slavery, the likelihood is that many new questions will take the place of the one settled.

Chief Justice Marshall, in a seminal interpretation of the nation's charter, emphasized that "we must never forget, that it is a constitution we are expounding." The observation has been belittled by some critics as an overly grand statement of the obvious. Marshall's point in fact affords no instruction with respect to how the Constitution should be interpreted. Implicit in Marshall's comment, disclosed by the process of judicial review as it has evolved and heightening the significance of debate over constitutional principles, is the reality that definition of the Constitution itself is more a competitive than a conclusive exercise.

INDEX

About the Author

DONALD E. LIVELY is Professor of Law at the University of Toledo College of Law. He is the author of *Modern Communications Law* (Praeger, 1991), *Essential Principles of Communications Law* (Praeger, 1991), and *The Constitution and Race* (Praeger, 1992).